# Christian Morality:
## Biblical Foundations

*Raymond F. Collins*

UNIVERSITY OF NOTRE DAME PRESS
Notre Dame, Indiana 46556

**Library of Congress Cataloging-in-Publication Data**

Collins, Raymond F., 1935–
  Christian morality.

  1. Christian ethics — Biblical teaching.  2. Christian
ethics — Catholic authors.  I. Title.
BS680.E84C65  1986        241.5         85-41020
ISBN 0-268-00758-6

Manufactured in the United States of America

IN HONOR OF FATHER AND MOTHER

# Contents

# Acknowledgments

With gratitude do I express my appreciation to the editors and publishers of those journals who so willingly gave me permission to have reprinted within the covers of this book material which had originally appeared in their publications: *Proceedings of the Catholic Theological Society of America* (29 (1974) 215–241) for "Scripture and the Christian Ethic"; the *American Ecclesiastical Review* (161 (1969) 169–182) for "The Ten Commandments in Current Perspective"; *Louvain Studies* (3 (1970–1971) 308–322) for "The Ten Commandments and the Christian Response"; the *Living Light* (14 (1977) 219–233) for "The Fourth Commandment — for Children or for Adults?"; *Laval théologique et philosophique* (35 (1979) 235–261) for "'A New Commandment I Give to You, That You Love One Another . . .' (Jn 13:34)"; *Emmanuel* (87 (1981) 107–113) for "Paul's First Reflections on Love," reprinted, with footnotes added, in *Studies on the First Letter to the Thessalonians.* BETL, 66 (Louvain: University Press, 1984) pp. 346–355; the *Biblical Theology Bulletin* (7 (1977) 149–167; 8 (1978) 3–18) for "The Bible and Sexuality"; *New Testament Studies* (29 (1983) 420–429) for "The Unity of Paul's Paraenesis in 1 Thess 4:3–8: 1 Cor 7:1–7, a Significant Parallel"; and the *Andover Newton Quarterly* (10 (1969) 19–30) for "Christian Personalism and the Sermon on the Mount."

# On the Use of the Scriptures in Moral Theology: A Roman Catholic Perspective

Special attention needs to be given to the development of moral theology. Its scientific exposition should be more thoroughly nourished by scriptural teaching. It should show the nobility of the Christian vocation of the faithful, and their obligation to bring forth fruit in charity for the life of the world.[1]

## A CHALLENGE

With these words, taken from the conciliar Decree on Priestly Formation, the Fathers of the Second Vatican Council formulated their only explicit statement on moral theology. Their statement constituted a challenge for moral theologians and biblical scholars alike; indeed it was a challenge for the Catholic theological community. The challenge addressed to the moralists was twofold. On the surface of things, that is, initially and obviously, Roman Catholic moral theologians were urged to enrich their presentation of traditional moral teaching with teaching on the Christian way of life drawn from the Scriptures. Essentially this implied that the scriptural teaching was to inform, almost in a Scholastic sense, the development and presentation of moral theology in a way that had not been common at the time of the conciliar statement.

During the first part of the twentieth century the use made of the Scriptures in most Roman Catholic treatises of moral theology found the Scriptures at the periphery of the exposition. To the extent that it was used at all, the Bible was generally introduced into moral theology in one of two ways. Sometimes appeal was made to a scriptural passage, taken out of its biblical context, in order to provide a biblical warrant for or a scriptural confirmation in support of a moral judgment which had been essentially elaborated by means of a merely rational process.[2] Sometimes the Scriptures were used as a principle of organization in the exposition of moral theology. Typically, the commandments of the decalogue were used to provide chapter headings[3] for treatises of moral theology in such a way that the uncritical reader was led to believe that the specific moral injunctives advanced in the text were sanctioned by the word of the Lord.

When the Scriptures were used by moralists in either of these ways the use of the Scriptures did not really enter into the exposition itself. Their use was more like the icing on the cake or the package in which it was to be delivered than an essential ingredient of the cake. In calling for the exposition of moral theology to be more thoroughly nourished by scriptural teaching, the Council Fathers expressed the wish that the scriptural teaching play an essential part in the exposition of moral theology itself.

More profoundly, however, the challenge addressed by the conciliar fathers to moral theologians was one which urged them to think about the nature and task of moral theology. Unfortunately the presentation of moral theology in many of the manuals in use in the early sixties was little more than an analysis of sin in its many forms. This situation was due to the history of the manuals. To a great extent they represented a development of the handbook for confessors, a *genus litterarium* which was a byproduct of the early medieval *libri penitentiales*.[4] Because of this history the manuals of moral theology in common use at the time of the Council typically focused on specific human acts, judged to be sinful, in order to assist penitents to make a confession of "each and all mortal sins . . . and the circumstances which alter the nature of sin" as the Council of Trent required.[5] The common exposition of moral theology in the nineteenth and twentieth centuries was thus oriented toward the sacrament of penance. The manuals of moral theology were prepared for the benefit of future confessors, whose role would also include the formation of the Christian conscience. As such these manuals were individual oriented, act oriented, and sin oriented. To a large extent they lacked the positive thrust of the great medieval *summae* in which a good part of the exposition focused on the theological virtues of faith, hope, and charity. The concentration on individual acts and their sinfulness in the manuals of moral theology was also, to some extent, accentuated by the systematization of theology.

Moral theology was separated from ascetical theology.[6] It was the province of the latter to focus on the Christian way of life, presumably the vocation of a select few Christians.

The Council's call for the more thorough nourishment of moral theology by scriptural teaching in order to "show the nobility of the Christian vocation of the faithful and their obligation to bring forth fruit in charity" implied a radical recasting of moral theology. Rather than focus on sin, moral theology was to focus on charity. Rather than focus on acts, it was to focus on vocation. The Council's call was for a radical renewal of moral theology. It was an appeal for moral theology to be renewed by means of a fresh contact with the scriptural roots of the Christian tradition. If moral theology was to be so renewed, it would once again show forth its continuity with the great medieval treatises on moral theology where charity was clearly presented as the sum and summit of the Christian life.

A significant byproduct of the conciliar appeal for the renewal of moral theology by means of reflection on the scriptural teaching would obviously be the possibility of a truly ecumenical dialogue on ethical issues. In the 1960s there was a great difference between the way in which moral theology was taught in Roman Catholic institutions and the way in which Christian ethics were presented in other Christian schools. Instead of the confession-individual-sin approach found in Roman Catholicism, a gospel-social-virtue approach was highlighted in non-Catholic schools of theology.[7] If Roman Catholic moral theology were to be renewed by means of a return to the Scriptures then ecumenical dialogue on moral issues could be engaged in more easily because a common ground work for moral judgment would have been laid. This common ground would provide a terrain for dialogue, but it would not offer ready-made solutions. The Council Fathers took note of the fact in the very passage in which they formulated their plea for ecumenical dialogue on moral issues. In the Decree on Ecumenism they wrote:

> And if in moral matters there are many Christians who do not always understand the gospel in the same way as Catholics, and do not admit the same solutions for the more difficult problems of modern society, nevertheless they share our desire to cling to Christ's word as the source of Christian virtue and to obey the apostolic command: "Whatever you do in word or in work, do all in the name of the Lord Jesus Christ,

giving thanks to God the Father through him" (Col 3:17). Hence, the ecumenical dialogue could start with discussions concerning the application of the gospel to moral questions.[8]

The ecumenical dialogue on moral issues proceeds from an understanding of the gospel. The conciliar text appropriately noted that many Christians do not always understand the gospel in the same way as Roman Catholics, but it failed to take note of the fact that there is no single understanding of the gospel among non-Catholic Christians. Indeed there is no single understanding of the gospel among Roman Catholic Christians. Nonetheless the conciliar challenge to Catholic biblical scholars was that they should interpret the Scriptures in such a way that the biblical tradition sheds light on the Christian way of life. Within a month's time after their plea for the renewal of moral theology the council fathers urged Catholic exegetes and other students of theology to devote themselves:

> . . . to an exploration and exposition of the divine writings. This should be done in such a way that as many ministers of the divine word as possible will be able effectively to provide the nourishment of the Scriptures for the People of God, thereby enlightening their minds, strengthening their wills, and setting men's hearts on fire with the love of God.[9]

For Catholic biblical scholars, this was an enormous challenge. For years they had oriented their exposition of the Scriptures to the development of Christian doctrine. They were directed in this approach by many magisterial pronouncements which placed the investigation of the Sacred Scriptures in the service of the Church's doctrinal teaching.[10] Only recently had the ecclesial context of their biblical study become such that they were able to approach the Scriptures of both the Old and New Testaments with the tools of the historical critical method in hand.[11] Now, along with their non-Catholic colleagues, Catholic scholars were able to study the Scriptures with the insights provided by form-criticism and redaction-criticism. The freedom to pursue the task of the interpretation of the Scriptures which Catholic biblical scholars then enjoyed brought them into ecumenical dialogue with their colleagues of other Christian traditions. They could be, and were, devoted to the exposition of the meaning of the Scriptural texts in their own right.

Freed from the constraints which forced them to exercise their métier as the servant of the theological disciplines, Catholic exegetes quickly turned their attention to the historical and literary questions whose resolution was necessary for an understanding of the biblical texts. They studied the composition of the texts, the history of the texts, the traditions behind the text, and the meaning of these texts in their respective historical contexts. Yet all that was a far cry from the application of these texts to the Christian life. Exegesis is not biblical theology.

Some Catholic exegetes eschewed the elaboration of a biblical theology as a matter of principle. Still more were reluctant to glean from their exegetical endeavors even a sketch of that scriptural teaching, which would "show the nobility of the Christian vocation of the faithful, and their obligation to bring forth fruit in charity for the life of the world." Yet the challenge which the council fathers addressed to Catholic exegetes was to do just that. Some Catholic exegetes attempted to respond to the challenge, but they were relatively few. Still fewer were the Catholic exegetes who made the attempt in English language publications. Although some major works by German and French language authors (e.g. Schelkle, Schnackenburg, and Spicq)[12] were translated into English, other major works never made their way into English (e.g. Spicq, Lazure).[13]

## SCRIPTURAL TEACHING

There are, to be sure, theoretical and methodological questions of major moment for which some response must be found before the exegetes and/or moral theologians can focus on that "scriptural teaching" which can serve to show forth the nobility of the Christian vocation and highlight the need for the faithful Christian to live a life of charity. The very first question to be posed is what is meant by "scriptural teaching." For the systematic theologian and the Christian ethicist "scriptural teaching" may well represent a univocal concept; for the exegete "scriptural teaching" is at best an equivocal concept, if indeed it is a concept at all. For the exegete, the ambiguity revolves around both terms in the expression. What does "scriptural" mean when the topic is "scriptural teaching"? What does "teaching" mean when the subject under discussion is "scriptural teaching"?

Scripture is an ambiguous term. Quite generally, the term connotes writing that enjoys authority in the religious domain.[14] Among the Christian churches "scripture" has sometimes been used to designate an individual passage in the scriptures; while at other times "scripture" is used for the entire collection of scriptural texts, namely, the Bible itself. Among the various Christian traditions discussion continues to the present day as to which books legitimately comprise the canon of the Scriptures.[15]

If one focuses on a single passage of the Bible as the key to understanding what is meant by "scriptural teaching," the attempt to provide nourishment for the exposition of moral theology by means of scriptural teaching is fraught with difficulties. First of all there arises the possibility of mere proof-texting. In this case the elaboration of moral theology is a datum; scriptural texts are introduced in order to provide one's moral reasoning with scriptural authority, be it divine, prophetic, or apostolic. A current agenda, fixed without reference to the Scriptures, determines the selection of the scriptural texts.

Virtually everyone who has entered into a discussion of moral problems with committed and biblically oriented Christians has had the experience of a single biblical text being quoted out of context as a support for a given moral posture.[16] Some scriptural passages are cited more frequently than others—the Ten Commandments, for example— but one must ask whether the frequency of citation in modern times is an adequate indication of the importance of the dictum in the development and presentation of the biblical tradition itself. Moreover, one must ask whether there exists a real analogy between the situation addressed by the biblical text and the modern context with regard to which it is quoted.

The proof-texting method of dealing with the Scriptures in view of developing "scriptural teaching" highlights another weakness in the single text approach. That is its selectivity.[17] There are, literally, thousands of biblical texts which relate to human conduct, to the type of life that was to be lived in Israel, or to the life style that is appropriate to discipleship. Were one to approach moral theology on the basis of individual scriptural passages which have been collated and organized, the danger is very great that some significant scriptural passages would be omitted from one's process of selection. In the almost unthinkable hypothesis that all of the relevant scriptural passages were collected, there is the danger that in the very process of organization a lesser authority would be accorded to some of them than to others.

On what grounds? To pick and choose from among the biblical texts those that suit one's own fancy is simply to allow the scriptures to tickle one's own fancy.[18]

To the exegete, however, it is the third potential danger that makes it most difficult to develop scriptural teaching on the basis of individual texts. Exegetes prefer the explication of texts to the exposition of biblical teaching precisely because texts must be interpreted in context. The isolation of even a single most significant verse from its scriptural (and historical) context so easily leads to misrepresentation. The primary meaning of the biblical texts is their literal meaning. Literal meaning is much more than the sum total of the dictionary definitions of the several words of a text; the literal meaning of a text has to do with the significance of a text in its historical and literary context.

In this regard, the New Testament scholar will surely note that the sayings of Jesus which are commonly understood to have been taken over by Matthew and Luke from the Q-source have been preserved only within the context of the Gospel format development by Mark. While many of the sayings in the Q-source enjoy a relatively high claim to represent the dicta of the historical Jesus, their present gospel situs is a dramatic reminder that these sayings have acquired meaning within the Christian tradition because they come from the one who died and was raised.[19] Sayings taken from the Q-source enjoy authority within the Christian tradition and have gospel significance precisely because the death and resurrection of Jesus of Nazareth puts them in a new light.

If one begins one's reflection on "scriptural teaching" from the point of view that "the scriptures" comprise the entire Bible, and even if agreement could be reached as to how many books belong to that Bible, the development and diversity of biblical teaching must still be taken into account. Today it is commonly asserted that there are as many biblical theologies as there are books in the Bible.[20] The Christology of Mark is different from the Christology of Matthew, and his Christology is, in turn, different from that of Luke, John, or Paul. Were one to develop a systematic presentation of New Testament Christology, attention to the diversity of New Testament Christologies would certainly require that each New Testament book be accorded sufficient attention in its own right. A harmonized presentation of New Testament Christology does not do justice to the faith witness of any single New Testament author, nor does it do justice to New Testament Christology itself. New Testament Christology is an abstraction; the reality is the several different Christological viewpoints of which the several different New Testament books give respective evidence.

That there exists a similar diversity of viewpoint within the Scriptures with respect to morality must also be acknowledged. This diversity relates both to the composite behavioral profile and to its component parts. The topic of agapeic love might be cited as one example. Agapeic love is a key feature of the New Testament teaching on morality, yet there are different understandings of love evident in the writings of Matthew, Mark, Luke, John, and Paul, not to mention the other authors whose work has been incorporated into the canonical New Testament.[21] A real difference exists between the Johannine teaching on the love of one another and the teaching on the love of enemies contained in Matthew's version of the Sermon on the Mount. Nonetheless, despite some significant differences in insight and presentation, there is essential compatibility between the respective points of view. Indeed on the topic of agapeic love the thought of one New Testament author is essentially compatible with that of the other New Testament authors. When one turns to other ethical topics, that is often not the case. Compatibility is often difficult to obtain; indeed sometimes differences between two points of view can be such as to preclude compatibility. How, for example, does one reconcile Matt 5:32 with Luke 16:18?

Should one attempt a systematic presentation of a specific theme related to moral theology from the biblical perspective, one must take into account not only the diversity of biblical teaching but also the development of that teaching. In his classic criticism of the methodology employed by the authors of the articles in the *Theological Dictionary of the New Testament*,[22] James Barr[23] correctly noted that even the meaning of terms varies considerably from generation to generation. This statement of principle is also applicable to the terms which relate to human behavior. The exegete may not uncritically presume that *porneia* (unchastity) has precisely the same meaning in Acts 15:20 as it does in 1 Thess 4:3.

Beyond the development in the meaning of those terms which have a place in moral discourse, there is also the evolution of moral standards which must be taken into account. A comparison of some of the Pentateuchal traditions about the patriarchs is illustrative in this regard. For example, according to the Yahwistic narrative recounting Abram's sojourn in Egypt (Gen 12:10–30), Abraham lied about the nature of his relationship with Sarah with the result that she entered the pharaoh's harem. In the parallel Elohistic account (Gen 20:1–18) Abraham explains that Sarah is his half-sister. A divine intervention prevents the innocent Abimelech from having sexual intercourse with her. The modification of the tradition was due to Israel's developing moral standards.

The evolution of Israel's moral standards is also reflected in the legal traditions. Comparison of parallel norms occasionally show a change in vocabulary that reflects a more insightful social and moral sensitivity. For example the shift from the use of *sheqer* in Exod 20:16 to the use of *shaw'* in Deut 5:20 in the formulation of the decalogue's "Thou shalt not bear false witness against thy neighbor"[24] indicates that it is not only blatantly perjurious testimony that is harmful to the neighbor but all talk about him that does not convey "the truth, the whole truth, and nothing but the truth."[25]

That such diversity and development exists should not be surprising since the biblical texts were written at various points throughout an entire millennium. Yet, if the exegete who wants to develop "biblical teaching" on a specific theme or subject must take both the diversity and development of biblical teaching into account, the moral theologian who would attempt a comprehensive presentation of the biblical teaching inevitably confronts these factors as major obstacles to a systematic exposition which does justice to the reality of biblical teaching on morality. The underlying difficulty is that each of the books of the Bible is a historical text. Each of its moral statements must be understood within a historical context, if it is to be understood at all. The historical framework within which the biblical traditions were formulated and then committed to writing that makes a simplified systematic presentation of the biblical teaching a virtual impossibility.

Nonetheless we must return to the initial query, namely, the meaning of "biblical teaching." To the exegete the expression seems to come from another age, one in which the scriptures were scrutinized for their doctrinal content. In medieval times the study of the scriptures focused upon their four senses: the literal, the allegorical, the tropological, and the anagogical.[26] The tropological sense yielded the moral teaching of the Scriptures. Since the rise of the historical-critical method of interpretation,[27] whose roots go back to the period of the Enlightenment and even before, the question which the biblical interpreter generally poses to the scriptures is not a doctrinal one. The exegete's question is essentially a historical one. For this reason many practitioners of the art and science of biblical exegesis, including many believing exegetes, simply avoid doing biblical theology altogether.[28]

If it is granted that the interpreter no longer commonly approaches the biblical text from the standpoint of the doctrinal question, it is nonetheless possible for the interpreter to do so. When a biblical scholar approaches the Scriptures with the doctrinal question as the leitmotiv of research he or she must take into immediate consideration the diversity of literary forms within which the biblical message is expressed. Relatively few scriptural pericopes have teaching as such as their principal focus. Only a few passages in the Bible have the literary form of *didache* (teaching). There are many different forms of moral discourse contained in the Scriptures.[29] There are moral commands, and prohibitions. There are laws, the examples of persons, narratives of actions that are judged to be faithful or unfaithful to God's moral will, parables, and allegories. There are paraenetic instructions, proverbial sayings, and community traditions. The different forms within which moral discourse is conveyed imply different modes of scriptural authority with regard to human conduct.[30] The authority of personal example functions in one way, the authority of traditional wisdom in another way, and the authority of explicit command or prohibition in yet another way.

## MORAL THEOLOGY

This reflection leads to still other concerns, namely, those which bear upon the authority of the Scriptures in the exposition of moral theology and the authority of the Scriptures in the process of a Christian's making ethical decisions. To the extent that it is possible to elaborate scriptural teaching in moral matters, to what extent is that teaching normative? How does its authority operate in practice?

These are questions which the ethicist must answer. The moral theologian can legitimately expect the exegete to give a descriptive presentation of "scriptural teaching" in its different forms. The theologian can even expect the exegete to treat of the way that teaching functioned in the life of Israel and/or the earliest Christian communities. The ethicist can expect the exegete to raise the issue of the authority of moral dicta, traditions, and examples in the historical past. However the moral theologian cannot expect the exegete to apply the results of his or her research to moral theology today; neither can the theologian expect the biblical scholar to pronounce on the normativity of the biblical tradition for contemporary ethical decision making. These types of considerations belong to the province of moral theologians.

Some years ago James Gustafson wrote a seminal article on the place of Scripture in Christian ethics.[31] Two distinct foci emerge in the article. One focal point centers on the use of the Scripture in the determination of ethical principles, with their eventual use in the formulation of ethical judgments upon human behavior. The use of the Scriptures in this fashion highlights the biblical texts and traditions insofar as they have a more or less explicitly ethical interest. We might call this the specifically ethical use of the Scriptures.

Gustafson has suggested[32] that the most stringent use of Scripture in this vein, that is, as revealed morality, is had when the actions of persons or groups which violate the moral law revealed in Scripture are judged to be morally wrong. Gustafson has noted that this use is difficult for Christian ethics, implicitly because of the tension between the law and the gospel. One might add that this use is also difficult to manipulate because reliance upon the mere text of a law sometimes overshadows the abiding question of its permanent and/or contemporary validity.

A second use of Scripture as revealed morality is had when the actions of persons and groups which fall short of the moral ideals given in Scripture are judged morally wrong, or at least morally deficient. One can certainly speak of the moral values and the moral ideals to which the Scriptures attest, but there remains the problem of formulating concrete moral norms which promote these values and pursue these ideals.[33]

A third use of Scripture is had when those actions of persons and groups are judged morally wrong because they are similar to actions judged, according to the Scriptural evidence, to be contrary to God's will. Here the crucial issue is that of relevant analogy. The choices made by people in the past may remind us of the choices to be made today, but to what extent are the circumstances of today truly similar to the circumstances about which the biblical authors wrote?

Gustafson's fourth use of the Scriptures in ethical discourse is one which takes into account the variety of literary forms and the difference of historical circumstances in which the ethical material was formulated. It is one in which the Christian community judged the action of persons and groups to be morally wrong, or deficient, on the basis of reflective discourse about present events in the light of appeals to this variety of material as well as to other principles and experiences. In this instance the appeal to the Scriptures is somewhat looser than in the first three cases. Here use is made of the Scriptures because they are one of several elements which can help to clarify the ethical dimension of a given course of action.

This fourth use of the Scriptures in ethical discourse easily leads into Gustafson's second focus on the Scriptures as formative for Christian ethical discourse. In this mode the study of the Scriptures focuses on what God is doing.[34] Attention to the biblical God requires not only that one ask who is this God who acts, it also demands that one ask what kind of things has he said, what kind of things has he done. Attention to what God has done and is doing can provide clues as to how the God-fearing moral agent should act.[35] This mode of using the Scriptures in ethical discourse might be described as the specifically theological use of the Scriptures in moral discourse.

To the extent that Jesus of Nazareth is recognized in faith as the personal embodiment of the revelation of God, the judgments and activities of Jesus can provide clues as to how the Christian moral agent should act. If a biblical text is to be cited in this regard, appeal could be made to the Pauline dictum, "Have this mind among yourselves which is yours in Christ Jesus" (Phil 2:5). This text is almost programmatic for this Christian use of the Scriptures in ethical discourse.

A moralist might well object, however, that proper methodology requires that one first deal with the nature of moral theology and only then proceed to the methodological issue of the use of the Scriptures in moral theology.[36] There are, in fact, different ways of doing ethics, even among Christian ethicists.[37] A first way of proceeding to the formulation of an ethical norm is the deliberative motif, the use of the categories of philosophical thought as a means for stating Christian imperatives. Moral theology in this mode is quite familiar to most Roman Catholic thinkers because it is to this mode that the natural law approach to moral theology essentially belongs. A second ethical mode is one which focuses on the prescriptive motif. It is a matter of concepts of law and application of rules. The casuistic approach to moral theology certainly reflects this mode of elaborating Christian ethics, but so too do Gustafson's suggested first and second uses of Scripture in Christian ethics. A third ethical mode is relational. It focuses upon relationships and situations. A Christian ethic which recalls God's actions in history fits well within this approach to ethics. Indeed the appeal to a contemporary expression of a Jewish or Christian ethos which is implicit in Gustafson's third and fourth uses of the Scriptures in Christian ethics suggests that this third mode of doing ethics is one which provides space for a rather significant use of the Scriptures in Christian ethics.

## CONCLUSION

This rapid review of the principal modes of doing Christian ethics highlights the complexity of the situation of the Roman Catholic ethicist who wishes to respond effectively to the conciliar challenge to nourish moral theology more thoroughly by scriptural teaching in order that "it show the nobility of the Christian vocation and the obligation to bring forth fruit in charity." The challenge which the council Fathers addressed to exegetes was that they provide some elements for that nourishment.

The series of studies which follows does not attempt to offer a full analysis of scriptural teaching on matters of ethical interest. What this volume seeks to provide is an understanding of some ethical themes taken from the Scriptures and the clarification of some biblical texts in their historical context.[38] Hopefully, it might help to make the use of the Scriptures more profitable for Christians and Christian moral theologians who want to appreciate the nobility of the Christian vocation and the consequent obligation to bring forth fruit in charity for the life of the world.

## NOTES

1. *Optatam Totius*, 16. The conciliar Decree on Priestly Formation was promulgated on October 28, 1965. The citation of the text is taken from Walter M. Abbott (ed.), *The Documents of Vatican II* (New York: Guild Press, 1966), p. 452.

2. Essentially this use of the Scriptures is to be found in the work of Bernard Häring, *The Law of Christ*, 3 vols. (Westminster: Newman, 1963, 1964, 1967). At the time of its publication in English, this three-volume work was considered to be an outstanding example of Roman Catholic scholarship in the ethical field. One of its merits was the use of the Scriptures. The importance of the Scriptures is clearly more important in the later volumes than it is in the earlier volumes. Nonetheless

it must be acknowledged that, apart from some significant exceptions (e.g. on the love of neighbor), the use of the Scriptures did not really enter the fabric of the exposition.

3. See, for example, Henry Davis, *Moral and Pastoral Theology.* Volume Two: *Commandments of God, Precepts of the Church* (London: Sheed & Ward, 1935).

4. See Bernard Häring, "Historical Survey of Moral Theology," in *The Law of Christ,* vol. 1, pp. 3–33, especially pp. 15–17.

5. Heinrich Denziger–Adolf Schönmetzer, *Enchiridion Symbolorum definitionum et declarationum de rebus fidei et morum* (34th ed.: Barcelona: Herder, 1967) No. 1707. As background material to the seventh canon on the sacrament of penance (November 25, 1551), one should consult chapter seven of the decree on penance, D.S. 1680.

6. Adolphe Tanquerey's manuals were among the most popular theological manuals of theology in use in the United States. In 1953, for example, Benziger republished the twelfth edition of the second volume of Tanquerey's work on moral theology, even though the thirteenth edition had already been in print for ten years. Among Tanquerery's works are a three-volume *Synopsis theologiae moralis et pastoralis* (Tournai: Desclée, 1931 [Vol. 1: 13th ed.; Vol. 2: 9th ed.] and 1943 [Vol. 3: 10th ed.] and a thousand-page work, *Précis de théologie ascétique et mystique* (11th ed.: Paris, Desclée, 1958), an earlier edition of which was translated into English with the title *The Spiritual Life: A Treatise on Ascetical and Mystical Theology* (2nd ed.: Tournai: Desclée, 1930).

7. My experience as a visiting professor in the Andover Newton Theological School in 1969 provided a personal confirmation of the differences between the two approaches.

8. *Unitatis Redintegratio*, 23. The Decree on Ecumenism was promulgated on November 21, 1964, eleven months prior to the promulgation of the Decree on Priestly Formation (see above, note 1).

9. *Dei Verbum*, 23. The Dogmatic Constitution on Divine Revelation was promulgated on November 18, 1965, not quite one month after the Decree on Priestly Formation.

10. For example, in the encyclical letter *Spiritus Paraclitus*, ostensibly written to commemorate the fifteenth centenary of the death of St. Jerome, Pope Benedict XV stated that "it is from the Bible that we gather confirmations and illustrations of any particular doctrine we wish to defend" (*Spiritus Paraclitus*, 48; September 15, 1920; see Claudia Carlen, ed., *The Papal Encyclicals*, vol. 3: *1903–1939*, Wilmington: McGrath, 1981, p. 188). Even Pope Pius XII, in the very encyclical which served as a Magna Carta for Roman Catholic biblical scholars in recent decades, stated that "they should set forth in particular the theological doctrine in faith and morals of the individual books or texts so that their exposition may not only aid the professors of theology in their explanations and proofs of the dogmas of faith, but may also be of assistance to priests in their presentation of Christian doctrine to the people"

(*Divino Afflante Spiritu*, 24; September 30, 1943; see C. Carlen, ed., *The Papal Encyclicals*, Vol. 4: 1939–1958, p. 71).

11. See not only the aforementioned *Divino Afflante Spiritu* but also *Sancta Mater Ecclesia*, the April 21, 1964, Instruction of the Pontifical Biblical Commission concerning the Historical Truth of the Gospels. On the evolution of the ecclesial context within which Roman Catholic biblical scholars worked, see Raymond F. Collins, *Introduction to the New Testament* (Garden City: Doubleday, 1983) pp. 370–384.

12. Karl Hermann Schelkle, *Theology of the New Testament*. Vol. 3: *Morality* (Collegeville: The Liturgical Press, 1973); Rudolf Schnackenburg, *The Moral Teaching of the New Testament* (Freiburg: Herder, 1965); *Christian Existence in the New Testament*. 2 vols. (Notre Dame: University of Notre Dame Press, 1968); Ceslaus Spicq, *The Trinity and Our Moral Life according to St. Paul* (Westminster: Newman, 1963); *Agape in the New Testament*. 3 vols. (St. Louis: B. Herder Book Co., 1963–1965).

13. Ceslaus Spicq, *Théologie morale du Nouveau Testament*. Etudes bibliques. 2 vols. (Paris: Gabalda, 1965); Noel Lazure, *Les valeurs morales de la théologie johanniques*. Etudes bibliques (Paris: Gabalda, 1965).

14. See David H. Kelsey, *The Uses of Scripture in Recent Theology* (Philadelphia: Fortress, 1975) pp. 89–94.

15. See G.L. Robinson–R.K. Harrison, "Canon of the OT," in Geoffrey W. Bromiley, ed., *The International Standard Bible Encyclopedia*. Vol. 1 (Grand Rapids: Eerdmans, 1979) 591–601, esp. pp. 594–595; James C. Turro, "Canonicity," in Raymond E. Brown, Joseph A. Fitzmyer, Roland E. Murphy, eds., *The Jerome Biblical Commentary* (Englewood Cliffs: Prentice Hall, 1968) 515–534, p. 524.

16. Fundamentalists particularly have a very selective way of choosing and dealing with biblical texts. An example of this highly selective use of the Scriptures is to be found in J. J. Vellenga, "Christianity and the Death Penalty," in Hugo A. Bedau, ed., *The Death Penalty in America* (Garden City: Doubleday, 1964) pp. 123–130.

17. Selectivity is often a matter of the selection of one text with the relative neglect of others. Perhaps even more often it is a matter of the selection of texts bearing on a particular theme or advancing one point of view at the expense of the total witness of the Scriptures. The Roman Catholic Bishops of the United States were widely praised for their issuance of "The Challenge of Peace: God's Promise and Our Response," a pastoral letter on nuclear armament, the final text of which appeared in *Origins* 13 (1983) 1–32. Nonetheless one member of the body of Bishops, Richard Sklba, a biblical scholar, criticised the document because of its selective use of scriptural texts. See Richard Sklba, "Bishops' Open Forum," *Origins* 12 (1982) p. 406.

18. See 2 Tim 4:3.

19. With specific regard to the collection of sayings used by Mark, see Martin Hengel, *Studies in the Gospel of Mark* (London: SCM, 1985) p. 40.

20. On this point see, for example, James D. G. Dunn, *Unity and Diversity in the New Testament: An Inquiry into the Character of Earliest Christianity* (London: SCM, 1977).

21. On this point see, for example, not only the aforementioned work by C. Spicq (above, note 12) but also Victor Paul Furnish, *The Love Command in the New Testament* (Nashville: Abingdon, 1972). Spicq's work retains its value but the reader should be aware that Spicq uncritically mixed subsequent theological reflection and his exegetical analysis.

22. Gerhard Kittel and Gerhard Friedrich, eds., *Theological Dictionary of the New Testament*. 10 vols. (Grand Rapids: Eerdmans, 1964–1974).

23. James Barr, "Some Principles of Kittel's Theological Dictionary," chapter eight of *The Semantics of Biblical Language* (London: Oxford University Press, 1961), pp. 206–262.

24. This catechetical formulation repeats the translation of the commandment found in the Douai-Rheims version of the Bible. This version gives the same translation for Deut 5:20 as it does for Exod 20:16. Although their translations differ somewhat from that of the Douai-Rheims version, the Revised Standard Version, the New English Bible, and the Jerusalem Bible (1966 edition) offer the same translation for Deut 5:20 as they do for Exod 20:16. The New American Bible, however, respects the difference between the Hebrew texts, translating Deut 5:20 as "You shall not bear dishonest witness against your neighbor," and Exod 20:16 as "You shall not bear false witness against your neighbor."

25. See below, essay 2, "The Ten Commandments in Current Perspective."

26. See Henri de Lubac, *Exégèse mediévale: les quatre sens de l'écriture.* 3 vols. (Paris: Aubier, 1959–1964).

27. See chapter two, "Historical Critical Methodology," of my *Introduction to the New Testament*, pages 41–74. The issue of the possibility of biblical theology is a moot question which deserves to be treated in the appropriate forum.

28. See, among others, Brevard Childs, *Biblical Theology in Crisis* (Philadelphia: Westminster, 1970).

29. The significance of this phenomenon is succinctly cited by James M. Gustafson in "The Place of Scripture in Christian Ethics: A Methodological Study," *Interpretation* 24 (1970) 430–455, pp. 431, 444.

30. See David L. Bartlett, *The Shape of Scriptural Authority* (Philadelphia: Fortress, 1983) esp. pp. 11–130.

31. See above, note 29.

32. *Art. cit.*, pp. 439–445.

33. On the formulation of concrete moral norms, see Louis Janssens, "Norms and Priorities in a Love Ethics," *Louvain Studies* 6 (1976–1977) 207–238.

34. See J. Gustafson, *art. cit.*, pp. 439, 445–447, and "Christian Ethics" in Paul Ramsey, ed., *Religion* (Englewood Cliffs: Prentice-Hall, 1965) 285–354, esp. pp. 301–306, 316–320.

35. See, for example, Luke 6:36 "Be merciful, even as your Father is merciful."

36. See, especially, Charles E. Curran and Richard A. McCormick, eds., *The*

*Use of Scripture in Moral Theology*. Readings in Moral Theology, 4 (New York-Ramsey: Paulist, 1984).

37. See Edward LeRoy Long, Jr., *A Survey of Recent Christian Ethics* (New York: Oxford University Press, 1982), especially chapter one, "Norms," pp. 1–46.

38. Modern texts must also be interpreted within their own historical contexts. From today's perspective it is quite clear that the language of some of the essays which follow is manifestly sexist. This is especially true of the older essays in the collection. I would beg the reader's indulgence and ask that the hermeneutic endeavor which is always to be made with regard to biblical texts be applied likewise to my twentieth-century texts.

# PART ONE

## Scripture and Christian Ethics

# 1

# Scripture and the Christian Ethic

THE QUESTION THAT LIES before us for our general consideration is, in fact, a double question. On the one hand, we might well ask, "Is there a Catholic moral theology?" and thereby raise the issue of pluralism in moral theology. On the other hand, we can ask "Is there a Catholic moral theology?" and thereby inquire whether or not there is a specifically religious (i.e., Catholic or Christian) dimension which can be brought to bear upon ethical questions. It is obvious to all of us that there is a factual pluralism in Catholic moral theology.[1] There is not now nor has there ever been a single Catholic moral theology. Not even during those centuries when natural law methodology was enjoying its heyday nor during those more recent times when Catholic moral thinking was largely influenced by magisterial statements and the formulations of Canon Law was there a single Catholic answer to any but the most obvious ethical questions, and even then we were confronted by more moderate opinions, pastoral judgments, the limitation of human freedom, and the subjectivity of the human conscience as the consensus opinion was brought to bear upon a specific case. The recognition of the factual pluralism in Catholic moral theology over the centuries means that a question such as the one I have cited, "Is there a Catholic moral theology?" can yield fruitful dialogue not on the issue of fact, but only on the issue of the value of this pluralism. We might then consider the utility of such pluralism or the relationship between the magisterium and Catholic moral theology.

It is likewise obvious to all of us that the inquiry as to the specifically religious dimension attaching to a Catholic moral theology is one of the most vigorously debated questions in fundamental ethics today. Even a general discussion of this question necessarily involves some consideration of the use to be made of the Scriptures, and more particularly the use to be made of the New Testament Scriptures, by Catholic and other Christians in the formulation of their ethical positions.

For those of us who belong to the Roman Catholic tradition, it is but recently that the issue of the use of the Scriptures in moral theology has become particularly important. For years, the Scriptures — more specifically the decalogue — were used to provide categories within which it was possible to elaborate a moral theology. Alternatively the Scriptures were used to provide proof texts of ethical positions developed on the basis of a natural law methodology. In more recent times, however, we have come to recognize the importance of the Scriptures. Thus, Bernard Häring's *The Law of Christ*, standing at the end of the line of the manual presentation of moral theology, took the cue for its title from Rom 8:2 and attempted to utilize the Scriptures more thoroughly in its presentation of moral theology than did the generations of authors who preceded him. It was, in fact, this turning towards the Scriptures which largely contributed to the renewal of moral theology in the past two decades.

Vatican II's *Optatum Totius* drew from the developing renewal to urge that those who teach moral theology should more thoroughly nourish the scientific exposition of their subject matter by scriptural teaching.[2] On the other hand, *Gaudium et Spes* has reminded us that morality must keep pace with scientific knowledge and an ever-increasing technology.[3] That ethicists, Christian and non-Christian alike, have done so has made the study of ethics something of a challenge in so far as the ethicist is confronted by and must deal with the knowledge explosion in the behavioral sciences, economics, political science, medicine, law, and ever so many other scientific disciplines whose data must necessarily provide some of the information to be weighed by the ethicist as he attempts to do ethics in the modern world. The dialogue between ethics and the sciences is challenging and even difficult at times; nonetheless I think it is safe to say that most ethicists find it easier to incorporate the data furnished by the modern sciences into their ethical reflection than it is to use the insights of the Scriptures.

Those who attempt to use the Scriptures in the doing of Christian ethics inevitably encounter the difficulty that the Bible does not address itself to the great ethical questions of modern man. Even "the problem of war does not allow of a direct solution from the Bible."[4] Much less do the problems of abortion and polygamy, of genetic engineering and *in vitro* fertilization, and the ethical problems related to the establishment of multi-national corporations and world-wide political alliances admit of biblical solutions. The great ethical problems of modern man were unknown to the biblical author; indeed the major issues of social ethics were beyond his comprehension. By and large the vision of the biblical author looked to the rather narrow arena of the relationship between one man and his neighbor. Since, however, the complexity of contemporary society weighs heavily upon the Christian person in his relationships with others, can it be said that the moral norms contained in the Scriptures retain their validity as principles for the Christian person to use in his relationships with his fellows?

Despite this question and the limitations to which I have just pointed, it seems imperative that we raise the question of the relationship between the Scriptures and ethics if we are going to consider the issue of the possibility of a Christian ethic with the breadth which is its due. Indeed, for Catholic ethicists, it is imperative that the relationship between the Scriptures and ethics be considered. Theologians have long spoken of the Scriptures as the norm and source of theology. *Dei Verbum* has proclaimed that the study of the Scriptures is the soul of sacred theology.[5] If little or no use of the Scriptures is made in the doing of moral theology, is it possible to speak of a Catholic moral theology? More generally, given the unique and normative role of the Bible in the Christian tradition, is it possible to speak of a Christian ethic without giving serious consideration to the relationship between the Scriptures and ethics?

Those who are inclined to opt against the possibility of a Christian ethic generally raise the issue of the relationship between the Bible and ethics. Two methodological questions are immediately raised. The first question concerns the way in which Christian ethicists should employ the Scriptures. The second question focuses upon the relationship obtaining between the content of the ethical teaching in the Scriptures and the content of non-biblical ethical teaching. Not finding an answer to the first question which will satisfy Christian ethicists as a group and finding little specific content which is proper to the Judeo-Christian tradition, some ethicists give a negative answer to the question, "Is there a Christian ethic?"

On the other hand, those ethicists who give a positive answer to this question inevitably do so on the basis of a Christology and/or the teachings of Jesus. Such is the point of view adopted by James M. Gustafson[6] and Karl Rahner,[7] among others. These authors, too, must confront the methodological question. Still maintaining that there is indeed a Christian ethic, Professor Gustafson has again raised the issue of the scriptural contribution to the Christian ethic in a recent article by asking a series of questions. He writes: "Is Scripture primarily a resource for theological reflection, and its consequences for ethics through its consequences for theology? Or are there ways in which Scripture has more immediate and direct authority for ethics? How does one choose within the richness of Scripture? Are there themes which are more persistent, and thus have more authority in Christian ethical thinking? What principles govern the use of Scripture by the moral theologian (or theological moralist)?"[8]

These questions are questions which the moralist legitimately addresses to the biblicist. Unfortunately most of the studies on ethics in the Bible do not give an answer to these questions. Rather these studies, many of which are excellent, give a systematic presentation of the content of the Bible's moral teaching. Thus even Karl Hermann Schelkle systematically presents the basic concepts, basic attitudes, objectives and various areas for consideration in the third volume of his *Theology of the New Testament*. Rather than give such a survey or comment on the methodological questions which ethicists raise, I would rather reverse the question and consider how the biblical authors treat ethical issues. Such a consideration should not only shed some light on the factual pluralism of Catholic moral theology, but should also serve as a contribution to the ongoing dialogue centering around the issue "Is there a Catholic and/or Christian ethic?" How, then, do the scriptural authors respond to ethical questions?

## THE SYNOPTICS

A brief consideration of three aspects of the Synoptic problem will help us to discern something of the way in which the Synoptists or the tradition which lies behind them responded to ethical questions. Thus we will treat the Sermon on the Mount (Mt 5:1–8:1), the parables of Jesus, and the great commandment (Mt 22:34–40; Mk 12:28–34; Lk 10:25–28).

Matthew's Sermon on the Mount constitutes the Magna Carta of the Christian Life. Matthew's sermon is roughly parallel to Luke's Sermon on the Plain (Lk 6:20–49), although substantial portions of Matthew's Sermon find their closest parallel in the other sections of Luke's Gospel, notably in chapters 11 and 12. On the other hand, Matthew's sermon does not appear in Mark on whom the Matthean text is dependent. Matthew has, in effect, added to the Markan Gospel "teachings of Jesus" which have come to him from another source. Thus he is able to constitute a lengthy and principally ethical exhortation for the Christian community to which his Gospel is addressed. An analysis of the context of the sermon reveals that it partially replaces the Markan pericope of Jesus in the synagogue of Capernaum (Mk 1:21-28).[9] Mk 1: 21-22 simply states that "on the Sabbath he entered the synagogue and taught. And they were astonished at his teaching, for he taught them as one who had authority, and not as the scribes." Matthew has taken over the passage as the conclusion to the Sermon on the Mount (Mt 7:28b-29), but whereas Mark had failed to give the content of Jesus' teaching, Matthew offers us three chapters of teaching. This teaching is clearly presented as the scribal teaching of Jesus, since Mt 7:29 contrasts Jesus and "their scribes." This scribal teaching is apparently addressed to the crowds,[10] a group whom Matthew distinguishes from the disciples as well as from the Jewish authorities. Demonstrating a favorable attitude towards them, Matthew gives the crowds a prominent place within the universal missionary mandate of the Church.

Thus, when dealing with the extension of the gospel message beyond those to whom Jesus preached during his historical ministry, Matthew is able to offer what he considers to be a Christian ethic, yet he is not restrained by the paradigm of Mark's Gospel which serves as his principal source. For the instruction of his Church, a divided community,[11] he freely adds material that comes to him from another source. This material is presented on the authority of Jesus, the teacher, who has an authority which can be compared to that of the scribes, but which is, in fact, greater than that of the scribes and even greater than that of Moses himself.[12]

But isn't Matthew's additional source the famous "Q" (*Quelle*), which has as much claim to reflect the authentic tradition about Jesus as the Gospel of Mark itself?[13] A quick look at the antitheses of Mt 5: 21-48 offers some valuable insights. Considerations relative to the form, content, and source of these antitheses lead us to divide them into two groups.[14] The first (vv. 21-26), second (vv. 27-30) and fourth antitheses (vv. 33-37) seem to radicalize the demand of the Law; whereas the third (vv. 31-32), fifth (vv. 38-42) and sixth (vv. 43-48) antitheses seem to imply that the Law is no longer valid. Each of the antitheses in the second group have a parallel in Luke, namely, Lk 16:18, 6:29-30, and

6: 27–28, 32–36. This is an indication that they have come to Matthew from the Q-source. Indeed on the basis of the principle of dissimilarity they have some claim to being authentic sayings of Jesus. On the other hand, the antitheses of the first group have no parallel in Luke[15] which leads us to suspect that they have not come to Matthew from his Q-source. The catechetical material which they contain bears the imprint of material found in the Jewish catechism[16] and thus is of questionable authenticity. For our purposes, it is important to note that Matthew of the Jewish Christian catechetical tradition from which he draws has developed a context for this first group of antitheses in which Jesus is featured as the lawgiver, superior to Moses himself. As far as their pertinence for the Christian ethic is concerned, it is not their distinctive content which makes them appropriate to the Sermon on the Mount, but rather the fact that they are cited by Matthew who calls upon Jesus as the one in whose name this catechetical material is promulgated. Material from the Jewish catechetical tradition, taught within that tradition on the basis of its proper authority has been assimilated into Matthew's Christian tradition and been promulgated on the authority of Jesus, the Supreme Lawgiver, who urges radical obedience to the demands of the Law. In a word, what is otherwise ethical for Matthew's Church has become a norm for the life of the disciple of Jesus.

The second group of antitheses has come to Matthew from the tradition of Jesus' sayings contained in Q. Nonetheless the presentation of these sayings in Matthew bears traces of Matthean redaction in so far as each of the sayings is preceded by the introductory *lemma*, "You have heard that it was said," a formula not found in the parallel version of the sayings found in Luke. Thus Matthew has taken over a traditional group of Jesus' logia and inserted them into his own catechetical framework. At the very least this is a change in format; at the most it is a change in form which underscores the authority with which Jesus uttered the ethical statements attributed to him, a point dear to Matthew, the redactor, as Mt 7: 28b–29 clearly indicates.

It is within this second group of antitheses that we find the statement of Jesus' logion on divorce (Mt 5: 31–32). Matthew's version of the logion differs notably from the Q version of the saying (Lk 16: 18), in that Matthew has inserted the famous exception clause: "except on the ground of unchastity" (Mt 5: 32a). There is no doubt that the presence of this clause results from Matthew's redactional activity. On the one hand, the exception is not found in the parallel text of Luke nor is it found in the indirect reference to Jesus' logion found in 1 Cor 7: 10.

On the other hand, a similar exception is found in Matthew's version (Mt 19:3–9) of Mark's conflict story on divorce (Mk 10:2–12). Moreover the literary form of the logion in the Sermon on the Mount, as well as its context, and the literary form of the conflict story militate against the presence of an exception in the tradition lying behind Mt 5:31–32 and 19:3–9. Finally we would note that although there is a difference in the phraseology of the exception clause in 5:32a and 19:9 a similar exception is made in both instances and both focus upon the presence of unchastity (*porneia*) in the wife. Exegetes have long discussed the significance of the exception and this is not the occasion to further extend the debate on the matter. For the purposes of this presentation, it is sufficient to note that Matthew has introduced a "pastoral adaptation" into the tradition of Jesus' logion on divorce. By so doing, Matthew has maintained the common tradition, based on Jesus' authority, according to which fidelity in marriage is an expression of the will of God, but also renders his judgment that in a particular instance some exception to the ideal can be deemed legitimate. Unlike Paul, he does not attribute the exception to his own authority, albeit based on that of the Spirit (1 Cor 7:12, 40b), but to the authority of Jesus. In ethical terms, Matthew has maintained as a formal norm the ideal of fidelity in marriage, but has developed a concrete norm which is in apparent opposition to that otherwise held by the Christian communities of his generation.

Before turning from the divorce pericopes, we should again turn our attention to the Markan conflict story. The Matthean version of the story has no parallel to Mk 10:12, "and if she divorces her husband and marries another, she commits adultery." The absence of this clause from Matthew and the fact that it is not present in the Q version of Jesus' logion on divorce give us every reason to suspect that it did not originally belong to the tradition which Mark had used. In fact, the divorce of a Jew by his wife was unknown to first-century Palestinians. Since, however, the divorce of a husband by his wife was known to the Greco-Roman world, Mark or the tradition which he was following developed the logion of Jesus so that it would be more fully relevant to the Hellenistic world in which the Gospel was preached. In other words, sensitivity to the formal norm of fidelity in marriage to which the concrete norm of Mk 10:11 bears witness led to the development of a new concrete norm (Mk 10:12) so that the formal norm might not lose any of its binding character.

When we turn our attention to the parables of Jesus, we are re-

minded of the words of Charles Dodd who wrote: "the Church, look-
ing for guidance in the teachings of the Lord, would naturally tend
to re-apply and re-interpret His sayings according to the needs of the
new situation; and that in two ways (i) they would tend to give a general and permanent application to sayings originally directed towards
an immediate and particular situation; and (ii) they would tend to give
to sayings which were originally associated with the historical crisis of
the past an application to the expected crisis of the future."[17] For our
purposes, it is the first type of re-application of the parables which gives
some indication as to how the biblical authors approached ethical issues.
The parables of Jesus are the segment of Jesus' teaching which is most
widely accepted as authentic by today's scholars.[18] Yet we might note
that the axiology of the early Church has had its influence on the fashion in which the parables appear in the written gospels. Thus many
writers would speak of the hortatory use of the parables by the Church
in so far as the parable tradition was used to inculcate moral values.
Among the moral values to which the Synoptic tradition of the parables bears witness are fidelity to commitment and authenticity. It is
in terms such as these that contemporary axiologists might speak, but
the appreciation of these values and their relevance for the life of the
Christian was already sensed by the biblical authors. They taught these
values by expanding the tradition of Jesus' parables. A couple of examples will suffice to make the point clear.

    One of the few parables which stands in all three of the Synoptic
gospels is the parable of the sower (Mt 13:1-9; Mk 4:1-9; Lk 8:4-8)
which is accompanied by an interpretation in each of the three Synoptic
accounts (Mt 13:18-23; Mk 4:13-20; Lk 8:11-15). Scholars such as
Jeremias and Linnemann[19] have clearly shown that the interpretation
did not belong to the original strand of the parable tradition. Among
the several arguments which can be cited are the inconsistency of the
interpretation itself—does the seed represent the word (Mk 4:14) or
those who hear the word (Mk 4:15ff)? Moreover, the language of the
parable itself bears the characteristics of translation Greek from an earlier Aramaic version, whereas the interpretation is written in ordinary
Koine Greek. Finally, the language and interest of the interpretation
is largely that of the primitive Church.

    The point made by the appended interpretation is fidelity to the
word of God which has been received. As such it is a religious value
which is expressed by the explanation of the parable. However this re-

ligious value is a specification of the moral value of fidelity to commitment. In its somewhat allegorical interpretation of the parable, ecclesial tradition also alluded to some of the counter-values which can militate against fidelity to commitment, e.g. riches (Mk 4:19). Moreover an appreciation of the value of fidelity to commitment and the necessity of patient perseverance as a quality of fidelity has apparently even led to a change in the parable narrative itself. Mk 4:5b, 6b, and 8b are apparently redactional insertions made to facilitate the hortatory use of the parable preserved in Mark's Gospel.[20] The few additional words are somewhat redundant in the narrative, but point to the importance of perseverance in fidelity, the point explicitly made in the interpretation which follows.

To cite another example of ethical sensitivity impinging on the tradition of the parables, we can refer to the parable of the Pharisee and the publican. This parable is almost as well known as that of the sower even though it stands only in the Gospel of Luke (Lk 18:9–14). The parable shows every evidence of having been conveyed through a period of oral transmission. Its claim to authenticity is very strong in so far as the setting of the parable is clearly Palestinian and the point of the story is at odds with the position generally accepted in the Judaism of the times. The point of the story is that it is the publican rather than the law-abiding Pharisee who is justified. The original conclusion is found in Lk 18:14a, "I tell you, this man went down to his house justified rather than the other." The tradition of the Church added to the original conclusion a moralizing exhortation, "for every one who exalts himself will be humbled, but he who humbles himself will be exalted" (Lk 18:14b). "Thereby the parable received a commonplace ethical meaning which is far removed from its wording."[21] writes Martin Dibelius. In fact the moralizing conclusion is inconsistent with the parable and those who interpret the parable on the basis of the final conclusion present in Luke's text invariably miss the very point of Jesus' parable itself.

The moralizing conclusion ultimately expresses the value of human authenticity. What is most significant to our purposes is that, in both the case of the parable of the sower and the case of the parable of the Pharisee and the publican, tradition has added to a parable of Jesus a moral exhortation which is foreign to the point of the parable itself. In this way the axiology of the early Church receives expression. In this way, too, the values held by the early Church are endowed with a new authority in so far as they are proclaimed as the teaching of Jesus himself.

The third passage to which we can turn our attention is the pericope on the great commandment (Mt 22:34–40; Mk 12:28–34; Lk 10: 25–28). According to the Markan schema, this is the fourth of the Jerusalem conflict stories. According to its literary form, it is a classical example of the conflict story in that (1) the occasion of the story is presented; (2) a question is asked by the opponent(s); and (3) the response of Jesus is given.[22] The question put to Jesus, "Which commandment is the first of all?" must be understood according to its Palestinian setting. Rabbinic tradition sets the number of commandments at 613.[23] Within this context it was not unusual for Jews to ask about the chief commandment. Nor was it unusual for rabbis to summarize the commandments, even if the summary offered varied from rabbi to rabbi.

The Markan version of the story is somewhat longer than its parallels in Matthew and Luke. Moreover it tends to make a point somewhat different[24] from that underscored by each of the other evangelists. Its length is due, on the one hand, to Mark's citation of the *Shema* (Dt 6:4) as the first element of Jesus' response (Mk 12:29), and, on the other hand, to the scribe's acceptance of Jesus' response—an acceptance which merits Jesus' praise (Mk 12:32–34). The emphasis on the oneness of God, recapitulated in the scribe's response, is an indication that the Markan version of this pericope has particular significance within the context of the Christian mission to the Gentile world. The present formulation is directed against Hellenistic polytheism and thus has acquired an apologetic character. The general point of the Markan text, as this is underscored by the scribe's response, is that what is essential to true religion and salvation is the worship of the one true God and obedience to the moral law. That obedience to the moral law is essential to the worship of the one true God and that such obedience is related to the kingdom of God is the key point of Mark's narrative. Thus the moral life is qualified by Mark as having a religious dimension.

However, it should be noted that, strictly speaking, Jesus does not answer the scribe's question. The scribe has asked about the first commandment. In reply Jesus offers both a first and second commandment. In effect the scribe is told that there is no single commandment that can be ranked above the others. The two commandments (Dt 6:5 and Lev 19:18) together are greater than the other commandments. Although Mark tends to separate the two commandments by listing them as first and second, Jesus' response (vv. 30–31) and that of the scribe (v. 33) indicate that the one cannot be placed before the other in the religio-salvific order.

The Matthean and Lukan versions of this pericope are obviously derived from the Markan version. By deleting from and adding to the Markan tradition, each of the other evangelists has somewhat modified the point of the Markan story. Matthew's version reflects Matthew's concern with the law (Mt 22:36, 40). Among the Pharisaic rabbis it was commonly understood that the written and oral Torah together constituted the content of divine revelation and that the individual precepts of both the written and the oral Torah were of equal obligation.[25] Thus for Matthew, the lawyer's question was ultimately concerned with whether Jesus accepted this unitary vision of the Torah. By choosing but two precepts of the Torah, Jesus sets his opinion over against the common interpretation of the Law. Thus we find that in Matthew, unlike Mark and Luke, no agreement of the lawyer with Jesus is reported. While contrasting Jesus with the other interpreters of the Law, Matthew is able to affirm that there is a similarity between the first great commandment and the second great commandment. The double commandment of love is the hermeneutical key to the interpretation of the many precepts of the Law. Matthew does not intend to imply that all moral precepts can be derived from the twofold commandment of love; but that the twofold command of love must serve as the interpretative key of all the norms formulated in the twofold Torah. In a sense, Matthew's Jesus rejects here, as in the Sermon on the Mount, a legalistic approach to the concrete moral norms set down in the Torah.

Luke's version of this incident differs sharply from that of Mark and Matthew in that the focus of the story has been shifted away from the precepts themselves to the person who is confronted by moral demand. This is apparent from the beginning of Luke's account when the question put to Jesus is, "Teacher, what must I *do* to inherit eternal life?" The emphasis on doing rather than on speculating continues through v. 28 and receives illustrative confirmation in the parable of the Good Samaritan with its forceful conclusion. "Go and do likewise" (Lk 10:37). In fact, Luke has taken the Markan tradition and reinterpreted it in a rather personalistic sense. According to Luke's version, the questioning lawyer is already aware of the twofold commandment of love, which is conflated by Luke into a single precept (Lk 10:27).

His question then becomes, "And who is my neighbor?" (v. 29), a formulation which calls for a determination (i.e., limitation) of the concept of neighbor. By offering a parable instead of a legal answer to this question, Luke's Jesus engages the inquisitive lawyer in a concrete situation. As the parable develops, the emphasis seems to lie on the concrete acts of compassion extended to the man who had fallen among robbers. It is his personal needs that must be attended to if the single commandment of love (v. 27) is to receive a faithful response. The legalism implicit in the lawyer's question is broken through still further in the counter-question which concludes the parable, "Which of these three, do you think, proved neighbor to the man who fell among the robbers?" (v. 36). The Lukan response shows that the moral question does not ultimately resolve itself in the formulation of norms to be rigorously adhered to, but by the adoption of a personal attitude in which each man sees himself as a neighbor to others. The focus is no longer upon the law itself but upon the person in relation to another person.

Despite the shift in emphasis which the parable entails, its force is somewhat lost if the religious and Christian context of the entire discussion is overlooked. The introduction to the parable has raised the eschatological question (v. 25), and thus the urgency of the discussion which follows is underscored. The statement of the lawyer (v. 27) prefaces the discussion with the presupposition that the moral life is part of the fabric of the religious life. In a word, there is a religious quality to the ethical quest. When we shift our attention from the introduction to the conclusion of the parable, it becomes quite clear that Luke's Jesus is not simply a teacher who interprets the Law but is one who authoritatively commands that the Law be kept: "Jesus said to him, 'Go and do likewise.'" Luke's vision of Jesus is that of a "sovereign commander"[26] who authoritatively demands of his followers that they live the ethical life in its fullness.

Before moving on to some of the other books of the New Testament, in an attempt to appreciate something of their approach to ethical questions, we might briefly summarize some of the key features of the Synoptists' treatment of ethical questions. First, it appears that each of these evangelists sees the moral life as integral to the Christian life. To follow Jesus is to live ethically. This is so true that the evangelists, particularly Matthew and Luke, present Jesus as the one who commands his followers to live the ethical life. For the disciple of Jesus there is a note of urgency that attaches to the ethical life in that it is related to the kingdom of God and/or eternal life. Secondly, the content of Jesus' ethical teaching, as proposed by each of the Synoptists, does not derive exclusively from Jesus himself. The greater part of that teaching is taken over from the precepts of the Law and Jewish catechetical material. Even the twofold commandment of love derives from the Old Testament, even though it is promulgated anew on the authority of Jesus. Thirdly, formal moral norms seem to be much more significant for the evangelists than concrete norms. It is not that concrete norms are unimportant, but that the evangelists add to or delete from concrete norms as the circumstances warrant. Thus the evangelists attest to a certain pluralism in the solution of concrete moral problems. Finally, there is a decided shift in the solution of ethical problems from reliance upon traditional norms to a more personal response to personal needs. Ultimately this can be seen as true discipleship, i.e., the following of Jesus who ministered to the needs of men rather than limit his actions to those explicitly required according to traditional norms.


## PAUL

Again it might prove useful to study the ethical approach of Paul from several different points of view. We can, as Victor Furnish[27] does, begin with a survey of the sources of Paul's ethical thinking. His review of the Jewish, Hellenistic, and "Christian" sources used by Paul has led to the conclusion that Paul does not hesitate to borrow his material from secular sources, the Old Testament and the tradition of Jesus' sayings. Beyond that Paul's ethical teaching contains material similar to that offered by the rabbis, Jewish apocalyptists, and Hellenistic popular philosophers. Indeed, in his paraenesis, Paul constantly showed himself to be an eclectic. It is the tradition of Jesus' words which he proclaims in 1 Cor 7:10. It is the decalogue which he cites in Rom 13:9. Yet much more frequently he borrows his ethical material from "secular" sources. This is most notable in Phil 4:8: "Finally, brethren, whatever is true, whatever is honorable, whatever is just, whatever is pure, whatever is lovely, whatever is gracious, if there is any excellence, if there is anything worthy of praise, think about these things." None of these terms is specifically Christian and some of them do not appear in any other part of the Pauline corpus, nor even in any other book of the New Testament. It is as if Paul had taken a list of virtues from some philosopher and incorporated it into his text.[28] In any event Paul exhorted the Philippian Christians to pursue those moral values which were counted honorable by men at large.

Even more clearly indicative of the fact that Paul borrowed his ethical material from secular sources is the presence in his letters of the so-called catalogues of vices and virtues. Among the former we can note Rom 1:29-31; 13:13; 1 Cor 5:10-11; 6:9-10; 2 Cor 12:20-21; Gal 5:19-21; Eph 4:31; 5:3-5; and Col 3:5-8. Among the latter we find Gal 5:22-23; Eph 4:2-3; Col 3:12-14. These catalogues are similar to those found in Stoicism and first-century philosophy and may well have their origin in the Stoic-cynic diatribe.[29] In the form in which they are found in Paul, however, these catalogues show lexigraphical similarities with similar catalogues found at Qumran and among the other writings of late Judaism. Thus it is quite legitimate to enter into a debate on the issue of whether Paul borrowed these catalogues directly from the Hellenistic world in which he preached or whether they came to him via the route of Hellenistic Judaism. In either event, Paul essentially incorporated secular ethical materials into his letters. We should take particular note of the fact that catalogues of this type are not limited to one or another of Paul's letters but are found in each of the major Pauline letters.

The use of these secular materials implies that Paul has adopted essentially secular standards as the material out of which his paraenesis is formed. Man's common moral estimation is that which Paul adopts and proposes to his essentially Gentile Christian audience. On occasion Paul cites the judgment of other Christian communities (1 Cor 11:16), but more frequently he cites the moral standards of men at large as a source of reflection for his churches. Thus he chides the church at Corinth for tolerating the presence of evil whose presence would not be tolerated by non-Christians (1 Cor 5:1). The post-Pauline Church followed the example of the master by citing the estimation of men as a standard for the Christian. Thus 1 Tim 3:7 writes of the qualities of the man who aspires to the office of bishop that "he must be well thought of by outsiders."

If Paul employs secular categories as the content of his paraenesis, further attention ought to be paid to the manner in which he uses this material. First of all, we might note that there is a wide diversity in the virtues and vices cited in the different catalogues. Thus the catalogues of vices in the major letters cite some thirty-nine different vices.

Moreover, Paul adds an *et cetera* to the catalogues of vices found in Gal 5:19-21 and Rom 1:29-31. A similar phenomenon is found in Rom 13:9 where the reference to the decalogue concludes with "and any other commandment." It is as if Paul is implying that the moral demand cannot be limited to predetermined categories, no matter how traditional or authoritative they may be. This implies a certain openness in his ethical sensitivity. A similar openness is implicit in his frequent reference to *agape*. The Christian is exhorted to walk in love (Eph 5:2). Love is the fulfillment of the law (Rom 13:10). Love, with its many qualities, should be the moral aim of the Christian (1 Cor 13:1–14:1). Thus, Paul presents *agape* as the norm of the Christian life but does not define its content.

Another characteristic of Paul's use of his "borrowed" ethical material is that it places a heavy emphasis on the community and its needs. The community orientation of the Pauline ethic appears very clearly in those chapters of the first letter to the Corinthians which deal with the Eucharistic celebration and charismatic gifts (1 Cor 11–14). However this community orientation is also present in Paul's presentation of secular ethical material. For example, the lists of vices which appear in his letters contain a heavy preponderance of those social vices which disrupt the life of the community. Thus Rom 1:29-30 cites envy, murder, strife, deceit, gossip, and slander among the vices present in those who do not acknowledge God.

Furthermore, although the letters of Paul occasionally contain a concrete moral norm — e.g., "Pay taxes to whom taxes are due" (Rom 13:7) or "Let the thief no longer steal" (Eph 4:28) — the emphasis of his paraenesis lies on the proclamation of moral value and the presentation of formal norms. Inversely, his tendency is to cite the vices which should have no place in the lives of Christians rather than to cite and condemn specific immoral actions. It is to be granted that this is a matter of emphasis, but it is an interesting emphasis. To some extent the phenomenon is to be explained by the simple fact that Paul is a founder, builder, and leader of congregations. He is an apostle who evangelizes and exhorts his congregation in a general sort of way. However, the Pauline letters are of an occasional nature. They generally respond to the problems of the communities which Paul has evangelized. Yet, whereas he tends to be more specific in dealing with ecclesial problems and the interpretation of his *kerygma*, he tends to speak of ethical matters in a more general and formal manner.

Finally we must turn to a brief consideration of the trait which most sharply distinguishes Paul's use of ethical material from that of his non-Christian contemporaries. This trait is the Christological and soteriological character of Pauline ethics. This characteristic is clearly manifest in Paul's use of a catalogue of vices and a catalogue of virtues in Gal 5:16–25. The entire passage lies within the scope of the great Pauline antithesis between *sarx* and *pneuma*. As is well known the Pauline *sarx* does not so much describe man in his corporality, as it describes man in his creatureliness and proneness to sin. The sarkic man is one who has not yet come under the power of the Spirit of God. Subsequently Paul is able to use a catalogue of vices (vv. 19–21) to describe the condition of man who is still alienated from the power of God's spirit. Idolatry, selfishness, envy and the like are not characteristic of those who are heirs to the kingdom of God. On the other hand, Paul is able to use a catalogue of virtues (vv. 22–23) to describe the condition of those who have received the Spirit. These virtues are so many charisms, or gifts of the Spirit, to those who belong to Christ Jesus. Broadly considered, it is not only ecclesial ministry which is charismatic by nature, but it is also the moral life which is essentially charismatic. For Paul, the gift of the Spirit is the ground of the moral life. This Spirit is, of course, the Spirit of Christ.

Thus far we have not made mention of the household codes found in the late Pauline and post-Pauline literature. Such a code appears in Col 3:18–4:1, which has more developed parallel in Eph 5:21–6:9. Even in the simpler version of this code in Colossians it is service of the Lord which is cited as the principle motivation for the faithful fulfillment of one's duties as a member of a household. "Wives, be subject to your husbands, as is fitting in the Lord. . . . Children, obey your parents in everything, for this pleases the Lord. . . . Slaves, obey in everything . . . in singleness of heart, fearing the Lord." In the middle of this household code, Paul inserts a statement which summarizes to some extent his approach to human responsibility in ethical matters: "Whatever your task, work heartily, as serving the Lord and not men, knowing that from the Lord you will receive the inheritance as your reward; you are serving the Lord Christ" (Col 3:23–24). As Paul consistently makes use of the title Lord (*Kurios*) in this context, it is clear that he understands the moral life to be not so much a response to a traditional mandate coming from the earthly Jesus, but that he would rather understand the moral life as a response in service to the risen Lord.

A variation on this theme appears in Eph 5:2, "And walk in love, as Christ loved us and gave himself up for us, a fragrant offering and service to God." This concludes the paraenesis found in Eph 4:25–5:1. It indicates that Christ is the exemplar of the moral life or more precisely it indicates that Christ's loving sacrifice is the exemplar, ground, authority and norm for the love which should characterize the life of the Christian.[30] Despite the secularity of its content, Paul's ethics are decidedly Christian precisely in so far as Christ can be cited as exemplar, ground, authority and norm of the moral life.[31] This notion receives striking expression in Phil 2:5–11. Few passages in the New Testament have received as much study as the Christological hymn of vv. 6–11. The specific exegesis of the hymn cannot be our concern here. What is of concern to us is that Paul has made use of a pre-Pauline soteriological hymn to ground his ethical appeal.[32] For Paul it is not the human personality of Jesus which is the ground of his ethical appeal. It is not even the mere fact that Jesus is Lord, with the concomitant notions that the Lord is one to whom service is due and that Jesus as Lord is one who will return at the Parousia in his capacity as judge, which ultimately grounds the Pauline ethic. Rather it is the Christosalvific mystery in its entirety that grounds Paul's ethical appeal to the churches. Within this context it should not be overlooked that it is precisely as risen Lord that Jesus the Christ is able to give the vital Spirit who is the enabler of the moral life.

Admittedly this survey of Pauline ethics is all too brief. I have not considered in any detail the content of Paul's ethics,[33] the issue of natural motivation in ethical matters,[34] the question of conscience,[35] the relationship between the sacraments (Baptism and Eucharist) and the ethical life,[36] Pauline mysticism and the significance of the "In Christ" formula,[37] the rich Pauline notion of love,[38] and so very many other significant aspects of Paul's ethics.[39] Each of these justly requires a presentation in themselves and such a presentation would, I suggest, be of value to Catholic ethicists. What I have rather chosen to do is to dwell on those features of the Pauline ethic which indicate that Paul has essentially adopted secular standards — standards that in some instances prove a scandal for the men of our times, particularly when we consider Paul's reflections on the responsibilities "in the Lord" of women and of slaves.[40] He has taken these secular standards and inserted them in a theological context which in fact gives new meaning to the ethical life. That context is the Christ event in its fullness. Finally, we should note that Paul is less inclined to stress the growth of the individual than he is to stress the growth of the community and that he is more inclined to stress moral value (or disvalue) than he is to propose concrete norms.

## JAMES AND JOHN

Before bringing this presentation to a conclusion, it would seem that I ought to address myself to the approach to ethics found in the Letter of James and the Johannine corpus. I do so not only because the names of James and John are linked together by the gospel tradition, but also because they stand at opposite ends of the spectrum when we consider the books of the New Testament. The Gospel of John, in particular, has traditionally been considered the most theological of all the gospels. Christology is its touchstone; and its Christology is certainly among the most sophisticated Christologies of the entire New Testament. Because of its theological character and its Christological emphasis, John is among the least of the books of the New Testament as far as the *quantity* of its ethical content is concerned. On the other hand, the letter of James is among the least theological of the books of the New Testament. Its Christology is so little in evidence that some would doubt its right to belong to the canon and others would doubt its Christian origin. What it does contain is a great quantity of ethical material.

Among the New Testament books James is, in fact, unique precisely by reason of the quantity of ethical material which it contains. It is clearly not a letter, even though the opening verse gives the appearance of a letter. What it reminds us of is not the letters of Paul, but the sermons of Hellenistic literature and the exhortations of some of the Hellenistic Jewish writings. It belongs to the literary genre of paraenesis.[41] As such it is characterized by a thorough-going eclecticism, drawing its materials from many diverse sources. In a sense, the letter of James is almost the *Poor Richard's Almanac* of the first Christian century. Yet to a large degree its content is similar to that of the Sermon on the Mount. It draws from the Old Testament, the Stoics, and the traditions of the sages. Drawing from these different traditions, it contains what Dibelius has rightly called "a conventional ethic."[42] It contains no program for world reform nor does it offer any radically new approach to morality. Its Christian character comes not so much from the fact that the name of Jesus is cited in 1:1 and 2:1 nor from the fact that it is a document which attests to the presence in the early Church of a dispute deriving from a misunderstood Paulinism (Jas 2: 18–26), but from the fact that the expectation of the Parousia is cited as a basic motivation for the practical Christian life (Jas 1:2–4; 12; 5: 7–11). As is the case with most Christian ethics of the New Testament period, eschatology[43] is a significant factor in shaping the form of concrete norms and providing a motivation for the moral life.

If the letter of James can be compared with the other ethical sections of the New Testament by reason of its eclectic content and its theological context, it nonetheless is distinct from other New Testament writings by reason of the quantity of the former and the paucity of the latter. Hence it appears somewhat out of place in the New Testament. From the standpoint of the canon of Scripture, the letter of James stands in a relationship to the rest of the New Testament somewhat analogous to the relationship that exists between the Canticle of Canticles and the Old Testament. The presence of each of these books is somewhat anomalous in the canon. Yet it is this very fact that should hearten moralists. The presence of a book such as that of James in the New Testament attests in a most striking fashion that the moral life is indeed integral to the Christian life. In its singularity the canonical letter of James indicates that the study of ethics is to be ranked as a theological enterprise, despite the particularity of its object and the distinctive quality of its methodology.

As we now turn our attention from the most ethical to the most theological book of the New Testament, the Gospel of John, we are confronted by the fact that the keeping of Jesus' commandments is presented as the means by which Jesus is loved (Jn 14:15). Yet the Gospel of John does not long dwell with explicit attention on the commandments of Jesus. The Gospel speaks to us of moral values, truth, fidelity, friendship, etc.[44] — all of which must be understood in their specifically Johannine sense. Nonetheless, the sole commandment presented *expressis verbis* is the new commandment of Jn 13:34, "A new commandment I give to you, that you love one another; even as I have loved you, that you also love one another." The commandment receives a slightly different qualification in Jn 15:12 where it is described as "my commandment": "This is my commandment, that you love one another as I have loved you." The presence in the Johannine text of two versions of what is essentially the same commandment is part of the great problem of the multiplicity of Johannine sources, and, more specifically, the problem of the two farewell discourses in John (Jn 13-14; Jn 15-17). Each formulation of the commandment must be interpreted within its own context. Thus the new commandment of Jn 13:34 must be related to the footwashing of Jn 13:1-20 and the commandment of 15:12 must be related to the vine and the branches of Jn 15:1-11.

There are four points upon which our attention should rest for a moment as we consider the new commandment of John's Gospel. First of all, it is a matter of a commandment (*entole*). The term reflects the authority of the one who commands. In the circles within which the Johannine tradition was developed the commandment of Jesus recalled the commandments of Deuteronomy, when Yahweh commanded his people. In keeping with the high Christology of the Fourth Gospel it is now Jesus, about to be glorified, who commands his disciples. That Jesus is the one who commands is fully emphasized in Jn 15:12, where the Johannine Jesus speaks of *my* commandment.

Secondly, the commandment of Jesus is a *new* commandment. The commandment which Jesus gives is qualitatively different from those commandments with which it is compared. As a new commandment, it is a commandment that is proper to the eschatological era and is radically different from the commandments of the old dispensation. Thus the Johannine commandment of love cannot be equated with the Synoptic love command. The perspective of the Synoptics is that of the Old Dispensation and the manifold prescriptions of the Torah, from among which Jesus chose the principal commandments. Now we have a new perspective, the reality of the eschaton which has dawned with the ministry of Jesus.

Thirdly, the commandment of Jesus is that his disciples should love one another. Love of those belonging to the Christian brotherhood is the hallmark of the Johannine love command. Indeed the love which the disciples bear for one another should serve as a witness to those who do not belong to the brotherhood: "By this all men will know that you are my disciples, if you have love for one another" (Jn 13:35). The content of the love command is not further spelled out except to the extent that the footwashing pericope gives an indication that this love is a love which manifests itself in service. This fact and the indication that the disciples of Jesus should *love one another* is an indication that the Johannine tradition does not view love as a vague disposition of heart, but that it presents love in its concrete reality. The love which Jesus commands takes the form of service to those who are in close relationship with the disciple of Jesus.

Finally, and most distinctively, the Johannine love command offers Jesus himself as the *exemplar* of love. Thus the Christology which characterizes the entire Gospel also characterizes the Johannine ethic. Christian love as the norm of discipleship (friendship) is a love which is to be patterned after Jesus' own love. His was a love of service; his was a love unto the end. Yet it is not a matter of simply following the example of the historical Jesus, not even to the extent that some glimpse of the historical Jesus can be obtained from the Fourth Gospel. Rather Jesus' love for his disciples is a response to and manifestation of his Father's love for men (Jn 15:9). The contextual relevance of the parable of the vine and the branches is thus clear. The Christian loves because he abides in Jesus and is thereby enabled to love with the very love of the Father himself, for Jesus and the Father are one. In a word, Christian love is a participatory love, of which the human love of Jesus for his disciples is a model and exemplar.


## CONCLUSION

The literature on ethics in the New Testament is quite vast and it has not been my intention to make a summary of this literature in this presentation. Indeed, it would have been both foolhardy and impossible to do so. Nor have I intended to resolve the methodological questions which ethicists raise when they deal with the Scripture and ethics. Just as certainly I have not attempted to give an overview of the content or general characteristics of New Testament ethics. Such overviews are readily available in a much more comprehensive fashion than these few brief pages allow. What I have presented is simply a brief essay on the way that some of the authors of the New Testament books addressed themselves to the ethical issue. Hopefully such an essay can make some small contribution to the ongoing question about the existence or nonexistence of a Christian ethic.

From this rapid survey, it appears that each of the New Testament authors considers ethical teaching as an *integral part of the gospel message*. Each in his own way incorporates ethical content into his work. In a very unique way the presence of the letter of James in the New Testament canon attests to the belief of the patristic Church that ethics is a part of the Christian message considered in its totality.

Secondly, there is an eclecticism that characterizes the New Testament ethic. The sayings of the sages, the ethics of the Stoic philosophers, contemporary ethical standards, the teaching of the rabbis, the Jewish catechism, the texts of the Bible, and the good sense of the New Testament authors each contribute to the content of New Testament ethics. The result is that there is both an *openness* and a *pluralism* in New Testament ethics. Consequently it is not easy to, nor is it legitimate to, reduce the ethical teachings of the New Testament to a single ethical view.

Thirdly, *formal norms* seem to predominate over concrete norms in the ethical teaching of the New Testament authors. The axiology of the different New Testament authors is readily manifest. Nonetheless the New Testament authors are well aware that formal norms can only be implemented by *concrete action*. Thus an occasional concrete norm is introduced into the biblical text. A solution is given to a concrete problem. Concrete examples are given to "flesh out" the formal teaching of the biblical writings. Even the catalogues of vices and virtues which appear in Paul's letters are a literary device used to concretize the ethical demand for the Christian.

Fourthly, *"agapeic love"* is the single thread that links together the ethical teaching of the various New Testament authors. But each of the New Testament authors approaches the matter of love in a different way. The ones show that it must be expressed in action. Others show that it can sum up all ethical norms. Still others propose that it is the gift of the Spirit of God. Love is related to the personal needs of those with whom the Christian comes into contact; thus, love is concretized and personal. Ultimately John will present Jesus himself as the exemplar and more than exemplar, of love as the norm of the Christian life.

Finally, the New Testament authors present their eclectic and somewhat divergent views in a *theological context*. It is this context which makes the ethic of the New Testament a Christian ethic. In summary fashion, it can be said that this context is *Trinitarian*. Ethics are Christian in so far as the living of the ethical life is a way of being a disciple of Jesus. Love is a Christian virtue in so far as it is a matter of loving as Jesus loved. Ethics are Christian in so far as to love as Jesus loved is to respond to the command of the Father and to love with the love of the Father himself. The ethical life is a necessary response to the presence of the kingdom of God among us. This quality underscores the *urgency of the ethical demand* as it relates to the Christian. Moreover it explains why the ethical demand of the New Testament is open-ended. Man's response to the kingdom of God can be no more limited to *a priori* categories than can the kingdom of God itself be so characterized. Finally there is a pneumatic dimension to Christian ethics in so far as the Spirit of God, given to the children of God, is the power wherewith they are enabled to respond to the ethical demand. The Spirit is himself both the gift of power and the source of demand. The command of the Lord Jesus, the presence of the kingdom and the gift of the Spirit are so many ways of saying that there is a Christian motivation for living the ethical life.

In a word, it is this theological context that makes of the New Testament ethic a Christian ethic. Its content is essentially secular, but could we expect more of a God who has chosen to enter into our history and who sent his Son to be one of us?

## NOTES

1. Cf. Charles E. Curran, "The Present State of Catholic Moral Theology," in *Transcendence and Immanence: Reconstruction in the Light of Process Thinking. Festschrift in Honour of Joseph Papin*, ed. by Joseph Armenti, vol. 1 (Saint Meinrad: The Abbey Press, 1972), pp. 13–20, esp. p. 13; Roderick Hindery, "Pluralism in Moral Theology," in *CTSA Proceedings* 28 (1973), 71–94.

2. *Optatum Totius*, 16.

3. *Gaudium et Spes*, 62.

4. Karl H. Shelkle, *Theology of the New Testament*, vol. 3: *Morality* (Collegeville: The Liturgical Press, 1973), p. 235.

5. *Dei Verbum*, 23.

6. Cf. James M. Gustafson, *Christ and the Moral Life* (New York: Harper and Row, 1968).

7. Cf. James F. Bresnehan, "Rahner's Christian Ethics," *America* 123 (1970), 351–4; Jeremy Miller, "Rahner's Approach to Moral Decision Making," *Louvain Studies* 5 (1974–1975), 350–59.

8. James M. Gustafson, "Toward Ecumenical Christian Ethics: Some Brief Suggestions," in *Festschrift in Honour of Joseph Papin*, p. 36.

9. Cf. Frans Neirynck, *Duality in Mark. Contributions to the Study of the Markan Redaction*, Bibliotheca Ephemeridum Theologicarum Lovaniensum XXV (Louvain: Leuven University Press, 1972), pp. 41–2.

10. Cf. Mt 7:28 but compare with Mt 5:1. For a reflection on the significance of the crowds in Matthew, cf. J. D. Kingsbury, *The Parables of Jesus in Matthew 13* (London: SPCK, 1969), p. 27.

11. Cf. William G. Thompson, *Matthew's Advice to a Divided Community, Analecta Biblica*, vol. 44 (Rome: Biblical Institute Press, 1970).

12. Cf. Mt 5:21ff.

13. A paper of this length does not permit an adequate consideration of the use of Q in Mt 5–7, nor of the authenticity of the Q tradition. Some pertinent remarks are given by Vincent Taylor, "The Order of Q," in *New Testament Essays* (London: Epworth Press, 1970), pp. 90–7, esp. pp. 92–3; and "The Original Order of Q," in *ibid*, pp. 95–126, esp. pp. 98–104. Cf. also T. W. Manson, *The Sayings of Jesus* (London: SCM Press, 1950), pp. 15–26.

14. Cf. D. M. Albertz, *Die synoptischen Streitgespräche* (Berlin, 1931).

15. I.e. with the exception of Mt 5:23b–26 for which a parallel can be found in Lk 12:57–59.

16. Cf. Krister Stendahl, *The School of St. Matthew* (Philadelphia: Fortress Press, 1968), p. 137. It may well be that the material contained in the first antithesis and parallel to Lk 12:57–59 was added by Matthew to the material which he had taken over from his source. Thus T. W. Manson is led to conclude that the original form of the first antithesis probably consisted of vv. 21–22a. The Matthean expansion of v. 22a is in keeping with Matthew's style, which often groups material by threes. Cf. Manson, *The Sayings of Jesus*, p. 155.

17. C. H. Dodd, *The Parables of the Kingdom* (London: Fontana, 1961). p. 100.

18. Cf. James M. Robinson, "Jesus' Parables as God Happening," in *Jesus and the Historian (Colwell Festschrift)*, ed. by F. T. Trotter (Philadelphia: Fortress Press, 1968), p. 134; Gunther Bornkamm, *Jesus of Nazareth* (New York: Harper and Row, 1960), p. 69.

19. Cf. Joachim Jeremias, *The Parables of Jesus*, rev. ed. (New York: Scribner, 1963), pp. 77–9; Eta Linnemann, *Jesus of the Parables* (New York: Harper and Row, 1966), pp. 117–9.

20. Cf. John D. Crossan, "The Seed Parables of Jesus," JBL 92 (1973), 244–66, esp. 244–51.

21. Martin Dibelius, *From Tradition to Gospel*, rev. ed. (New York: Scribners, n.d.), p. 253.

22. Cf. Albertz, *Die synoptischen Streitgespräche*, p. 6, who cites the characteristics of the conflict story. According to Rudolf Bultmann, the Markan version belongs more properly to the genre of (rabbinic) scholastic dialogue. Bultmann willingly admits, however, that the Matthean and Lukan versions are conflict stories. Cf. Rudolf Bultmann, *The History of the Synoptic Tradition* (New York: Harper and Row, 1963), p. 22.

23. Cf. Abraham H. Rabinowitz, "The 613 Commandments," in *Encyclopedia Judaica*, vol. 5 (Jerusalem: Macmillan, 1971), pp. 759–83.

24. Cf. Victor P. Furnish, *The Love Command in the New Testament* (Nashville, Abingdon Press, 1972), p. 29.

25. Cf. George F. Moore, *Judaism in the First Centuries of the Christian Era*, vol. 2 (Cambridge: Harvard University Press, 1927), pp. 5–6.

26. Cf. Furnish, *The Love Command in the New Testament*, p. 39.

27. Cf. Victor P. Furnish, *Theology and Ethics in Paul* (Nashville: Abingdon, 1968).

28. Cf. F. W. Beare, *The Epistle to the Philippians BNTC* (London: A & C Black, 1959), p. 148.

29. Cf. S. Wibbing, *Die Tugend- und Lasterkataloge im Neuen Testament und ihre Traditionsgeschichte unter besonderer Berücksichtigung der Qumran-Texte*. Beihefte zur Zeitschrift für die neutestamentliche Wissenschaft, vol. 25 (Berlin: Topelmann, 1959).

30. Cf. Heinrich Schlier, *Der Brief an die Epheser* (Dusseldorf: Patmos-Verlag, 1957), p. 232.

31. In this regard it is interesting to note that it is only in Phil 4:8 that Paul speaks of virtue (*aretē*). It is not the notion of virtue which grounds his ethics, but the notion of the Christian's existence in Christ.

32. Cf. Beare, *The Epistle to the Philippians*, p. 75.

33. Cf. Rudolf Schnackenburg, *The Moral Teaching of the New Testament* (New York: Herder and Herder, 1965), pp. 261–306; etc.

34. Cf. Robert C. Austgen, *Natural Motivation in the Pauline Epistles* (Notre Dame: University of Notre Dame Press, 1966); etc.

35. Cf. C. A. Pierce, *Conscience in the New Testament, SBT*, vol. 15 (London: SCM Press, 1955); M. E. Thrall, "The Pauline Use of *Syneidēsis*," *New Testament Studies* 14, No. 1 (1967), 118–28; etc.

36. Cf. Rudolf Schnackenburg, *Baptism in the Thought of Saint Paul* (New York: Herder and Herder, 1964), pp. 187–96.

37. Cf. Albert Schweitzer, *The Mysticism of Paul the Apostle* (London: A & C Black, 1931); Alfred Wikenhauser, *Pauline Mysticism. Christ in the Mystical Teaching of St. Paul* (New York: Herder and Herder, 1969); etc.

38. Cf. Ceslaus Spicq, *Agape in the New Testament*, vol. 2 (St. Louis: B. Herder Book Company, 1965); etc.

39. Cf. Otto Merk, *Handeln aus Glauben: Die Motivierung der Paulinischem Ethik* (Marburg: N. G. Elwert Verlag, 1968); etc.

40. Cf. W. J. Richardson, "Principle and Context in the Ethics of the Epistle to Philemon," *Interpretation* 22 (1968), 301–16.

41. Cf. Martin Dibelius, *Der Brief des Jakobus, KEK*, vol. 15, 11th ed. (Göttingen: Vandenhoeck & Ruprecht, 1964), p. 19.

42. *Ibid.* p. 71.

43. Cf. C. H. Dodd, *Gospel and Law. The Relation of Faith and Ethics in Early Christianity* (New York: Columbia University Press, 1951), pp. 25–32.

44. Cf. Noël Lazure, *Les Valeurs morales de la théologie johannique, Études Bibliques* (Paris: Gabalda, 1965).

PART TWO

# The Ten Commandments

# 2

# The Ten Commandments
# in Current Perspective

ARE THE TEN COMMANDMENTS relevant to contemporary Christianity and today's world? This is a question which the Christian church has always addressed to itself, and one which it has always answered in the affirmative—but for a variety of different reasons.

For the early Christian community, the key to the issue of the decalogue's relevancy would be found in the memory of the episode of the rich young man (Mk 10:17–22 and par.) and the response offered to that disconcerting question "which is the first of all the commandments?" (Mk 12:28). It was within the context of the ministry of Jesus who had come to complete the Law and the prophets (Mt 5:17) that the early Church found an answer to the question of the relevancy of the ten commandments. The decalogue was relevant because it was a condition of discipleship. It was, however, not self-sufficient because the entire Law and prophets were completed in Jesus. Only in discipleship of Jesus was to be found the completion of the decalogue. In brief, the Church found the key to the decalogue in its basic approach to life.

The question of the relevancy of the ten commandments was again posed by later generations of Christians, by those whose outlook on life and the world was somewhat different from that of their first-century Christian ancestors. When the Christian of the thirteenth century asked the question of the relevance of the ten commandments, he phrased his answer from the standpoint of his world view and his conception of ethics. Rather than speak of the decalogue's relevancy in terms of discipleship, St. Thomas spoke of the relationship between natural law and the commandments of the Old Law. "All the moral precepts belong to the law of nature; but not all in the same way. For there are certain things which the natural reason of every man, of its own accord and at once, judges to be done or not to be done: e.g. 'Honor thy father and thy mother,' and, 'Thou shalt not kill,' 'Thou shalt not steal'; and

49

these belong to the law of nature absolutely.—And there are certain things which, after a more careful consideration, wise men deem obligatory. Such belong to the law of nature, yet so that they need to be inculcated, the wiser teaching the less wise: e.g. 'Rise up before the hoary head,' and 'honor the person of the aged man' (Lv 19:32 and the like).— And there are some things to judge of which, human reason needs Divine instruction, whereby we are taught about the things of God: e.g. 'Thou shalt not make to thyself a graven thing, nor the likeness of anything; Thou shalt not take the name of the Lord thy God in vain'" (Thomas Aquinas, *Summa Theologica*, I–II, 100, 1,c.).

To the conservative Christian of a somewhat fundamentalist inclination the ten commandments are indeed relevant. To him they form the touchstone of the only sound morality in a world whose sense of morality has become somewhat awry. This traditional Christian desires that the moralist turn from the vagaries of his moral speculations and return to the sources—the ten commandments, in strict and traditional interpretation.

To the secular Christian of a somewhat humanistic bent, however, the ten commandments seem somewhat out of touch with today's world and its moral vision. For some, the decalogue is a woefully inadequate formulation of moral demands in today's society. For others, the ten commandments are considered merely moral demands based on a mythical world view and a belief in a "God out there." These Christians desire nothing more than that the Church demythologize its moral formulations and return to the fundamentals—the law of love which Christ gave as the new commandment to his disciples.

That today's secular Christian and today's traditionalist Christian give such sharply divergent responses to the question of the relevancy of the decalogue—a question to which other generations of Christians gave still other answers—leads me to believe that the question of the relevancy of the ten commandments for today's Christian is a question which must be posed in earnest. It is not merely the precepts of the decalogue which are at issue: it is ultimately the entire Christian moral tradition which is at stake.

Moreover, the fathers of the Second Vatican Council urged that the scientific exposition of moral theology be "more thoroughly nourished by scriptural teaching" (*Decree on Priestly Formation*, 16). If the ten commandments themselves have lost their note of authenticity and relevancy, then it is difficult to imagine how moral theology can be nourished by scriptural teaching. Hence I judge the question of the relevancy of the ten commandment's for today's Christian to be a matter of urgency as well as interest.

It is the consideration of human rights which forms the context within which today's ethical decision-making takes place. If the decalogue is to have a message for today's society it will only be because it strikes a chord that harmonizes with the ethos of the day. The familiar "Thou shalt not" of Semitic apodictic law is hardly consonant with today's quest for authentic self-fulfillment. The casuistic formulation of some of the Bible's moral positions is not much better suited to today's thought. A commandment, expressed in absolute and negative terms, hardly appeals to a world of change and relativity in which positive self-fulfillment is the goal to be realized, both on the individual and national levels.

Traditionally the decalogue has been presented as consisting of two tables, one of which contains the commandments relating to God, and the other containing the commandments related to one's neighbor. Although the division is facile and eminently suited to catechesis, it is hardly based on the Scriptures themselves. Dt 4:13 does indeed mention "two tablets of stone" but it might well be that the verse implies that there were two copies of the decalogue rather than two tablets, each of which contained part of the decalogue. The Deuteronomic tradition seems to present the decalogue as covenant prescriptions and it was common, then as now, to make two copies of every contractual agreement, one for each of the contracting parties. Thus it is more than likely that Deuteronomy's reference implies a second copy of the entire decalogue than it does a division of the commandments. Moreover, not a few exegetes have pointed out that the Hebrew text would not easily lend itself to a division between God-directed and neighbor-directed commandments. Neither the present Hebrew text nor any of the several emendations which have been proposed provides for a balanced textual division of the decalogue's commandments into two groups.

Be this as it may, our Roman Catholic tradition dating well into patristic times has promoted a catechesis of the decalogue based on a God-neighbor division of the commandments. Since this is so, it might be well for us to consider the commandments according to the traditional division. This accommodation of tradition will enable me to quickly pass over the complicated issue of the proper division of the "ten" commandments. That there are ten is indisputable (Dt 4:13; 10:4

and Ex 34:28); how the exact breakdown into ten is to be made is still the subject of exegetical interpretation.

My own preference is for a division of the decalogue which makes two commandments of our traditional first commandment and which looks to Ex 20:17 as an indication that our ninth and tenth commandments were but one precept during the early stages of the decalogue tradition. Hence, to combine my exegetical position with our traditional enumeration I will consider the ten commandments as Ia, Ib, II III, IV, V, VI, VII, VIII, and IX–X.

Of these the first four (Ia, Ib, II, III) relate to God and the last six (IV, V, VI, VII, VIII, IX–X) to one's neighbor. Some consideration of each is in order, and I should like to base my thoughts on the Deuteronomic text which, by and large, reflects a later stage of the decalogue tradition.

## Ia

*You shall have no gods except me. You shall not bow down to them or serve them. For I, Yahweh your God, am a jealous God and I punish the father's fault in the sons, the grandsons and the great-grandsons of those who hate me; but I show kindness to thousands of those who love me and keep my commandments* (Dt 5:7, 9–10). This first commandment (Ia) is not an abstract affirmation of monotheism. Rather it imposed a unique demand upon Israel. It required the nation to recognize in its worship its unique relationship with Yahweh. Rather than teaching orthodoxy, it demands orthopraxy. Thus the commandment would be equally at home in a society whose credal formulas were an expression of henotheism as in that later Israelite society which had arrived at a true monotheism.

To twentieth-century man, the acknowledgment of Yahweh's jealousy is a myth to be rejected. To him the thought that man's fault should warrant the punishment of his sons is as cruel as it is subhuman. To ancient Israel, however, the jealousy of Yahweh was an anthropomorphism which pointed to the uniqueness of the relationship between Yahweh and his people. (And is not jealousy today always predicated upon some actual or desired unicity of situation?) Similarly, the traditional formulation of reward and punishment could hardly have been taken literally by Israel after the time of Ezechial and Jeremiah, but it did inculcate the traditional urgency with which Israel felt itself obliged to recognize the uniqueness of its position vis-a-vis Yahweh.

Thus the point of the commandment is that it is urgent and most important that man recognize, in his practice and his worship, the uniqueness of his relationship to Yahweh, his God.

## Ib

*You shall not make yourself a carved image or any likeness of anything in heaven above or on earth beneath or in the waters under the earth* (Dt 5:8). Commandment Ib also bears upon Israel's practice and its liturgical forms, but the point of reference is quite different from that of commandment Ia. If commandment Ia is predicated upon the thought that Yahweh stands in a unique relationship with Israel, commandment Ib says something about Yahweh himself. It implies that Yahweh is a transcendent God, who reveals himself in man's history, when and where he wills.

As a matter of fact, this commandment is best seen against the background of those traditional forms of worship which employ various media as means of contact with the deity. The use of such media indicate that divine-human contact is limited to a prescribed format. The erection of sanctuaries and temples implied the localization and limitation of a deity's power. Israel, of the Deuteronomic tradition, could not countenance such a circumscription of Yahweh's power. Permanent sanctuaries were not to be erected, oracular media were not to be employed, idols (not as substitutes for, but as means of contact with Yahweh) were not to be found within Israel. Why? Because Yahweh was the Lord of history, who revealed himself in human acts, whose revelation followed no predetermined pattern, whose lordship was not restricted to any one locale or any single sanctuary. Thus, by implication, commandment Ib inculcates a belief in the transcendence and utter freedom of Yahweh, the Lord of history.

## II

*You shall not utter the name of Yahweh your God to misuse it, for Yahweh will not leave unpunished the man who utters his name to misuse it* (Dt 5:11). The second commandment is one which is, perhaps of all the commandments, most often misrepresented. The reason is simply that twentieth-century Western man cannot fully appreciate the value which the Semites ascribed to the "name."

The Semites, however, did not look so casually upon the name. To them, the name was intimately linked with the person who bore it. To give a name to an infant was to say something about the infant, perhaps even to determine a program for his life. The biblical narratives on the change of name (Jacob-Israel, Simon-Peter, to mention just two) dramatically indicate the significance of the name for the person. The name was not accidental to the person, it belonged to his essence and his function. It represented the person, almost to the point of being an hypostasis of the person.

Thus, at root, the second commandment inculcates a reverence for the reality of Yahweh himself. Yahweh was the holy one, the totally other, who was not to be implicated in the sin of his people, nor was he to be subject to the volatile will of a single Israelite.

Given the Semitic mystique of the name, the very mention of a name was to implicate the one so named in one's own activity. Since Yahweh was the holy one, he was not to be implicated in those activities related to which Israel might be inclined to utter oath or curse. Yahweh's sovereignty was such that he was not to be fettered by the misplaced invocation of his name; his sanctity was such that he was not to be implicated in the profane and the commonplace.

## III

*Observe the sabbath day and keep it holy, as Yahweh your God has commanded you. For six days you shall labour and do all your work, but the seventh day is a sabbath for Yahweh your God. You shall do no work that day, neither you nor your son nor your daughter nor your servants, men or women, neither your ox nor your donkey nor any of your animals, nor the stranger who lives with you. Thus your servant, man or woman, shall rest as you do. Remember that you were a servant in the land of Egypt, and that Yahweh, your God, brought you out from there with mighty hand and outstretched arm; because of this, Yahweh your God has commanded you to keep the sabbath day.* (Dt 5: 12–15.) This commandment, the longest in both Deuteronomic and Elhoist (Ex 20) versions of the decalogue, is one whose two biblical versions differ significantly from one another. The Exodus version cites the creation motif as the reason for the sabbath rest, whereas the later Deuteronomic version cites the reminiscence of the Exodus event as the reason for the sabbath rest. Each version thus bears witness to the fact that when reasons were to be cited for Israel's moral and social laws, these reasons were always of a religious nation. Why? Because Israel was essentially a religious nation, a theocratic society, which existed by reason of the divine election. Without this election, Israel would simply not exist as a nation and its social and ethical codes would be without substantive foundation.

Thus Israel came to ascribe a religious value to each of its ethical precepts, including that which prescribed rest for all who belonged to the Israelite household (even though the wife is not explicitly mentioned) on the seventh day of the week. Eventually this day of rest, required for social purposes, saw the religious motivation so predominate that the day of rest became a day of cult.

Thus, in the so-called "first table of the Law," there is contained a series of laws which implicitly say something extremely significant about the God-man relationship. They reveal that there is but one God who is significant for man, and that this God reveals himself in his action in man's history. He is a God who is holy and free from human control. What man does, he does as a response to God. It is nonetheless most fitting that man celebrate his relationship with God in worship since worship is a celebration of those acts by which man's existence has come to be valued. The sabbath observance not only provides opportunity for necessary physical rest; it also provides opportunity for the celebration of those divine acts which lie at the source of man's basic dignity and value.


*IV*


With *Honour your father and your mother, as Yahweh your God has commanded you, so that you may have long life and prosper in the land that Yahweh your God gives to you* (Dt 5:16), the so-called "second table of the Law" begins. In traditional catechesis, the precept is generally considered as addressed to children; by extension it is applied to man's attitude towards authority. The catechetical emphasis is undoubtedly misplaced since the decalogue is addressed to the entirety of Israel, rather than to just a segment of its population. A child-directed commandment might well have found its way into a household code in the wisdom literature or in the New Testament; it would not have found a place in a covenant-form code, which served as something of a basic law within Israel.

As a matter of fact, the extended application can well be the more pertinent interpretation. Within Israel of the period during which the decalogue tradition developed, the basic structure of the Israelite society was patriarchal. The basic unity of society was the clan. The family did not consist of a husband and wife with their youngsters, but of a paternal elder with all his progeny. In such a context, honor for the patriarch would imply respect for order and authority within the clan.

Yet each of the more popular interpretations of the fourth commandment may well be slightly off target. The language of the precept does not urge obedience, it urges honor. Moreover it requires that honor be paid not only to a paternal figure, but also to a mother. Such terminology evokes other dicta of the Biblical tradition such as Dt 27:16, "A curse on him who treats his father or mother dishonorably" and all the people shall say "Amen" and Lv 20:9, "Anyone who curses father or mother must die. Since he has cursed his father or mother, his blood shall be on his own head." Such passages indicate that dishonouring one's parents, and specifically with a curse, is a capital crime. That cursing one's parents merits death is understandable, but what form of dishonour could possibly warrant the curse of Dt 27:16?

It may well be that the fourth commandment like the curse of Dt 27:16 envisions the situation in which an Israelite would refuse to give his aged parents the bread necessary for their subsistence or would force them to leave the house. Such a situation would implicitly be the cause of death and would be, therefore, a veritable capital crime. That Israel was obliged to regulate such situations is manifested by the saying of the wise man preserved in Prov 19:26. "He who dispossesses his father and drives out his mother is a son as shameless as depraved."

Thus the fourth commandment would be one which demands support for one's aged parents in lieu of causing their death by non-support or banishment. With this understanding of the precept the balance between crime and punishment, of which the law of talion is the most common expression, and between good deed and reward, so much a part of Israel's ethical perspective, is admirably preserved. He who so honors his parents as to provide a long life for them is to be rewarded by Yahweh with the gift of longevity.

That the commandment is to be so interpreted is further demanded by the New Testament: "For God said: 'Do your duty to your father and mother' and 'Anyone who curses father or mother must be put to death,' But you say, 'If anyone says to his father or mother: "Anything I have that I might have used to help you is dedicated to God," he is rid of his duty to father or mother'" (Mt 15:4–6; par. Mk 7:10–12). The Gospel links the precept on honor with the curse and applies them to the care of one's parents.

Thus the fourth commandment stands rightly at the head of the neighbor-oriented commandments, not so much because it inculcates obedience to societal authority, as because it indicates that human value lies in something other than human function. The temptation was strong in ancient Israel as in other primitive societies to banish or destroy those humans who were not functional, the aged, the weak, the sick, the orphans, etc. With the fourth commandment Israel radically banished the concept of function-based worth. Might one not say that the fourth commandment is based on a view which sees man's worth in his innate and God-related human dignity rather than in his societal or functional value?

## V

*You shall not kill* (Dt 5:17) is a word of Yahweh which the Israelite male could accept with religious reverence even as he entered battle. The demands which the precept placed upon him were, to his mind, consistent with a national ethos which accepted the killing of one's enemies in wartime. Such consistency was easily affirmed since the notion of the sacral war made warfare a religious act and the killing of the enemies of Israel an act sanctioned by Yahweh himself, the living God, who had given the gift of life. Even within the nation itself, the fifth commandment was consistent with the taking of life as a punishment for a capital crime or within the ambit of the laws on vengeance. In a word, "You shall not kill" did not originally convey the idea that all forms of killing were an affront to Yahweh's lordship over life.

Part of the difficulty in understanding the original significance of the precept is that the Hebrew verb cannot be precisely translated by one English verb. The meaning of the Hebrew term is somewhat more restrictive than "kill," and somewhat more extensive than "murder."

We simply don't have a word that fills the bill, but the Hebrews did, and it was this word which appears in the decalogue.

As a matter of fact, the commandment prohibits not only murder but accidental homicide. Thus the point of the precept is clear enough: the faithful Israelite is prohibited from taking unto himself the right of life or death over a fellow Israelite. The commandment expressly forbids all forms of taking of life which are not sanctioned by the religious-social code of behavior within Israel.

Thus the positive value which the precept seeks to protect is man's right to life, a right which must be protected, but not at the expense of society's need to protect itself nor of Yahweh's claims over human life. The fact that the commandment prohibits even the accidental taking of life indicates that it is directed more towards the protection of Israelite life than it is to the exclusion of certain limited forms of human behavior.

## VI

*You shall not commit adultery* (Dt 5:18) is undoubtedly one of the most intelligible of the commandments. Its significance is best appreciated when it is interpreted rather restrictively than generically. What the commandment forbade in biblical times was sexual intercourse between a man and a married woman. The Hebrew male did not sin against his own marriage by his extramarital sexual activity; rather he sinned against the marriage of another Israelite. Thus the commandment did not forbid a sexual liaison between an Israelite and a woman taken in war or a prostitute. In these cases there was no aggrieved spouse whose marriage had been violated by what we would call sexual misconduct.

To this extent Israel viewed the sin of adultery in much the same way that Roman law considered the crime of adultery. Yet the commandment was particularly significant in that it indicated that the whole sphere of sexual activity and family was subject to regulation by Yahweh's instruction. The nature of its application within Israel was such, however, that it makes us realize that the Israelites considered their sexual ethic in a much more relational manner than do we. Sexual misconduct was not so much a matter of being "unchaste" (in the abstract) as it was a manner of violating relationships upon which certain be-havioral demands were predicated.

At any rate, the positive content of the commandment is respect for the marriage of another man. Marriage, so sacred in ancient Israel because it was the means by which the blessing of Abraham was made effective, was the positive value which lay behind the sixth precept of the decalogue.


## VII


*You shall not steal* (Dt 5:19) contains a verb which was rarely fol-lowed by a physical object. Moreover were the commandment merely a prohibition of theft, it would make the tenth commandment (IX–X) virtually redundant. It is this latter commandment, as we shall see, which prohibits stealing.

What, then, can be the significance of the seventh commandment? Inserted as it is among those "words of Yahweh" which are concerned with the relationships among the Israelites, it might be conjectured that the commandment pertains to a human relationship. The conjecture proves to be more than mere conjecture when it is determined that the verb of the Hebrew text is one which is normally followed by a human object. So strong is the connotation of the verb that not a few scholars have reconstructed the precept to read "Thou shalt not steal a man or a woman," "Thou shalt not steal any man from thy neighbor," or some-thing of this order.

Although a precise textual emendation is a matter of scholarly con-jecture, the exegesis which it implies is quite solid. What the seventh commandment forbids is nothing other than kidnapping the free Israel-ite. The kidnapping of a free man was sufficiently commonplace to be featured in the Joseph story of the patriarchal saga (Gen 37). Kidnap-ping was, moreover, so much a real possibility within Israel that it was made the object of a special prohibition in the Book of the Covenant: "Anyone who abducts a man—whether he has sold him or is found in possession of him—must die" (Ex 21:16), a precept which the Deu-teronomic reform was quick to reiterate (Dt 24:7).

The human value upon which the commandment is based is quite obviously the value of human freedom. Man's right to be free was so sacred in Israel that its protection was mandated by Yahweh; and supported by other elements of the Torahitic teaching.

## VIII

*"You shall not bear false witness against your neighbor"* (Dt 5:20) is a commandment whose original significance can be appreciated only against the background of Israelite jurisprudence. The administration of justice lay within the hands of every male Israelite since all could be called upon to give testimony, and the elders of an Israelite village served as judges. The trial of the accused was conducted at the gates of the town. Since the sentence was immediately executed, there was no appeal from a punitive judgment in a capital case. Since the accused was presumed guilty upon the testimony of two witnesses, the testimony of the witnesses was of great importance.

It is this primitive legal system which gives to "You shall not bear false witness against your neighbor" its original significance and intense urgency. The burden of the precept is to ensure that no Israelite be subject to a false judgment due to erring testimony about himself. That this is so is vividly revealed by a comparison of the two versions of this precept which appear in the biblical text. Unfortunately most of the common English translations of Ex 20:16 and Dt 5:20 do not reflect a very significant refinement of meaning introduced by the choice of a different term in the more recent Deuteronomic text. The earlier text employed a noun whose strict connotation was "lying." Thus the situation was created in which an ingenious and clever witness could inflict an injustice upon his neighbor without rebelling against the word of Yahweh — simply by irrelevant testimony and trite remarks which could not be construed as "lies" in the strict sense. Thus he could convince himself that he would escape Yahweh's judgment even if he were the source of a condemnatory judgment upon his neighbor. The later text sought to protect the rights of the accused more fully by obviating such devious attempts to circumvent the law of Yahweh. Thus the Deuteronomic text employed a term whose more common meaning was "evil, wickedness, vanity, worthlessness." It was broad enough to include the telling of lies, but also provided a condemnation of other forms of devious testimony.

The refinement of the law protected the value which lay at the basis of the word of Yahweh, namely, the rights of the Israelite to his reputation and autonomy. That these rights were in danger of peril in the trials at the town gate is graphically illustrated by the Old Testament story of Jezreel and Naboth (1 Kgs 21:8–16). The false testimony which was uttered against Naboth at the order of the wicked queen was nothing other than a means to murder the innocent and usurp his property rights.

### IX–X

To speak of property rights is, however, to speak of the tenth word of Yahweh: *You shall not covet your neighbor's wife, you shall not set your heart on his house, his field, his servant — man or woman — his ox, his donkey, or anything that is his.* (Dt 5:21.)

A comparison of this "word of Yahweh" with the earlier version of Ex 20:17 shows traces of a significant development. The neighbor's "wife" now assumes the first place among the properties over which he exercised lordship. Indeed, the author of Deuteronomy bore further witness to the singular significance of woman among man's possessions by employing one verb, "covet" (the verb used by the Elohist author of Exodus), with reference to the neighbor's wife, and another verb, "to set one's heart on," with reference to the rest of the neighbor's property.

Yet, the precept does not have the narrow, restrictive meaning that our English text would seem to imply. By no means does it specifically and exclusively prohibit sins of the mind, sins of thought and desire. To the Semitic mind merely internal realities are nonentities. His epistemology was of the concrete. Something unseen was real to the extent that it became externalized. It is true that the heart was the core element in moral or immoral action, but the significant point is that the heart produced results according to its goodness or badness. The merely internal was really a non-category for ancient Israel. The reality of the immaterial is affirmed only within the framework of those philosophies which have a dichotomous view of the human reality. Israel's philosophy was not one of these.

What is thus prohibited by the tenth commandment is the usurpation of what belongs to another, whether this be his wife or his house (tent), his donkey or anything else that is his. Yet to give proper thrust

to the biblical text, it might be noted that the language of the Hebrew
text encompasses within the scope of the precept not only the theft
itself but all the intrigue which preceded the act of theft and which
is part of the act in its fullest human reality. Thus the precept is concerned with the world of thought, but only insofar as this world of
thought becomes externalized in the world of act.

Negatively, therefore, the last of the commandments prohibits
theft; positively it inculcates a respect for the property rights of another.

## CONCLUSION

Within these words of Yahweh spoken "when all were assembled
on the mountain" there is thus contained a primitive but very realistic
teaching on human values. The last five commandments point to the
value of human life, family, freedom, justice, and property. Given the
Semitic penchant for placing the more significant item at the head of
a listing, it is quite legitimate to look to each of these five as being
valued by ancient Israel in proportionate fashion. First in the hierarchy
of values comes man's life, then his family, his freedom, justice, and
in the last place, his property.

Should the interpretation of the commandments focus more on
the values which they protect than upon the negative prohibitions, one
might well say that the second table of the decalogue implicitly contains a bill of rights which even twentieth-century man can proclaim.
The final precepts protect man's right to life, family, liberty, justice,
and property. It is, moreover, indeed noteworthy that ancient Israel which
considered "peace" (*shalom*) as the content of Yahweh's beneficence but
which described it chiefly in terms of material prosperity would give
to man's right to personal property a place subordinate to the more fundamental and inalienable human rights.

If the last five words of Yahweh contained in the decalogue implicitly contain a bill of rights, the first five words of Yahweh provide
the context within which this bill of rights becomes fully meaningful.
The fourth commandment graphically reminds us that man's rights are
not based on his utilitarian value. The precept resolutely eschews such
pragmatism. It points to something other than function as the basis
of human rights, and it might be suggested that this something other

is human life itself, which the man of biblical faith considers as the gift of the living God.

Thus man's awareness of his own rights and those of others should incline him to think of the living God whose relationship to man constitutes the foundation and source of his rights. The God from whom man's living reality derives has an ontic, and historical precedence over man. Thus the decalogue would not be entirely consistent if it did not consider first the nature of man's relationship with Yahweh, the living God, before it pointed to those rights which accrue to man in relationship with the living God.

Man exists in a unique relationship to Yahweh God, who is sovereign and free, who reveals himself in man's history, whose very person is to be honored and respected by man, not only or especially by cult, but by the way man acts and the way he treats his fellow man. The third commandment ultimately places man's action and interaction with others within the framework of response to the God of creation and salvation.

Thus the decalogue proclaims that man's rights are founded upon his relationship to Yahweh. His respect for the rights of others is his response to the living God, the God of creation and salvation. Such is the context within which ancient Israel declared its "bill of rights," the second table of the decalogue, as valid for man come of age as it was for the nation of promise.

# 3

# The Ten Commandments and
# the Christian Response

IN THE PREVIOUS ESSAY[1] I attempted to put the Ten Commandments in the perspective of the times in which they were first formulated and in the perspective in which we ought to understand them today. It would seem, however, that the Ten Commandments ought also to be examined from the standpoint of New Testament faith to determine whether or not they retain validity as a norm of morality for the Christian.

Surprisingly enough, there are more explicit references to the Ten Commandments in the New Testament than in the Old,[2] even though the latter is almost four times as long as the former. Of the seven New Testament passages which cite the Ten Commandments, three are in the Gospels and four in the Epistles: namely, the second section of the Sermon on the Mount (Mt 5:17–48), the dispute with the Scribes and Pharisees over ritual purification (Mt 15:1–9; Mk 7:1–13), Jesus' conversation with the rich young ruler (Mt 19:16–30; Mk 10:17–31; Lk 18:18–30), Paul's reflection on the function of the Law (Rom 7: 7–12), his presentation of the relationship between law and love (Rom 13:8–10), a section of the household code in the letter to the Ephesians (Eph 6: 1–4), and James' exposition of the fulfillment of the royal law (Jas 2:8–13).

In addition to these explicit references, a limited number of allusions to the Ten Commandments can be discerned in the New Testament. Thus in his narrative of what constitutes impurity, Matthew has reworked Mark's catalogue of a dozen vices (Mt 15:19; Mk 7:21) so that it bears a trace of the ordering of the Ten Commandments.[3] Luke's description of the visit of the women to Jesus' tomb mentions that they were careful to observe the requirements of the third commandment (Lk 23:56).[4] Apart from the Sabbath controversies,[5] the only Johannine allusion to the Ten Commandments is probably Jn 7:23. Paul's letters also contain some allusive references to the Ten Commandments. His

64

condemnation of the Jews who had violated the Law which had been given to them contains a reference to the sixth and seventh commandments (Rom 2: 21–22). Then in Col 3: 20, because of its similarity with Eph 6: 1–2,[6] we can find a reference to the fourth commandment. Beyond this, there are several sabbath controversies in the Synoptics,[7] and Paul's inclusion of disobedience among the vices,[8] but these are not directly related to the Ten Commandments.

A rapid overview of the New Testament's explicit references to the Ten Commandments leads to two significant conclusions. First of all, all the references are to the so-called Second Table of the Law. Each of the seven commandments dealing with man's relationship with his neighbor is cited in the New Testament, but the First Table of the Law, comprising the first three commandments, is not cited at all. Some commentators have suggested that the reason for this omission is to be found in the fact that the commandments ordering man's relationship to God were so obvious there was little need for Jesus to reiterate them. A much more likely explanation is that the written Gospels emanate from a time when the rupture between Church and Synagogue had become complete, so that the relationship between the Christian and the Father was no longer defined according to the First Table of the Law, understood in the manner of Jewish tradition. The moral responsibility of the Christian remained, however, no less serious than it was for those who still took part in a synagogue service.

Secondly, the New Testament passages which have been cited indicate that the Decalogue was considered as a consistent unit by the Christian churches. There are several indications to this effect. Mk 10: 19 offers as Jesus' response to his interlocutor the entire Second Table of the Law, combining the ninth and tenth commandments within a single injunction, "You must not defraud" (*mē apoterēsēs*).[9] Such a combination is in accordance with the primitive Old Testament tradition and the meaning of the expression chosen by Mark to complete the listing of the commandments well concurs with the original sense of the biblical precept. Secondly, Jas 2: 11 indicates that the binding force of the Law is to be considered as a unitary binding force. A man is guilty of breaking the entire Law if he has broken just one of its commandments, as, for instance, the fifth or the sixth commandment. Thirdly, Paul's exhortation to sons and daughters in Eph 6: 2 indicates that the fourth commandment cannot be dissociated from the context within which it has been handed down. It is the *first* commandment that has a promise attached to it. Finally, the order in which the Ten Commandments are listed throughout the New Testament indicates that the early Church did not consider these precepts as so many isolated injunctions but as an integral series.

It is, however, precisely this point which is troublesome. If Mk 10:19 offers the New Testament's most complete listing of the Ten Commandments in the New Testament, it follows an order to which we are not accustomed. The Second Gospel lists the commandments in the following order: V, VI, VII, VIII, IX–X, IV.[10] The parallel passage in Luke (Lk 18:20, Greek) lists the commandments in a different order, viz., VI, V, VII, VIII, IV. This second ordering of the commandments seems to underlie Jas 2:11. At any rate it is clearly found in Rom 13:9 which adds the ninth-tenth commandment, but omits the fourth.[11] Matthew (Mt 19:18) has followed the same order as Mark, but after the fourth commandment he adds Lv 19:18: "You must love your neighbor as yourself." The Matthean passage is the only New Testament witness to append this passage from the Code of Holiness (Lv 17–26) to the Ten Commandments, but both Paul (Rom 13:9) and James (Jas 2:8) introduce the "love your neighbor" precept into the context in which they treat the Ten Commandments.

The place of the fourth commandment after the eighth, found in all three Synoptics, is in accordance with Jewish catechetical tradition.[12] So also is the juxtaposition of Lv 19:18 and the Decalogue. Within Judaism, the Holiness Code was the main source of catechetical tradition. Thus it was not strange for Jewish teachers to combine other passages of the Old Testament, particularly a passage such as the second part of the Decalogue, with the Law of Holiness. In effect, the New Testament's use of the Ten Commandments seems to be a borrowing from Jewish catechetical practice.[13]

Other facts support this contention. First of all, the rich young ruler to whom Jesus quoted the Ten Commandments addressed Jesus as "Teacher" (Mt 19:16; Mk 10:17; Lk 18:18). In the first Gospel, the disciples of Jesus never call him "Teacher." Jesus is addressed as "Teacher" when he is called upon to make a rabbinic judgment (Mt 19:16, 22:16, 24:36). Jesus is described as a teacher in those passages in which he offers a rabbinic-type Scriptural response to a leading question addressed to his disciples (Mt 9:11; 17:24). Thus the very title by which the rich young ruler addressed Jesus indicates that we are dealing with a school setting. Similarly, Paul's allusion to the Ten Command-

ments in Rom 2: 21–22 indicates that memory of the Ten Commandments within the Christian Church was the memory of catechetical
material taught by Jewish teachers.

It is most probably this fact, that we are dealing with borrowed
Jewish catechetical material,[14] which explains the strange order of the
commandments in Lk 18: 20, Rom 13: 9, Jas 2: 11 and some manuscripts
of Mk 10: 19. The VI-V-VII-VIII ordering is found in many Jewish cate-
chisms. It even found its way into some Septuagint manuscripts of the
Ten Commandments.[15] This strange order is not, however, found in
Matthew. Undoubtedly, in his reworking of the dialogue, the evangelist conformed his material to the biblical texts. Thus Mt 19: 18 retains
the familiar order, that of the Hebrew text of the Old Testament and
the Palestinian manuscripts of the LXX.[16]

A reading of the New Testament's "Ten Commandments Passages"
draws attention to another feature of the early Church's use and understanding of the Ten Commandments. The precepts of the Second Table
of the Law are called "commandments" (entolai). In all three Synoptic
narratives of Jesus' conversation with the rich young ruler, the first phase
of the dialogue centered upon the "commandments" (Mt 19: 17; Mk
10: 19; Lk 18: 20). Obviously the term had a point of reference wider
than the seven commandments of the Second Table — wider even than
the Ten Commandments themselves. The young man's question indicates that Jesus' reply is one which offers a selection from among the
many precepts which can be called "commandments." Furthermore, there
are other bits of Old Testament legislation that are called commandments in the New Testament.[17] Nonetheless, despite its broad use, the
designation "commandments" for the precepts of the Decalogue is highly
significant. Of itself the term was not a religious one and covered a
whole range of meanings. However a rich Old Testament tradition lies
behind the use of the term. It was regularly used of an authoritative
command and, according to the tone set by the Deuteronomist, was
most especially used to designate divine ordinances. Thus when the
early Church continued to describe the ten precepts of the Second Table
of the Law as "commandments," it was doing more than adopting a
vapid epithet. It was indicating that the Ten Commandments were to
be considered as divine commands.

This impression is borne out by other New Testament passages.
Once again Jesus' dialogue with the rich young ruler is particularly in-
formative. The interlocutor had asked "What must I do to gain eternal

life?" It was a typical question in late Judaism which looked upon the life-to-come as a reward for the faithful accomplishment of human effort. Jesus' reply put the question in a context which was properly religious. He set the discussion against the horizon of the God who alone was good (Mt 19:17; Mk 10:18; Lk 18:19). Man's moral responsibility cannot be separated from his religious response. His destiny must be seen against the horizon of the Absolute and Unconditional.

This same attitude is evidenced in a variety of other ways. In the discussion about the traditions of the Pharisees, the fourth commandment is clearly labeled as "the commandment of God" (*hē entolē tou theou*) by Matthew and Mark. This sets up the tension between what is God's command and what is human tradition (Mk 7:8), a tension somewhat mitigated in Matthew's version of the incident. Yet the divine authority on which the commandment is based is also underscored by Matthew who introduces the commandment with the pregnant formula "God said" (Mt 15:4).[18] An earlier tradition, retained by Mark, had cited the commandment as a pronouncement of Moses (Mk 7:10).

Again it is Matthew who casts the Ten Commandments in the framework of divine pronouncement in the second section of the Sermon on the Mount. Instead of using the prophetic "God says," Matthew introduces the fifth and sixth commandments with the periphrastic "You have learnt how it was said to our ancestors" (Mt 5:21, 27).[19] The use of the third person passive form of the verb was a frequent Judaic periphrasis to avoid the name of God — one with which Christian tradition remains familiar because of the first petitions of the Lord's Prayer. "The ancestors" are most probably the generation that stood on Sinai.[20] For Matthew's Judaic readers there was no mistaking the import of his statement. God has spoken on Sinai; his authority was behind the fifth and sixth commandments.

The introductory lemma, "you have learnt how it was said to our ancestors," occurs a third time[21] in the Sermon on the Mount, namely to introduce "You must not break your oath, but must fulfill your oaths to the Lord" (Mt 5:33). The passage cited from the Torah is Lv 19:12. Once again a citation from the Holiness Code is used to fill out the Ten Commandments. This fact ought to serve as a confirmation that the early, Palestinian, church preserved the memory of the Ten Commandments within the context of catechetical material taken over from Judaism. Moreover, the formula "you have learnt" frequently means "you have received as tradition."²² The school setting and presentation of catechetical materials is never far removed from the New Testament's use of the Ten Commandments.

Hence another resonance of the designation "commandment" should not be overlooked as we attempt to share the early Christian's understanding of the Ten Commandments. The "commandment" (*entolē*) frequently connoted "instruction." Philo was tolerant of "commandments" because the immature and uneducated need admonition and instruction.²³ The Stoics looked to an ethic of "commandment" as a primitive form of morality. For the early Christians the Ten Commandments were a source of instructional or catechetical material. In the one word "commandment" they were able to indicate not only that divine authority grounded the Ten Commandments but also that these were a traditional source of catechetical material.

Thus far, it has been shown that 1) the early Church looked to the Second Table of the Law as the formulation of moral obligations that were incumbent upon Christians; 2) that the Church took over this material from Judaism and transmitted it in accordance with accepted Jewish catechetical practices; and 3) that it shared with Judaism the idea that these seven commandments expressed the will of God. Does this mean that the early Church accepted these commandments in the same way that Judaism did? Does the early Church's acceptance of these commandments rest on a tradition going back to Jesus? If so, does this mean that Jesus looked upon the Ten Commandments as did the rabbis of his day? To ask these questions is to raise the issue of the early Church's attitude towards the Decalogue which it had received from the Old Testament via Judaism. To answer these questions is to examine more closely the pericopes in which the New Testament deals with the Ten Commandments.

## THE SYNOPTICS

The first passage to be considered is that concerning the "rich young ruler" (Mt 19:16–30; Mk 10:17–31; Lk 18:18–30). The title is really a composite one. From Mark we learn that he was rich; from Matthew that he was young, and from Luke that he was a scion of a leading family, a magistrate, or a member of the local sanhedrin. Apart from

Matthew's thought about the call to perfection and the ordering of the commandments, the differences among the three narratives are not of particular interest for our concern.

All three give a portrayal of the incident that is true to life. The life situation is clearly that of late Judaism. Even Matthew's narrative of a second question posed by the interlocutor, "What more must I do?" (Mt 19:20) conforms to the pattern of rabbinic inquiry. In the rabbinic *halacha*, the determination of man's "ought" with respect to the kingdom of God or eternal life was a primary concern. The question "what must be done?" was posed within the context of a "*do ut des*," retributive form of justice. Moreover the rabbis compiled lists of supererogatory works which would merit a special reward in the world to come.[24] They sought to determine what had to be done to avoid even the trace of unhappiness in the future eon.[25] The underlying assumption was that man could do all that was commanded in the Torah.[26]

In his response to the question(s) of the rich young ruler, Jesus reiterates the Judaic tradition that the fulfillment of the Second Table of the Law is obligatory. He does not take issue with the contention that it is possible to fulfill these precepts. On the other hand, Jesus affirms that discipleship is something other than the fulfillment of these commandments. Discipleship is a matter of following Jesus according to the word of God that is addressed to man in concrete circumstances. It is a matter of radical existential obedience.

Of the three versions of the incident which have been preserved for us, Matthew's narrative brings this point out most clearly. One ought not to read Matthew's words as if they indicated the existence of a double standard within Christianity, one for the masses, and one for the perfect. "To be perfect" is not to belong to an elite class among the disciples of Jesus.[27] Such an interpretation would be contrary to the general tenor of the First Gospel. Moreover, Jesus' response in Mt 19:21 must correspond to the question asked. It concerns the attainment of the kingdom of God, not membership in a special class. Furthermore, Jesus' reply about "treasure in heaven" shows that he is keeping the discussion on the same plane as that of his interlocutor. From Matthew's use of the term "perfect" (*teleios*), it is clear that the call to perfection is addressed to all Jesus' disciples (Mt 5:48). In the Dead Sea Scrolls[28] "to be perfect" (*tamim*, the Hebrew equivalent of Matthew's term) is to be a disciple of Jesus and belong to the Church. This demands radical obedience. Discipleship is not merely negative blamelessness, not even perfect blamelessness, with respect to the law. In a word, the observance of the commandments should be considered as the presupposition of the Christian response, but even the perfect observance of the commandments cannot be equated with the demands of Christian responsibility.

In the second section of the Sermon on the Mount (Mt 5:17–48), Matthew offers an extensive commentary on the Christian's attitude towards the Law which is remarkably similar to his version of Jesus' reply to the rich young ruler. In one and the other passage we read of the commandments (in the Sermon only of the fifth and sixth, however), the injunction of Lv 19:18 to "love one's neighbor," and of "perfection" as the hallmark of discipleship.

In this section of the Sermon, the evangelist gives six antitheses, of which the first, second and fourth are remarkably similar in form and content. In each of the three cases, Jesus has taken a precept of the Torah and radicalized its demand.[29] Some authors contend that Jesus has spiritualized the content of the Old Testament legislation. To interpret the Sermon in this fashion is, however, to alter the meaning of the text. One should not interpret the antitheses as if Jesus were saying that the old law, as a law, could effectively control only man's external actions and that the new law, Jesus' demand, reaches down to the innermost part of a man and sanctions its demands with realities of the spiritual order. The Sermon is not a treatise on the virtues. The entire passage is much too concerned with human actions to be able to be interpreted according to the contrast between the letter and the spirit.

Rather we ought to understand the entire series of antitheses as six examples of Jesus' attitude towards the Law enunciated in Mt 5:17–20. On the basis of their similarity in form and content, their consistency with Jewish catechetical traditions, and their peculiarity in Matthew, the first (fifth commandment), second (sixth commandment) and fourth (Lv 19:12) antitheses should be considered as the most original examples cited as illustrations of Jesus' attitude. His statement of principle, illustrated by these antitheses, proclaims the lasting validity of the Law. The commandments, too, retain their validity.

Nonetheless the statement of principle is not as simple as it might appear at first reading. Mt 5:17, "Do not imagine that I have come to abolish the Law or the Prophets; I have not come to abolish but to complete them" implies the total rejection of an antinomian attitude. Mt 5:18–19 reflects a rejection of any attitude which could seek to sap the Law of its normative value by distinguishing weightier from lesser commandments or which would otherwise limit the extent of God's demand. The final thought in the statement of principle, "For I tell you, if your virtue goes no deeper than that of the scribes and Pharisees, you will never get into the kingdom of heaven" (Mt 5:20) is a Matthean construction and is clearly addressed to Jesus' disciples. Exegetes would have it that Mt 5:18–19 was found more or less intact in the tradition from which Matthew composed his Gospel. They consider, however, that Mt 5:17 is either a composition of the evangelist or, at the very least, an addition to Mt 5:18–19 taken from another source.

When this preamble to the antitheses is considered in its entirety, it appears that in Mt 5:18–19 and Mt 5:20 we have the same two-phase attitude towards the Law that we found in Mt 19:16–30: on the one hand, a strong conservatism towards the Law, and, on the other hand, a distinction between Jewish tradition and Christian discipleship in the framework of the kingdom of heaven. Thus, Mt 5:17, the opening declaration in the statement of principle, serves as Matthew's general reflection on Jesus' attitude towards the Law. In this introductory statement the key issue is the meaning of "complete" (*plēroun*). It is a typical Matthean expression, designating the fulfillment of what had been announced in the Old Testament. With regard to the moral demand addressed by God to man within the kingdom, it can only mean to confirm and bring to its full validity.

How does Jesus both reiterate the Law (including the commandments) and bring it to its full validity in such a way that there is a real contrast between the Law as it has been handed down and the demand which He, as the Messiah, addresses to his disciples? The hermeneutical principle in virtue of which the precepts of the Law are to be understood and the norm of conduct in the performance of which all other precepts are embraced is the two-fold commandment of love.[30] It is this principle which gives content to the injunction contained in Mt 5:20.

In the light of these considerations we can better understand Mt 5:21–26 on the fifth commandment and Mt 5:27–30 on the sixth commandment. The commandments themselves have retained their validity. They remain God's demand. Yet for the Christian within the kingdom of heaven, these commandments are not a self-sufficient norm of life, not even with respect to the spheres of life and human activity which they sought to regulate. For the Christian no commandment is a sufficient norm of life. Rather he ought to submit himself to the demand of Jesus: "But I say to you. . . ." His demand is addressed to the Christian with respect to the same areas of human activity once ruled by the commandments. The examples cited in Mt 5:22–26 and 28–30 are illustrations of the Christian *halacha*, radically reinterpreting the commandments themselves in terms of the fundamental law of love. Only in this way are the Ten Commandments "completed."

A pronouncement story of the traditions of the Pharisees (Mt 15: 1–9; Mk 7:1–13) provides us with our third Gospel witness to the early Church's appreciation of the Ten Commandments. Mark has appended to an original incident material from another source and context,[31] whose purpose is to illustrate the attitude of Jesus towards the oral law. According to this addition, Jesus assails the oral tradition, but reaffirms the binding force of the Decalogue. The situation envisioned is that of children who violate the fourth commandment because of "Corban." The expression might mean that resources which could have been used to support one's parents had been dedicated to God or it might simply mean that a child had sworn not to support his parents.

In keeping with his usual custom, Matthew has omitted the Markan explanations (Mk 7:3–4) and some of the Markan color (Mk 7:2, 12). Furthermore he has welded the two originally independent traditions into a single narrative unit. In this way he may have recaptured something of the real tension between the fourth commandment and the Corban practice. Ultimately the real-life tension in the situation described was not between a divine commandment and a human tradition (even though Mark understood the situation in this way). It was between two divine precepts: the fourth commandment and the obligation to keep an oath.[32] What Jesus takes issue with is the tradition according to which one divine precept is set against another to "exempt" the subject from the fulfillment of more fundamental responsibilities.[33] The practice could well have been used as an *ad hominem* argument against those who paid too close attachment to the oral law. At any rate it is clearly at variance with the hermeneutical principle for the interpretation of the divine Law proclaimed by Jesus.

At this point, two further reflections must be made. The first has reference to the immediate sense of the fourth commandment. The point of conflict in the Corban passage does not touch upon an immature person's formal disobedience to his parents. The issue is that of an adult person's failure to support his parents. As in the Old Testament, so also in the teaching of Jesus, the fourth commandment is construed as being principally addressed to full moral persons (adults) requiring them to honor their parents. Our present purpose does not allow us the opportunity to develop the several implications of this fact, but it does urge us to make another reflection. The attitude of Jesus cited in Mt 15:1–9 (Mk 7:1–13) makes a sharp distinction between one's attitude towards the Law (even divine Law) casuistically understood and authoritatively interpreted and one's moral responsibility before God. It is indeed possible to be irreproachable before the Law, yet morally culpable before God.

## PAUL

This naturally leads into a consideration of the two passages in the letter to the Romans in which Paul mentions the Ten Commandments: Rom 7:7 and 13:9. At first sight it appears paradoxical that these two passages should appear in the same epistle. In Rom 13:9 Paul reiterates the Ten Commandments as part of his Christian paraenesis. In Rom 7:7–8, he seems to ascribe to the ninth-tenth commandment an almost perverse function: "I should not have known what sin was except for the Law. I should not for instance have known what it means to covet if the Law had not said 'You shall not covet.'[34] But it was this commandment that sin took advantage of to produce all kinds of covetousness in me, for when there is no Law, sin is dead."

Before attempting to resolve the apparent conflict, it ought to be noted that Paul is indeed citing the ninth-tenth commandment. He is not writing of sexual desire specifically, but of the actual violation of the ninth-tenth commandment in its most generic sense.[35] A verbally identical reference to the ninth-tenth commandment appears in Rom 13:9 when Paul, citing the Second Table of the Law, states that all the commandments "are summed up (anakephalaioutai) in this single command: 'You must love your neighbor as yourself.'" The verb, "to sum up," used by Paul is derived from a noun which means the summit or main part. Seemingly, therefore, the verb signifies "to unite different elements under one heading."[36] It does not mean that a plurality is reduced to unity, but that several different things are united around a single point of reference. Paul's point is clearly that love of neighbor is the principal point of the Law and that all of the other precepts depend upon it. In his own way he has reiterated the primitive Christian tradition that the law of love is the norm of the Christian life and the hermeneutical principle for interpreting the Ten Commandments.

By so doing he has brought into even sharper focus the paradox between Rom 7:7 and 13:9. The paradox can and must be resolved on the basis of Paul's doctrine of Christian freedom.[37] Paul looks to the commandments of the Old Law, including the Ten Commandments, as having a function which is both revelatory of a state of sin and provocative to sin. The violation of the commandments unmasks man's sinful nature while their "thou shalt not" entices him to sin. Since the Christian is radically free from sin, he is free from the sin-related Law and its commandments. That is, he is free from the observance of the commandments as obligations imposed from without or from above. This does not imply that the Christian is immoral. He has within him the Spirit whose presence is the sign and source of love. By responding to his inspiration the Christian does all that the Law demands and more, even though he is not "bound" by the Law.

Within the Christian community the Ten Commandments can remain as an object of instruction since they are given for those whose conduct does not measure up to the standards of the Christian vocation.[38] Thus in the paraenetic section of the Epistle to the Ephesians, Paul[39] can return to the Christian's attitude towards the commandments. This time his thought focuses upon the fourth commandment (Eph 6: 1–2). Within the context of a household code, Paul cites the fourth commandment as one of the grounds for a Christian's obedience to his parents. As wives have been exhorted to obey their husbands, children are urged to obey their parents. Then Paul turns his attention to fathers, reminding them that they are not to discourage their children by acting severely or with tyrannical authority.

In the entire context, it is the Christian's being "in Christ" which determines the sense of the obedience which he owes as well as the manner in which a Father is to exercise parental (or conjugal) authority. The qualification "in Christ" not only gives the grounds of Christian obedience, but also its limitations. The Christian is to obey "in the Lord."

It is hardly certain that this demand is addressed only to those who are youngsters or adolescents. Children are always considered to be such by their parents, no matter their age. The Jewish tradition considered this commandment as applicable to children who had reached adult maturity. Paul's frequent use of the term "children" (*tekna*) hardly restricts its applicability to young children. Thus it is not unlikely that

Paul intends that this injunction would be taken to heart by all who are children, whether young or adult.[40] At any rate he parallels the position of children vis-a-vis their parents with that of wives towards their husbands (Eph 5: 22–33) and slaves towards their masters (Eph 6: 5–9). By so doing Paul specifies the honor required by the fourth commandment as that of obedience — obedience in the Lord.

If Paul's understanding of the Christian meaning of the fourth commandment is relatively clear, his reference to its being the "first that has a promise attached" is not quite so clear. "First" can mean "first in importance." If this is Paul's meaning, he would seem to be echoing the Jewish tradition which considered the fourth commandment the most difficult among the difficult commandments.[41] On the other hand, "first" can mean "first in a series." Then Paul would be implying that the fourth commandment is the first among the ten to have a promise attached. This interpretation must face the fact that in the Biblical tradition the first commandment[42] also has a promise attached — "I show kindness to those who love me and keep my commandments." Perhaps we have here another indication of the independent use of the Second Table of the Law as an instrument of catechetical instruction. Then the fourth commandment would indeed be the first with a promise.

The promise which Paul cites is literally[43] that found in Ex 20: 12 and Dt 5: 16, but its sense has been spiritualized. No longer is the long life on the land promised to those who remain faithful to the covenant and its demands construed as the extension of physical life in the Promised Land of Palestine. Hardly would the Ephesians look to life in Palestine as God's gift to those who are faithful. Rather in Eph 6: 3 we have a traditional formula of covenant blessing which had come to mean eternal life and the inheritance which the Father gives to those who are his own. In the New Testament the same spiritualization of covenant blessing is found in the third beatitude (Mt 5: 5). To those who are faithful to the commandments "in the Lord" is promised the fullness of covenant blessing, understood according to the eschatology of the new covenant.

## JAMES

Finally, from the standpoint of its composition, Jas 2: 11 represents the New Testament's final explicit reference to the Ten Commandments. The fifth and sixth commandments are cited, in reverse order, as examples of the demand of God to which Christian man must be totally responsive. He cannot pick and choose from among the divine commands. It is the demand of God to which man must respond. Individual precepts and specific demands are but different expressions of God's fundamental sovereignty over man. Man ought to submit himself totally to this sovereignty. To choose from among God's demands those that are to be followed is to reject God's absolute sovereignty and his final claim to man's total service.

Thus the individual commandments cannot be understood apart from the radical demand of God. Therefore James places the keeping of the commandments within the context of the eschatological judgment and the fulfillment of the royal law of freedom (Jas 2:8, 12–13). Man's fidelity to the demand of God is not a matter of mere obedience to a positive statute, but a matter of his ultimate destiny to be achieved in freedom before the absolute demand of a sovereign Lord.

From the context, it would appear that those to whom the epistle is addressed were rigid with accepting God's demand under the sixth commandment, but less inclined to pay deference to those without wordly honor. The author of the epistle, however, considers this to be a specific demand of the fifth commandment, radicalized according to the norm of love. The problem to which he responded is always with us. We are always tempted to be severe in some areas and self-justifying in others, forgetting that Christian fidelity to any one of the Ten Commandments ought merely to be the expression of a more radical obedience.

## CONCLUSION

With James our survey of the New Testament teaching on the Ten Commandments can be brought to its conclusion. This might well be expressed in Ten New Testament Thoughts on the Ten Commandments:

1. The Ten Commandments are a useful instrument for the catechesis of moral demand within the Christian Church.

2. It is the Second Table of the Law which served as a basic instrument of moral formation in the early Church.

3. The early Church understood the Ten Commandments according to their primitive meaning. It looked to the fourth commandment, not as a child's commandment, but as the word of God addressed to

adults. It regarded the ninth commandment not as a specific prohibition of sexual fantasy and feeling, but as a broad obligation according
to which man should not seek that which is not rightfully his to have.

4. Since moral responsibility cannot be separated from religious
response, the Ten Commandments must be understood as an expression
of God's radical claim to man's service, a claim whose validity must
be maintained.

5. A distinction must be made between responsibility under the
Law and responsibility before God.

6. The Ten Commandments point to areas of life in which man
has a variety of responsibilities before God, but their negative formulations do not exhaust the scope of man's positive response to the will
of God.

7. Since each of the commandments is but a specification of God's
ultimate moral demand, the commandments cannot be set over against
one another nor can a selection be made from among them.

8. The observance of the Ten Commandments should not be understood as the norm of the Christian life; they are the presupposition
of the Christian life.

9. The two-fold law of love is the norm of the Christian life and
the hermeneutical principle for interpreting the Ten Commandments
"in the Lord."

10. The Christian is freed from the commandments as alien and
coercive demands, but ought to fulfill them by living according to the
Christian norm of life.

## NOTES

1. "The Ten Commandments in Current Perspective," *supra* essay 2.

2. Outside of Ex 20 and Dt 5, the only sure allusions to the Decalogue are
Ho 4:1–2 and Jer 7:9. Ps 81:10–11 contains a clear reference to the prologue of the
Decalogue.

3. This verse belongs to the pericope which contains Jesus' dispute with the
scribes and Pharisees over ritual purification (Mt 15:10–20). It is joined to a passage
(Mt 15:1–9) which contains an explicit reference to the Ten Commandments.

4. On the basis of the Old Testament, it would seem preferable to refer to
the Sabbath precept as the fourth commandment. In deference to readers, I will use
the numbering which is most familiar within the Catholic tradition.

5. Jn 5:9–18 (cf. 7:23) and 9:13–17.

6. H. Schlier has rather conclusively demonstrated that Col 3:20 does not depend on Eph 6:1-2, nor vice-versa. Rather both passages are mutually dependent on a common tradition. See H. Schlier, *Brief an die Epheser* (Dusseldorf, 1963), p. 280.

7. Mt 12:1-14; Mk 2:23-28; 3:1-6; Lk 6:1-11; 13:10-17; 14:1-6.

8. Rom 1:30 and 2 Tm 3:2. In a similar vein, one might cite Gal 5:19, which lists homicide among the vices which are "works of the flesh."

9. See E. Lohmeyer, *Das Evangelium des Markus*. Kritisch-Exegetischer Kommentar über das Neue Testament, 1/2 (Gottingen, 1963), p. 210; D. E. Nineham, *Saint Mark*. Pelican Gospel Commentaries, (Harmondsworth-Baltimore, 1964), p. 274. This final negative injunction is not contained in Matthew or Luke. Moreover it is not found in several manuscripts of Mark. Some authors take the mss. evidence as an indication that the phrase is a scribal addition to the primitive text.

10. Some manuscripts add a second version of the sixth commandment to Mark's text, namely, "you must not commit fornication" (*mē porneusēs*).

11. C. Spicq, however, reads Paul's "and so on" (literally, "and if [there is] any other commandment") as an implicit reference to the fourth commandment, the sole positive precept in the Second Table. See C. Spicq, *Agape in the New Testament*, II (St. Louis, 1965), p. 58.

12. See Cf. K. Stendahl, *The School of St. Matthew* (Philadelphia, 1968), p. 62.

13. Stendahl also notes that the commandment "you must not defraud" was also well known in the Jewish ethical tradition.

14. The different forms of catechism would explain the different orderings of the Ten Commandments of which we find traces in the New Testament.

15. See the Chester Beatty and Nash papyri. This same order is also found in Philo. B. H. Woods and B. J. Roberts point out that the best mss. of the LXX have the VI-VII-V order for Ex 20 and the VI-V-VII order for Dt 5. They contend that the latter may have been original since it is also contained in Lk 18:20 and Rom 13:9. Cf. "Ten Commandments," in *Dictionary of the Bible*, F. C. Grant-H. H. Rowley, eds. (Edinburgh, 1963), p. 970. At any rate the Palestinian mss. of the LXX have either retained or have restored the order of the Hebrew text and this is preserved by Mt.

16. This order is also used by Josephus. Matthew's reworking of the tradition also led to his substitution of *ou* with the future indicative for the *mē* and the subjunctive. This conforms to the reading of the LXX.

17. Cf. Mt 22:36, 38, 40; Mk 10:5; 12:28; 31; Hb 7:5; 9:19 (possibly Hb 7:16, 18). There are other passages in which the term "commandment" is used without any Old Testament reference. Thus we may legitimately question W. A. Whitehouse's affirmation that "in the New Testament the term is used with special reference to the Decalogue." See W. A. Whitehouse, "Commandment" in *A Theological Wordbook of the Bible*, A. Richardson, ed. (New York, 1950), p. 50.

18. Cf. Jas 2:11.

19. Many manuscripts of Mt 5:27 read only "You have learnt how it was said." Several modern versions accept this short reading.

20. Thus A. Schlatter, E. Klostermann, J. Wellhausen, J. Schniewind, G. Barth, A. W. Argyle, W. D. Davies, etc.

21. That the same formula is used in Mt 5:21, 27 and 33 is an indication that Matthew considered the Old Testament passages cited as a consistent body of material. Again they are from the Decalogue and the Holiness Code.

22. G. Barth goes one step further to assert that "it was said" means "it was taught as tradition." See G. Barth, "Matthew's Understanding of the Law," in G. Bornkamm, G. Barth, H. J. Held, *Tradition and Interpretation in Matthew* (London, 1963), p. 93. Although this exegesis is enticing, it is not necessary to accept it. The Old Testament tradition (particularly Dt) looks to the Ten Commandments as the Words of the Lord and the New Testament elsewhere refers to them as having been spoken by God (Mt 15:4; Jas 2:11).

23. *Leg. All.* 3:90–95.

24. Cf. *Peah* 1:1 *(Mishnah).*

25. Cf. *San.* 101a

26. Cf. Phil 3:6.

27. Cf. F. V. Filson, *The Gospel according to St. Matthew*, Black's New Testament Commentaries (London, 1960), p. 210; D. E. Nineham, *o.c.*, pp. 272–273 and especially R. Schnackenburg, *Christian Existence in the New Testament*, I (Notre Dame, 1968), pp. 158–189; G. Barth, *art. cit.*, pp. 95–100.

28. Cf. I QS 1:8–9; 2:2; 3:3; 4:22; 5:24; 8:1, 9, 18, 20; 9:2, 5, 6, 8, 9, 19; 11:11, 17.

29. In the other three antitheses (divorce, talion, neighbor-love), Jesus takes an Old Testament saying, reverses the restrictive or permissive interpretation placed upon it in the schools, and radicalizes the demand for the values involved.

30. Cf. Mt 22:34–40; Mk 12:28–31; Lk 10:25–28 and the studies by G. Bornkamm, "End Expectation and Church in Matthew," in *Tradition and Interpretation in Matthew*, pp. 30–31; "Das Doppelgebot des Liebe," in *NT Studien für Rudolph Bultmann*, p. 93; G. Barth, *art. cit.*, pp. 75–85.

31. Note the use of another introductory formula in v. 9.

32. Cf. Dt 23:21–23; Nm 21:2; Mt 5:33; etc.

33. The same attitude may also lie behind the tradition on which Mt 5:19 is based.

34. This is a much better translation than that which renders the phrase "Thou shalt not lust."

35. The verb *epithumēseis* used in Rom 7:7 and 13:9 as well as twice in both Ex 20:17 and Dt 5:21 refers to any form of coveting. In the LXX, besides its use in the Decalogue, it is used to refer to the coveting of fields (Mi 2:2), gold (Dt 7:25) and land (Ex 34:24).

36. Cf. C. Spicq, *o.c.*, p. 59.

37. Cf. S. Lyonnet, "Saint Paul: Liberty and Law," in *The Bridge*, 4 (New York, 1961), pp. 229–251; R. Schnackenburg, "Freedom in the Thought of St. Paul," in *Present and Future* (Notre Dame, 1966), pp. 64–80.

38. Cf. 1 Tm 1:8–11.

39. The present context does not call for a discussion of the authenticity of the epistle.

40. Cf. A. Schlatter, *Die Briefe an die Galater, Epheser, Kolosser und Philomen.* Erlauterungen zum Neuen Testament, 7 (Stuttgart, 1963), p. 240.

41. Cf. p. *Peah* 1, 15d, 13, etc.

42. I.e., the second commandment according to the original division. Cf. Ex 20:6; Dt 5:10.

43. Paul's citation has, however, substituted the verb "to be" (*esē*) for the LXX's "to become" (*genē*).

# 4

## The Fourth Commandment – For Children or for Adults?

IN HIS CLASSICAL TREATISE on the 613 commandments of the Torah,[1] the great Jewish philosopher Moses Maimonides cites "honor and fear your parents" as the 210th and 211th precepts of the Law.[2] His combined reference to Ex 20:12, "Honor your father and your mother, that your days may be long in the land which the Lord your God gives you," and Lv 19:3a, "Every one of you shall revere his father and mother," was commonplace in rabbinical tradition. Jewish catechetical tradition frequently used the precepts of the so-called Holiness Code (Lv 17–26)[3] as a source of instruction on the Law. More specifically, in its exposition of the demands of filial piety, rabbinic tradition typically cited the *mitzwoth* (commandments) contained in Ex 20:12 and Lv 19:3 together and made them the source of the principal *halakhoth* dealing with the responsibilities of children towards their parents. A typical and salient example is contained in the Babylonian Talmud. The tradition maintains that "Our rabbis taught: What is reverence and what is honor?" Reverence means that he (the son) must neither stand nor sit in his (the father's) place, nor contradict his words, nor tip the scale against him. Honor means that he must give him food and drink, clothe, and cover him, and lead him in and out."[4]

*Honor thy Father and Mother*,[5] a recent book by Gerald Blidstein, professor of Jewish Thought at Ben Gurion University of the Negev, offers its reader an analysis of the rabbinic tradition which interpreted the two commandments of the law which serve as "the overriding foci of Jewish filial piety."[6] True to his tradition, Professor Blidstein carefully distinguishes *morah*, reverence, from *kibbud*, honor. It is the latter notion which is contained in the fourth commandment. In his exposition of the tradition commenting the biblical "Honor your father and your mother," Professor Blidstein indicates that the notion of honor is clearly rooted in *kbd*, that which is heavy and weighty. To honor a per-

82

son is to acknowledge him as a person of importance and of worth. It is a response to the weightiness of the person honored. As this might seem all too vague, rabbinic tradition from the Mishnaic to the contemporary era has sought to concretize the meaning of the biblical injunction, "honor your father and your mother," From their concretizing remarks, it is clear that the rabbis did not consider the fourth commandment to be incumbent primarily upon children. Indeed the honor of parents appears not to be so much a pattern of youth as it is the pattern of a lifetime.[7] Responsibility for the fulfillment of the fourth commandment lies not so much upon the young as it does upon adults.

## RABBINIC TRADITION

The importance of the fourth commandment is to be gleaned from its very position among the precepts of the decalogue; Rabbinic tradition normally divided the ten commandments into "two tables,"[8] the one bearing principally upon man's responsibilities to God (the first five commandments), the other bearing upon man's social responsibilities. The fourth commandment (the rabbinic "fifth" commandment)[9] lies at the juncture of the two tables of the Law. Why did this precept deserve a place of such singular importance? The rabbinic response is implicit in the motivations alleged as a basis for the observance of the commandment.

Why must one honor one's father and mother? First of all, parents are creators. The honor bestowed upon parents is consequently a continuation of the honor to be rendered to God himself. The notion was already current in tannaitic times (1st and 2nd centuries A.D.). The Babylonian Talmud narrates that "The rabbis taught: There are three partners (in the creation) of a man—the Lord, his father, and his mother."[10] To be sure the rabbis distinguished between the role of parents and that of God, nevertheless, they hold to the view that parents participate in the divine creative act. Because of the participatory relationship, the Talmud grounds the honor due to parents in the honor due to God. Thus, "When a man honors his father and his mother, the Lord says, 'I reckon it as though I abided with them and they honored me.'"[11] Another factor motivating the observance of the fourth commandment was the ethos of gratitude. Philo, the Alexandrian Jew and contemporary of Jesus, locates filial gratitude in the gratitude owed to benefactors. He writes, "who could be more truly called benefactors than parents in relation to their children? First, they have brought them out of non-existence; then, again, they have held them entitled to nurture and later to education of body and soul, so that they may have not only life, but a good life."[12] In citing gratitude as a motivation for filial piety, medieval rabbis were more inclined to focus upon gratitude for having been instructed in the ways of the Lord than upon gratitude for having received physical life.

According to Blidstein's study, the other two motivations for the observance of the fourth commandment cited by rabbinic tradition fall into what we might style categories of natural law.[13] Maimonides, for example, considers the family unit as the essential basis of social organization. Consequently proper observance of the commandment is necessary for the stabilization of society. In a word, his view is that structures of authority necessary for human life are dependent upon the model of filial piety. A variant on the theme is that the precept of the decalogue is necessary for the preservation of religious traditions. Thus a fifteenth century Rabbi, Joseph Albo, says that "The fifth commandment was given to urge respect for the tradition, that is to say, that a person should be drawn after the traditions of the fathers, for this is a main principle of all religions, the existence of which is inconceivable if men do not accept the traditions of the fathers and of the sages of that religion."[14] Thus societal and religious needs for authority can serve as a motivating force for the observance of the commandment. So, too, does the natural inclination of children to honor their parents. A medieval notion of *humanitas* undergirds some rabbinic comments on filial piety. In this respect it is interesting to note that although the rabbis did not draw examples from the animal world to show the natural quality of filial piety, as they did in presenting their views on modesty, fidelity, respect for property, etc., it was principally from among the Gentiles that they drew their examples of filial piety. First among those whose lives illustrated the quality of filial piety was the legendary Dama ben Netinah, a non-Jew from Ashkelon.


## A NORM FOR LIFE

Careful evaluation of these four types of response to the question, "Why honor one's father and mother?" already suggest that the fourth commandment is rather a norm for life than a child's commandment. In this regard, nevertheless, a consideration of the "whys" is not as determinative as is a consideration of the response to another question "What is the honor due to father and mother?" Preferably one ought to distinguish the haggadic tradition (narrative, inspirational material) from the halakhic tradition (casuistic, legal material). Rabbinic stories are told about the patriarchs and other heroes of Jewish history. Joseph is said to have had his life shortened by ten years because he did not reverence his father insofar as he allowed Jacob to be addressed as "thy servant." Dama ben Netinah is commended for not disturbing his father's sleep, albeit at great financial loss. Rabbi Tarfon is praised for allowing his mother who had lost her shoe to walk upon his hands until she had reached her couch. Yet the rabbinic tradition hardly commends his heroic efforts. It notes that "were he to do that a thousand times, he has not yet bestowed even half the honor demanded by the Torah."[15]

The examples of these first century (A.D.) heroes, the Ashkelonite and the Tannaitic rabbi, indicate that later rabbis basically understood the notion of honoring one's parents as the provision of personal service for them. Commenting the tradition, Blidstein concludes that "the talmudic realia of filial 'honor' focus on acts of service."[16] Indeed filial service is tantamount to the service which a slave performs for his master.[17] Nevertheless the slave performs out of obedience to authority; the dutiful son from his sense of responsibility. Indeed the rabbinic authorities do not cite the authority which parents exercise over their children as a motivation for the fulfillment of the precept; rather their concentration is upon the responsibilities which fall to children. The children in question, however, are not infants or youths. Rather the one whose duty it is to "honor his father and mother" is the adult who is *bar mitzwah*, a son of the commandment. Thus Blidstein correctly interprets the notion of "honor" in the fourth commandment when he renders it "personal service."

That the fourth commandment was interpreted by the rabbis as a command addressed to adults in order that they provide personal service to their parents readily appears from the survey of legal materials scanned in Chapters II–V of Blidstein's work. The most important aspect of filial responsibility discussed at length in the Talmud is the issue of parental support. Two passages, among others, from the Talmud get to the heart of the matter. The Babylonian Talmud juxtaposes the honor due to parents and that owed God, commenting: "It is stated: 'Honor your father and your mother.' And it is also stated: 'Honor the Lord with thy substance.' Just as one demands economic sacrifice, so does the other demand economic sacrifice."[18] In a similar vein, the tradition retains a saying ascribed to Simeon ben Yohai: "Great is the honor one must accord one's parents—for God elevates it even beyond the honor one must accord Him. Here it says, 'Honor your father and your mother'; there it says, 'Honor the Lord with thy substance, and with the first-fruits of thy increase.' How do you honor Him? With the wealth in your possession. . . . If you have the means, you are obliged to do all this—if you do not have the means, you are not. But with 'Honor your father and your mother' it is not so; whether you have the means or you do not, 'Honor your father and mother,' even if you must become a beggar at the door."[19]

These last few words show the extent to which the rabbis considered sons bound to provide care and support for their parents in order that the fourth commandment be fulfilled. A Talmudic story told of Rabbi Eliezer likewise points to the extent of service demanded by the honor of one's parents. He was asked "How far must one go in honoring one's father and mother?" He answered, "So that he throws a wallet into the sea before your very eyes and you do not shame him."[20] To honor one's parents is to provide them with the personal service necessary for their support. Honor might well be a matter of thought and of speech. Much more so is it a matter of deed, to give food and drink, to clothe and cover (i.e., to house), to lead in and out. Evidently such services could be rendered only by those "children" who had the wherewithal to support their parents; they would not be rendered by youths who were still dependent upon their own parents for the very necessities of life.

That such indeed is the importance of the fourth commandment is likewise clear from rabbinic discussions on the obedience which children owe to their parents. The rabbinic tradition cites Isaac as a model of obedience. The fourteenth-century "ethical will" of Kalonymus ben Kalonymus cites submission to one's mother as a Torah-commanded expression of filial piety. By and large, however, the rabbinic discussions on obedience show that filial submission to a parent's command is essentially a matter of respect for tradition, grounded in the wisdom of one's elders. Beyond respect for tradition the discussions found in the rabbinic casuistry show that obedience is generally not to be dissociated from honor rendered in the form of personal service. Are there any limitations to the obedient honor which a man owes to his parents? In response, the rabbis consistently affirmed that parents could not command their children to violate one of the commandments of the Lord. The casuistry of the thirteenth century proposed the following case: "You have asked: 'Can a father prevent his son from going to the land of Israel, since we rule that it is a *mitzvah* to go up to the land, and it is stated, 'I am the Lord,' that wherever a parental request conflicts with a *mitzvah* the parent is not to be obeyed, for the honor of God takes precedence over the honoring of parents." The response of Rabbi Moses of Trani was: "The son need not heed the command of his father and mother."[21] To be sure, casuistic efforts were made in order that both the command of the parent and the command of the Lord be honored, yet in a case of true conflict, it was the command of the Lord that took precedence.

An area of potential conflict was certainly the 212th precept of the Law, "You should perpetuate the human race by marrying," a precept based on Gen 1:28. Would not the housing and other economic support necessarily provided for a wife create a situation of conflict with the duty to provide for one's parents? How can one support both parents and a wife and children? A twelfth-century work, the *Sefer Hassidim*, attempts to balance the competing claims of filial piety and marital fulfillment: "Parents who command their son not to marry so that he might serve them make an inadmissible request: let him marry and live near them. But if he cannot find a wife in the town in which his parents live, and his parents are aged and need him to support them, let him not leave the town. And if he can earn only enough to support his parents, and would be forced—should he marry—to end this support, let him obey his parents. But if the son is wealthy and can have someone else serve his parents, he may then go to another town to take a wife."[22] It may well be objected that the *Sefer Hassidim* presents something of an unreal situation and that it does not establish the grounds for the norms which it cites. Nevertheless, the work does point to the singular importance of physical and financial support of aged parents as the sole appropriate way to faithfully fulfill the fourth precept of the decalogue.

That, indeed, is the essence of the commandment according to the rabbinic tradition. In support of this contention, Professor Blidstein notes that:

The entire talmudic discussion concerns, in fact, the obligation laid upon the child to render service to the parent—that is to say, to provide him with his needs, and to prevent his falling prey to those displeasures and pains to which he would otherwise be heir. What is essential, then, is that the claims of filial piety exist only in those areas in which the parent is inexorably involved—his own pleasure or pain. They do not exist in areas that are not of immediate personal concern to the parent, such as the behavior of his child, even if the parent chooses to involve himself and thereby make the issue one of parental pain or pleasure.[23]

## CARE FOR THE AGED

In point of fact, Blidstein's observations on the common thrust of talmudic discussion on the fourth commandment are an attestation that the rabbis were faithful to the spirit of the commandment as it was incorporated into the decalogue in biblical times and as it was interpreted in the first century A.D., a formative period for both Christianity and rabbinic Judaism. Exegesis of the pertinent Old and New Testament texts indicate that the fourth commandment was not a "child's commandment." A faithful interpretation of the traditions of both Old and New Testaments decisively shows that the commandment was not intended to require young people to obey their parents. Rather the fourth "word of the Lord,"—for it is thus that the Book of Deuteronomy would style the commandments of the decalogue—requires that adults, subject to the Law, provide support for their aged parents.

It is well-known that one of the most pressing problems to be faced by any people is that of the care of the aged and non-productive members of society. The problem is acute enough in modern times. It was even more acute in ancient times, among societies more primitive than our own. James Michener's best-selling *Centennial* provides a poignant case of the type of situation which lies behind the formation of the fourth precept of the decalogue. Michener tells the tale of Blue Leaf, an Arapaho squaw whose husband had just died. After his death, the family tepee was torn apart by scavenging squaws. Without husband and without tribal function, Blue Leaf was banished from the camp to die of exposure after three nights in the snow. Fictional though the narrative may be, Michener's narrative shows that utility is a major source of the valorization of human life. When man or woman is no longer useful, especially when advancing age has rendered him or her non-productive, it is the temptation of each society to cast him or her beyond the pale of society's protection and support. A nomadic tribe might well leave the elderly behind as it moves on; a sedentary group might cast them outside the city's gates.

It is to counter such barbarism that "honor your father and your mother" was formulated as a norm of social conduct, whence it was later incorporated into the convenantal stipulations of Ex 20 and Dt 5. Clear confirmation that such was the earliest significance[24] of the commandment is implied in the promise which is attached to it: "that your days may be long in the land which the Lord your God gives you" (Ex 20:12b).[25] It is not only the law of Talion which serves as a reminder of the strict commutative justice which reigned in Israel in biblical times. The "measure for measure" (*middah k'negged middah*) principle was applicable to a wide variety of situations. Thus, the promise of a long life is consistent with the command to honor your father and mother insofar as those who fulfill the commandment effectively procure a (relatively) long life for their parents.[26] The medieval rabbis were aware of the proportionality of the promise to the command to which it is appended. Thus the tenth-century rabbi Sa'adiah Gaon writes that "the reward for filial piety is 'length of days' . . . because it is destined to occur that parents will sometimes live for a long time with their sons."[27]

## THE NEW TESTAMENT TRADITION

Can it be said that the notion of financial support of one's aged parents remained the thrust of the fourth commandment even in New Testament times? It is to be noted that the commandments of the decalogue are more frequently cited in the New Testament than they are in the Old.[28] This apparently curious phenomenon is to be explained in terms of the catechetical function served by the decalogue in Jewish circles at the time of Jesus. Thus we should not be surprised to find the fourth commandment cited verbatim in two of the gospel pericopes. An examination of each of them will serve to help us understand the fourth commandment as it was interpreted by Jesus and his contemporaries.

It is to the Markan tradition (Mk 10:17–22) that we owe the narrative of the encounter between Jesus and the rich young man.[29] The evangelists, Matthew (Mt 19:16–22) and Luke (Lk 18:18–23), have taken over the narrative from their Markan source. Each of the later evangelists adopts the material in his own way. Thus Matthew identifies Jesus' interlocuter as "young" (Mt 19:20) and Luke describes him as "very rich" (Lk 18:23). In form the narrative is that of a pronouncement story. Jesus appears as a rabbi to whom the question is put "What must I do to inherit eternal life?" The Markan outline recalls the many rabbinic traditions about conditions to be fulfilled for entrance into the life-to-come. Thus the Mishnah would later list the honoring of father and mother, the doing of loving kindness, and bringing peace between man and his fellow as three acts "whose fruits a man enjoys in the world while the capital is laid up for him in the world to come."[30] In rabbinic fashion, Jesus cites the fulfillment of the decalogue's social commandments as conditions for the inheritance of eternal life. To a question posed in the context of the Old dispensation, he responds as a teacher of the law by citing the ten commandments. The five social commandments are cited in the usual order, whereupon they are followed by a mention of the "fourth commandment." The VI-VII-VIII-IX-X-V ordering of the commandments is somewhat unusual,[31] but is to be explained on the basis of Jewish catechetical tradition.

The point of the Markan narrative is obviously not an exposition of the ten commandments as such. Rather Mark's narrative is intended to contrast the faithful fulfillment of the law and the condition of discipleship. Jesus the rabbi is contrasted with Jesus who calls to discipleship. Consideration of this contrast is important but unnecessary for our present purpose. Rather we should note that the interlocuter's response to Jesus' listing of the commandments of the decalogue is "Teacher, all these I have observed from my youth." His words are significant for they indicate that the precepts of the decalogue have been kept from his youth—"from my youth" (ek neotētos mou). The implication is that from the time of his youth since he became a "son of the commandment" (bar mitzwah). At the age of thirteen the rich young man observed the precepts of the decalogue.[32] The response is not that of an arrogant opponent of Jesus, but the expressed conviction of a Pharisee who, like Paul before his conversion, could be found blameless under the law.[33] From the time when he was considered an adult and fully responsible for the observance of the covenantal prescriptions contained in the decalogue's social code, the rich young man faithfully observed the ten commandments. Mark's narrative does not imply that he was never disobedient to his parents, but that from the age of thirteen the young man had not failed to render faithful service to his parents. His reply is a sure indication that at the time of Jesus, the ten commandments, including "the fourth" were incumbent upon adult adherents to the faith of Israel.

Another Markan narrative which sheds light upon the early church's understanding of the fourth commandment is in the Corban pericope (Mk 7:9–13).[34] Although elements of the Markan setting (Mk 7:1–8) have been taken over by Luke (Lk 11:37–41), the discussion of Corban is reproduced only by Matthew (Mt 15:3–6). Matthew has reworked the Markan material somewhat. Rather than cite Is 29:13 prior to the Corban discussion—the sequence found in the Markan narrative—Matthew offers his readers the Corban discussion (Mt 15:3–8) and then quotes the saying of the prophet. Moreover, he has heightened the contrast between the "commandment of God" and "your tradition" by replacing Mark's "For Moses said" (Mk 7:10) with "For *God* commanded" (Mt 15:4). In any event the life-situation of the pericope is clearly Palestinian. It was the Palestinian church which had to deal with the problem of the relationship between the oral tradition and the written Law. Indeed the Markan narrative seems somewhat echoed by a Mishnaic saying attributed to the Rabbi Eliezer: "One may suggest to a man as an opening 'They may open for men the way (to repentance) by reason of the honor due to father and mother.'"[35] The Mishnah's tractate on vows, Nedarim, continues: "But the Sages forbid it. R. Zadok said: Rather than open the way for a man by reason of the honor due to father and mother, they should open the way for him by reason of the honor due to God; but if so, there could be no vows. But the Sages agree with R. Eliezer that in a matter between a man and his father and mother, the way may be opened to him by reason of the honor due to his father and mother." The Mishnah's judgment is that where the son has banned, by vow, the use of his property by his parents, an "opening" for the absolution of the vow may be found insofar as the son is otherwise incapable of properly honoring his parents.

The precise nature of the Corban vow remains the subject of exegetical dispute. Corban was a technical term used in two kinds of vows.[36] There is, however, no need for us to distinguish here between the different vows, since the point of the Markan controversy is clear enough. It contrasts tradition and the Law. In Deuteronomic fashion, it cites the fourth commandment as "the word of God" (Mk 7:13; Mt 10:6). The narrative speaks of him who fails to support his parents because the goods which ought to have been used for their support were in some way dedicated to God. The pericope does not focus upon a child's obedience; rather it has to do with the care and economic support of one's aging parents.

Consideration of these two New Testament pericopes clearly points to the fact that the oral tradition on which the gospel narratives rest considered "honor your father and your mother" as a commandment incumbent upon adults who were bound to the observance of the Law. It required them to provide financial support for their parents in their declining years. In this way they were not only to honor their parents, but also honor their God. If this be the constant teaching of the biblical, Judeo-Christian, and rabbinic tradition, how did it happen that the fourth commandment came to be considered as the "children's commandment" by medieval and modern catechetical tradition? Catechesis generally treats the fourth commandment as if it principally requires youngsters to be obedient to their parents. This use of the commandment is clearly foreign to the traditions which we have considered thus far. How did the catechetical application of the commandment to children come into being? A brief examination of Eph 6:2 may well provide some elements of the answer.[37]

## "RULES FOR THE HOUSEHOLD"

It is commonly asserted that Eph 6:1–3 is part of a collection of admonitions (Eph 5:22–6:9) whose literary genre is that of the *Haustafel*, "rules for the household." Collections of similar household rules are not infrequent in the New Testament. Col 3:18–4:1 contains a collection remarkably similar to that of Ephesians. Other collections are found in 1 Tm 2:8–15; 5:3–8; 6:1–2; Ti 2:2–10; and 1 Pt 2:13–3:7. The literary genre was developed in the Hellenistic world. Subsequently it was taken over by the Hellenistic synagogue and was eventually adopted by the Christian Hellenistic church. The collection of household rules found in Eph 5:22–6:9 is based upon juxtaposition of three pairs of relationships in which the mutual duties of wives and husbands (Eph 5:22–33), children and parents (Eph 6:1–4), and slaves and masters (Eph 6:5–9) are systematically expounded. The author is clearly concerned with the Christianization of the tradition which he has received. Since the obedience of children to their parents was a common element in popular moral instruction, it was not unusual for the *Haustafeln* to contain a section on the obedience of children to their parents. Popular ethics were concerned with the strengthening of family ties. The insertion of an exhortation to obedience in the household rules was just one expression of that deeply seated ethical concern. By inserting a household code into his letter, the author of Ephesians expressed a concern which was at once theological and ethical.[38] Theologically, he intended to affirm the lordship of Jesus over all human relationships. Ethically, he intended to strengthen family ties within the Ephesian community.

In articulating his double concern and making use of a household code as the framework for the expression of his theological conviction, the author of Ephesians borrowed Hellenistic and Jewish themes. From Hellenism and the traditional *Haustafel* came his thoughts on the obedience of children towards their parents. From Judaism and the biblical tradition came the citation of the Fourth Commandment. The author of Ephesians was not, however, the first to join these different traditions. Prior to him, Hellenistic Judaism had already joined the Hellenistic idea of filial obedience with the Jewish notion of honorful service. This development came about in response to the needs of the Jewish diaspora, namely, to reconcile an Hellenistic *Weltanschauung* with Jewish tradition. Philo's allegorical exegesis of the patriarchal narratives was one attempt to bring the two worlds together. His exegesis of the fourth commandment was another such attempt: "The fifth commandment, relative to the duty of honoring one's parents implicitly contains many necessary laws: those which touch upon the relations between the aged and the young, princes and subjects, benefactors and those indebted to them, slaves and masters. In the categories just named, parents occupy the superior rank, with the aged, sovereigns, benefactors and masters. Children are placed in the category of inferiors: the category of the young, subjects, the indebted and slaves. Many other maxims are added. The young have the duty of honoring the aged; the aged have the duty of taking care of the young. . . ."[39]

## COVENANTAL RESPONSIBILITY

In sum, it was Hellenistic Judaism's need to find some theological ground in support of a social norm which led to the fourth commandment's being cited as a motivation of youngsters' obedience to their parents. By so doing, one need was met and a catechetical tradition was established. Perhaps it is time to reevaluate that tradition. In his careful analysis of the rabbinic traditions which expound the fourth commandment, Professor Blidstein makes a number of judicious distinctions. Many of them are still useful for today's ethicists and catechists. Faithful to the rabbinic tradition, Blidstein distinguishes between reverence (*morah*) and honor (*kibbud*). The specific tradition which he weighs focuses upon a consideration of responsibilities rather than upon the determination of rights. Blidstein distinguishes between that which is legally binding and that which is ethically normative. The narrative which expresses an ideal is set off from the casuistry which formulates a rule of life. With Melden, Blidstein distinguishes between obligatory actions and actions which meet obligations. Such distinctions are useful for weighing an ethical tradition and forming the mature conscience. They pertain to the adult who must shape his pattern of life.

The formation of the child's conscience is most likely not to be found in fine distinction and ethical nuance. That is rather the stuff from which the more mature conscience takes shape. Consequently, it might be well for our catechetical tradition to abandon the hybrid formulations of Hellenistic Judaism (and Hellenistic Christianity). Let us acknowledge that "honor your father and your mother" is the word of God addressed to those who accept covenantal responsibility, admonishing them to provide care for their aged parents. There is a place in the divine dispensation for urging the obedience of young children to their parents. It is to be found in the need for education to values and respect for tradition so that a child, grown to maturity, can assume responsibility for himself and his world. It is to be found in parental love which seeks to prevent its God-given offspring from suffering physical, moral, and mental harm. It is to be found in a societal need for good order within the home and still larger communities. It may even be found in society's need for a positive response to authority so that the needs of the common good might be met for the betterment of all. The place which the divine dispensation accords to the obedience of young children is not, however, to be found in parental rights; nor is it to be found in the fourth commandment.

If catechesis were now to sunder what Hellenistic Judaism had joined, namely the fourth commandment and the due obedience of young children, we would take a great leap forward in our understanding of the commandments and their place within the covenantal tradition. Given the conventional catechesis on the fourth commandment, it is so easy to urge that youngsters obey their parents, and all the while to forget that the care of aged parents is the divine imperative of which the fourth commandment speaks. We, too, have tended to make void the word of God through the tradition which we hand on (cf. Mk 7:13). If we would but separate—at least in our catechesis, and only for an instant—the word of God and the needs of man, we would undoubtedly render greater honor to the God of the covenant and provide honorful service to all his children, the aged in our nursing homes as well as the young whose cries enliven the homes in which we live.

## NOTES

1. Rabbinical tradition distinguished 613 commandments in the Law. The 613 commandments included 365 proscriptions and 248 prescriptions. According to the Talmud, Rabbi Simlai is reputed to have stated that, "613 commandments were revealed to Moses at Sinai, 365 being prohibitions equal in number to the solar days, and 248 being mandates corresponding in number to the limbs of the human body." Cf. BT Makkoth, 23b. A modern reader might find the enumeration forced but he cannot argue with the basic insight—that evil is to be avoided all the days of man's life; and good is to be done with the whole of his being.

2. Cf. Abrahan H. Rabinowitz, "Commandments, The 613," Encyclopedia Judaica 5:760–783, cols. 769–770.

3. Esp. Lv 18–19. Cf. Krister Stendahl, The School of St. Matthew (Philadelphia: Fortress, 1968), p. 63.

4. BT Kiddushin, 31b. Significant parallels are to be found in PT Peah, 15c, Sif Lev 19:3, and a Tosefta on Kid 1:1. Cf. Raymond F. Collins, "Obedience, Children and the Fourth Commandment—A New Testament Note," Louvain Studies 4 (1972–1973), 157–173, p. 162.

5. Gerald Blidstein, Honor Thy Father and Mother; Filial Responsibility in Jewish Law and Ethics, The Library of Jewish Law and Ethics (New York: KTAV, 1975).

6. G. Blidstein, p. 37.

7. Thus, G. Blidstein, p. xii.

8. Eq. Perusha ha-Ramban, I, ed. by C. Chavel, pp. 403–404; Abarbanel, Commentary to the Torah (Warsaw, 1862) II, p. 38c. Other references may be found in G. Blidstein, p. 166, n. 73.

9. I have briefly treated the division of the decalogue's ten commandments in "The Ten Commandments in Current Perspective," supra essay 2. In the present article, "fourth" and "fifth" will be used interchangeably in keeping with the imme-

diate point of reference, our catechetical tradition or the biblical and rabbinic tradition, respectively.

10. BT Kiddushin 30b. Cf. PT Niddah 31a.

11. BT Kiddushin 30b.

12. Philo, *Spec. legg.* 2:229–231.

13. Blidstein offers some reflections on natural law and rabbinism, pp. 27–31.

14. "*Ikkarim*," III, p. 26.

15. PT Peah 1:1.

16. G. Blidstein, p. 51.

17. Professor Blidstein provides a comparison of the duties of slaves and those of children on pp. 47–51.

18. BT Kiddushin 32a.

19. PT Peah 15d. A discussion of this saying and of other rabbinic traditions on the matter of the financial support of parents is provided in my article, "Obedience, Children and the Fourth Commandment," pp. 160–163.

20. BT Kiddushin 32a.

21. Cf. G. Blidstein, p. 84; p. 196, no. 24.

22. *Sefer Hassidim*, Sec. 564, p. 371, as cited by G. Blidstein, p. 112.

23. G. Blidstein, p. 89.

24. This is not to overlook the fact that within Israel, particular significance was attached to parents insofar as they were the bearers of tribal and religious traditions. Anthony Phillips accurately notes however, that "it was the social purpose of the commandment which came to be stressed, rather than the original purpose of maintaining the ancestral religions. . . . " Cf. Anthony Phillips, *Ancient Israel's Criminal Law: A New Approach to the Decalogue* (Oxford: Basil Blackwell, 1970), p. 81.

25. Deuteronomy's parallel version of the promise is: "that your days may be prolonged, and that it may go well with you, in the land which the Lord your God gives you" (Dt 5:16b).

26. It is this promise which explains why the appropriate punishment for Joseph's lack of filial piety was the shortening of his life by ten years. Cf. *Pirke de-R. Eliezer*, Ch. 39.

27. Cited by the tenth century Rabbi Bahya ben Asher in *Hovot ha-Levavot*. The citation is given by G. Blidstein, p. 114.

28. Cf. Raymond F. Collins, "The Ten Commandments and the Christian Response," *supra* essay 3.

29. For further comments on the passage, reference may be made to my previous articles, "The Ten Commandments and the Christian Response," *supra* essay 3; and "Obedience, Children and the Fourth Commandment," p. 158.

30. *Peah* 1:1.

31. The displacement of "honor your father and your mother" may well lie behind Rom 13:9.

32. Cf. my "Obedience, Children and the Fourth Commandment," p. 167.

33. Phil 3:6.

34. Verses 9–13 had an independent existence in the early church. A fuller discussion of the pericope is provided in "Obedience, Children and the Fourth Commandment," pp. 158–159.

35. *Nedarim* 9:1.

36. Cf. J. D. M. Derrett, "*Korban, o estin dōron,*" NTS 16 (1969–1970), 364–68, p. 364.

37. Cf. "Obedience, Children and the Fourth Commandment," pp. 167–173.

38. Cf. Markus Barth, *Ephesians 4–6*, AB 34A. (Garden City: Doubleday, 1974), pp. 607ff.

39. Philo, *De decal.*, 165–167.

PART THREE

# The Love Command

# 5

# "A New Commandment I Give to You, That You Love One Another . . ." (Jn 13:34)

BY WAY OF CONCLUSION to an examination of the love ethic in the Johannine writings in the important monograph which he consecrated to the moral teaching of the New Testament, Rudolf Schnackenburg wrote that "St. John is not only a loyal guardian of Christ's inheritance preserving his spirit but also a disciple of the Lord illumined by the Holy Spirit, giving added profundity to the commandment of love and raising it to be the ruling principle of Christian morality throughout all ages."[1] Schnackenburg's enthusiastic praise of the Johannine endeavor is undoubtedly shared by most believers and teachers of morality who stand within the Christian tradition. It is, nonetheless, an enthusiasm which some contemporary exegetes refuse to share. Many of them see in the Johannine formulation of the love commandment, not so much a new profundity as a restriction of the commandment in view of the so-called sectarianism of the Fourth Gospel. Illustrative of this other position is the opinion offered by the Tübingen exegete, Ernst Käsemann. Käsemann claims that the Fourth Gospel was intended for a Johannine conventicle whose thought-patterns were decidedly gnostic. In view of this gnostic sectarianism, Käsemann proffers the opinion that "the object of Christian love for John is only what belongs to the community under the Word, or what is elected to belong to it, that is, the brotherhood of Jesus."[2]

This dichotomy of opinion is sufficient to indicate that the meaning of the Johannine "new commandment" is not as easy to ascertain as a first reading of the Gospel might suggest. In point of fact, the interpretation of Jn 13:34 raises a series of exegetical questions for which a response must be found if the Johannine version of Christ's command to love is to be understood fully. These questions are of a literary, linguistic, and theological nature.

From the standpoint of a literary consideration of Jn 13:34 the exegete must direct his attention to the appearance of the verse within the Johannine farewell discourse (Jn 13:31–14:31). Although the discourse apparently concludes at 14:31, it is followed by other farewell discourse material (Jn 15–16) which also includes the love commandment: Jn 15:12 and Jn 15:17. According to Raymond Brown, these verses are "related to and perhaps a duplicate of" 13:34.[3] In these passages, however, the commandment is not styled "a new commandment." This expression recurs in the New Testament only in 1 Jn 2:7–8 and 2 Jn 5. Given the rarity of the expression, some authors conclude that it is to 1 Jn 2:7–8 that we must go if we are to understand the meaning of the "new commandment" in Jn 13:34. This quickly brings one to a thorny aspect of the Johannine problem, namely the relationship between the Johannine epistles and the Fourth Gospel. When literary considerations are brought to bear upon the Gospel, considered as it were in isolation from other elements of the Johannine corpus, attention must be directed to the relationship between Jn 13:34–35 and the footwashing scene (Jn 13:1–20) as well as to the relationship between the love command of Jn 15:12, 17 and the parable of the true vine (Jn 15:1–11).

From the standpoint of a linguistic analysis of the text, two questions call for careful consideration. First of all, in what sense can the Johannine love command be styled a "new" commandment? Apparently the qualification was traditional within Johannine circles. Nevertheless it seems to have been problematic for the author of 1 Jn who writes, "Beloved, I am writing you no new commandment, but an old commandment which you had from the beginning; the old commandment is the word which you have heard. Yet I am writing you a new commandment" (1 Jn 2:7–8a). The author of the Fourth Gospel used the adjective *kainos* (new) but twice in his Gospel, namely in Jn 13:34 and again in 19:41. There the term is used with an obviously different meaning (the "new tomb"). Why, then, does the author use this adjective in Jn 13:34? The Fourth Gospel clearly stands within the Judeo-Christian tradition. Within Judaism the love command was at least as old as Lev 19:18; within Christianity the love command was at least as old as the Synoptic traditions reflected in the discussion on the greatest commandment in the Law (Mk 12:28–34 and par.) and those lying behind the Sermon on the Mount (Mt 5:43–48; Lk 6:27–28, 32–36). Why, then, is the Johannine formulation of the love command designated a "new commandment?"

In addition, attention must be directed to the very use of the term *entolē* ("commandment") in John's formulation of the Jesuanic logion. John uses the term in a sense different from that of the Synoptics. There *entolē* characteristically refers to the commandments of the Torah. As John uses the term, however, *entolē* refers to the commandments which the Father has addressed to the Son. It is also used of the commandments which Jesus addresses to his disciples. Does the use of the term imply an order issued from without? What is the relationship between the commandments (plural) of Jesus and his commandment (singular)?

From the standpoint of an analysis of the text which I would call theological because it has reference to the meaning of the Scripture as the "ruling principle of Christian morality," there are again two major issues to be raised. First of all, there is the matter of the object of love.[4] According to the Johannine version of the command, the disciples are to love "one another." The Synoptics characteristically speak of love of one's "neighbor" or love on one's "enemy." Albeit it from radically different perspectives, authors as different as William Wrede, Ethelbert Stauffer, Hugh Montefiore, Archbishop Bernard, Brown, and Käsemann indicate that the Johannine command has a scope more restricted than that of the Synoptics.[5] Is there truly a difference between the Johannine and Synoptic traditions?[6] If so, does this difference reflect an impoverishment or an intensification of the Johannine tradition as seen against that of the Synoptics? This question has been raised with renewed earnestness in recent years because of interest in the possible Gnostic background of the Fourth Gospel as well as in the comparison of John and the Qumran writings.

A second point to be considered is the Christological import of the "new commandment." The issue is all the more important in that there exists an ever-growing consensus which holds that the Christological and eschatological character of the New Testament ethic constitutes the hallmark of this ethic. Specifically the issue of the Christological import of the Johannine new commandment must be raised in view of the Christological insertion at Jn 13:34, "as I have loved you."[7] A similar insertion is not to be found in the Synoptic or Pauline versions of the love command. Granted the Johannine formulation of the insertion, some discussion must be had as to the nature of the Christological reference. Is Christ the exemplar of fraternal love or is he the source of fraternal love? Should we perhaps speak of both at once and of even more? Such are but some of the issues to which the remainder of this article will be devoted as it seeks to shed some light on Jn 13:34:

"A new commandment I give to you, that you love one another; even as I have loved you, that you also love one another."

## THE FAREWELL DISCOURSE

It is now commonly asserted that Jn 13:31–16:33 is written according to the literary genre of the farewell discourse.[8] Approximately fifty speeches ascribed to famous men in anticipation of their deaths have been preserved for us in biblical and extra-biblical sources. A most striking example of the genre is to be found in the speeches of the *Testaments of the Twelve Patriarchs*. Farewell discourses typically contain exhortations to keep the commandments of God, especially the commandment to love one another, and thus manifest the unity of the brethren. Indeed, in an unpublished dissertation, John F. Randall[9] has demonstrated that *agapē* (charity) is one of the most commonplace words in the whole literature. Love is sometimes expressed in service. Love serves as a sign for the nations. Joseph is the example or image of fraternal love. Randall's study thus points to fraternal charity as a characteristic trait of the farewell discourse genre. Consequently the appearance of the exhortation to fraternal charity in the farewell discourses of the Fourth Gospel is to be expected. In effect, the presence of the love motif in the Johannine farewell discourses is not as striking as is the specificity with which John casts his presentation of the love command.

That the exhortation to fraternal love is integral to the Johannine farewell discourses has been confirmed by André Feuillet's comparative structural analysis of Jn and 1 Jn.[10] Feuillet notes that whereas "light" and "life" are the key words of the first part of the Gospel, *agapē* (love) and *agapan* (to love) are the key words which characterize the second part of Jn. Of the thirty-six appearances of these two words[11] in the Fourth Gospel, thirty-one are found in the farewell discourses, where the verb is employed twenty-five times and the noun appears some six times. The verse which occupies our attention not only contains three of the verbal uses of *agapan*; it also makes use of a characteristic Johannine expression the *kathōs*-relationship formula, in a way which is restricted to the farewell discourses and the "high priestly prayer" which is appended to them.[12]

While a consideration of the literary genre of the farewell discourse and the use of agapeic vocabulary in Jn 13:31–16:33 confirm one another in the assertion that the theme of love is integral to John's farewell discourse, we may not overlook the fact that the extant text of Jn 13–17 gives evidence of having developed over a long period of time before reaching its present form.[13] The problematic "Rise, let us go hence" of Jn 14:31 as well as the many parallels between Jn 13–14 and 15–16 have led many authors to consider that the Johannine farewell discourse contains two editions of the same discourse or considerable secondary material (Jn 15–17) which have been added to an earlier text by a later redactor, a disciple of the evangelist.[14] Indeed Zimmermann has suggested that Jn 13–14 and 15–16 constitute two discourses.[15]

In any event the commandment of love, found at 13:34 and 15:12, is one of the duplicative elements which have led the majority[16] of Johannine commentators to conclude that the present text of Jn 13–17 is a composite whose present format results from a later redaction of the Johannine text. Within this perspective it has been suggested that the exhortation to love one another (Jn 13:34–35) is out of place in its present context and may well have been inserted into the farewell discourse from some other tradition of Jesuanic logia.[17] Analysis of Jn 13:31–38 reveals that the pericope has a structural pattern which recurs some six times in Jn 13–17.[18] The structural pattern consists of three elements: a revelation by Jesus, a question by his interlocutors who speak on a superficial level, and a response by Jesus to clarify his original revelation. Since the love commandment (vv. 34–35) is not alluded to within the context, it must be considered as an addition to the pattern.[19] Thus, the pericope within which the love commandment occurs, Jn 13:31–38, must be considered as a composite text with its own history. In this composite text the love commandment is situated within a frame of reference which has the departure of Jesus as its theme. By means of the sandwich technique,[20] a redactor has highlighted the love commandment as the legacy of the departing Jesus for the community which he has left behind.

By identifying six instances of the revelation-question-clarification pattern in Jn 13:31–14:31 and 16:4–33, Reese has called into question the broadly held theory that Jn 14 and Jn 16 are duplicate discourses. While accepting Jn 15:1–16:4 as a later insertion,[21] he has raised many questions, not the least of which is the unity of the present redaction of the farewell discourse. In an independent study,[22] Günter Reim has identified 15:18–16:4 as the later insertion and cites the changed situation of the community—namely, one of persecution—as its Sitz-im-Leben. Thus any attempt to explicate the farewell discourse in its present unity must take into account that the composite text is both a reflection upon the disciples' relationship to Jesus in his absence and a reflection upon the disciples' relationship to the world in its persecution. This is, of course, the point of Zimmermann's article, which so emphasizes the differences between Jn 13–14 and 15–16 as to conclude that they constitute two discourses, the first (13–14) expressing the significance of Jesus' departure and its bearing upon the situation of the Church while Jesus is with the Father, whereas the second (15–16) bears on the significance of Jesus' union with the disciples and their situation in the world. Despite the differences, we must note that the present text constitutes a unity[23] in which it is possible to discern an emphasis on the modality of Jesus' presence in his absence in the first part, and an emphasis on the recognition of the world in the second part. Within this unified body of material the evangelist and/or redactor have interspersed their version of traditions which are otherwise formulated in the Synoptic Gospels.[24]

When now we look to the Johannine formulation of the love commandment within the context of the farewell discourses, it is apparent that the author would have his readers understand the love commandment in specific reference to the Passion-glorification of Jesus. The *oun*[25] ("therefore") of 13:31 indicates that the entire pericope, consisting of vv. 31–38, must be considered in the light of the Passion. If Bultmann's suggestion to the effect that the *arti* ("now") of v. 33 relates in fact to the love commandment of v. 34,[26] then clearly the hour of the Son of Man gives urgency to the commandment itself. Now that he is about to depart in the hour of his exaltation-glorification, the Son of Man gives the new commandment of love to his disciples as his legacy and challenge. In Jn 15, the love commandment (v. 12) is followed by a passage which explicitly cites the Passion as an example of the love to be imitated by Jesus' disciples: "Greater love has no man than this, that a man lay down his life for his friends" (v. 13). Thus the reference to the Passion is a consistent and specifically Johannine element[27] in the presentation of the new commandment.

From the literary point of view, both Jn 13:34–35 and 15:12, 17 are joined to a symbolic narrative. The new commandment of Jn 13 is linked to the footwashing scene (Jn 13:1–20).[28] The composition of the scene owes to Johannine redaction. Whether it refers essentially to the Passion as a symbolic action or to baptism as a sacramental action remains, however, a moot question.[29] In any event, the present redaction of the scene offers Jesus' washing of his disciples' feet as a *hupodeigma*, an "example" (v. 15), to be followed by his disciples. The example shows that the love which the disciples are to imitate is the example of loving service, directed to one another. In its turn, the love commandment in Jn 15:12 has been linked to the parable of the vine and the branches (Jn 15:1–11).[30] Both the parable and the pericope which follows (15:9–17) are concerned with the fruitfulness of the word of Jesus. *Menein* ("abide") serves as the catch-word which links together the two inseparable pericopes. The catch-word demonstrably points to the intimate relationship among the Father's love for Jesus, Jesus' love for his disciples, and the disciples' love for one another. The pericope concludes with the refrain, "This I command you, to love one another" (v. 17). Although this verse was undoubtedly added to the narrative at a relatively late stage of composition,[31] it truly belongs to the narrative as presently edited. Indeed a quick look at the text shows that the thought of vv. 16–17 picks up the thought of vv. 7–8, albeit in reverse order.[32] Thus, the discourse material added to each of the symbolic narratives offers significant reflections on the Johannine notion of love as well as on the symbolic narratives themselves.

These brief reflections on the context of the love commandment in the Fourth Gospel have served to show that the evangelist and his disciple-redactor have truly integrated the theme of mutual love into the farewell discourses. Behind the farewell discourses of Jn 13–17 lies the history of the composition of the Johannine text. The pericopes in which the love commandment appears show clear and considerable evidence of Johannine composition/redaction. As a result, the entirety of the farewell discourses is encompassed by the theme of love, which occurs at their outset (13:1) and their conclusion (17:26). The most obvious lesson to be learned from the author's redactional efforts is that he would have the love command understood in reference to Jesus' Passion-glorification. It is the Passion-glorification which imparts meaning to the love commandment; the love commandment is Jesus' legacy for his own to be fulfilled during the period of his absence. Such are but a few elements connoted by the rich Johannine formulation of the love commandment.

## THE JOHANNINE EPISTLES

To speak of the love commandment as a "new commandment" is to speak the language of the Johannine school. The Johannine phraseology "new commandment" appears not only in Jn 13:34 but also in 1 Jn 2:7–8 and 2 Jn 5.[33] All three of these writings reflect a situation of tension within the Christian community. The tension present in the life situation of 1–2 Jn appears nevertheless to be more critical than that of the life situation of the farewell discourses.[34] It is to the situation of some crisis that John draws our attention when he writes of a commandment which is "no new commandment," the "old commandment," and yet "a new commandment" as he does in 1 Jn 2:7–8: "Beloved, I am writing you no new commandment, but an old commandment which you had from the beginning; the old commandment is the word which you have heard. Yet I am writing you a new commandment, which is true in him and in you, because the darkness is passing away and the true light is already shining." A similar assertion, but without the reversal of thought, is to be found in 2 Jn: "And now I beg you, lady, not as though I were writing you a new commandment, but the one we have had from the beginning, that we love one another."

The polemical aspects of each of these passages is clear enough. John affirms that the love commandment is not a new one because his correspondents have heard it "from the beginning." For John's correspondents, the love commandment cannot be considered a new revelation. The love commandment was part of their baptismal catechesis.[35] That is certainly the import of the explanatory formula, "the old commandment is the word which you heard" (v. 7).[36] For the recipients of the letter the commandment is not new, since they have received it as part of their fundamental catechesis, from the very beginning of their faith in Christ. Yet the author of the letter may well have intended to say even more. He may have intended to affirm not only that the recipients of the letter had received the love commandment along with the initial proclamation of the Gospel *to them*, but also that the love commandment is the commandment which Christianity has had from the very beginning, that is, from the first moment of the proclamation of the Gospel.[37] If this is indeed the case then John is both affirming his fidelity to the proclamation of the primitive Gospel and indicating that the primitive (i.e., in Johannine terms, the "old")

Gospel was actualized in the baptismal catechesis of the recipients of the letter.

The contrast between the old and the new makes sense only if we understand why the author makes pains to affirm that the love commandment of Christian tradition is not new. His concern is undoubtedly occasioned by the Gnostics who are the troublesome opponents for the author of both letters. It is hardly likely that the Gnostics had proposed any "new commandments." What is more likely is that they exploited a "new Christian experience" in the Spirit at the expense of Christian tradition.[38] Within that perspective, the Gnostics considered such commandments as the love commandment to be an outmoded part of tradition. In contrast the Johannine authors suggest that what is new is later and lacks the necessary authority to be an authentic part of the Christian experience. In this sense the love commandment is certainly not new—for it is the commandment of Jesus himself.[39]

Nevertheless the commandment which is not new in one sense is indeed new in another sense. Thus we have the paradox of 1 Jn 2: 7-8:[40] the commandment which is not new, but old, is, in fact, new. It is clear that the author of 1 Jn knew the logion of Jn 13:34; most probably his readers knew the logion as well.[41] His reference to the past, made in the heat of controversy, has brought him to consider the newness of the commandment which he is proposing once again.[42] The commandment of love has been given for those who abide in the light by none other than the Lord himself. The commandment is new because it is the commandment for the new age. Thus the author of 1 Jn affirms that the newness of the commandment owes to the fact that its truth[43] derives from Christ himself ("truth in him"—v. 8), and that its fulfillment is pertinent to the lives of Christians ("and in you") who live in the new age. In effect the love commandment is new because it is the eschatological commandment, the commandment for the new age,[44] ethics for the final times.[45]

In this new age love for one another is proof of one's love for God.[46] If one does not have mutual love, then one is only a liar. He belongs to the realm of darkness, rather than to the realm of light. Thus the love commandment is much more than one among the other Christian commandments. It is even more than the most important commandment in the Christian moral code. It is the decisive commandment.[47] For the Johannine authors, the fulfillment of the love commandment is the sign of true knowledge of God and the sign of belonging to the community of light. The one who does not practice brotherly love can no more claim to have true knowledge of God than membership in the brotherhood; he has cut himself off from one and the other. Thus the commandment of mutual love is "new" precisely insofar as it is the hallmark of the new age. 1 Jn, therefore, insists with even more emphasis than is found in the Gospel, that love for the brethren is the distinctive sign of belonging to the Christian community. The exercise of brotherly love is the essential manifestation of the Christian life. The commandment of mutual love is part of the traditional and authoritative proclamation of the Gospel. As such it is paradoxically old and new at the same time. It pertains to the traditional kerygma, and proclaims an ethic pertinent to the time of waiting for the end.

We must note, nevertheless, that it is on the commandment as such, as a precept demanding observance in behavior,[48] that the author of 1 Jn insists in the first pericope of his epistle in which he dwells upon the theme of love which pervades the entire document.[49] Subsequently[50] he will cite (1 Jn 3:10–24) the example of Christ as a model for love among the brethren. The author calls for a concrete expression of love: a love of one's "brothers" in mutual service.[51] Still later in the epistle (1 Jn 4:7–21) he will turn his attention to God as the very source of love. Thus while he chooses to counter the Gnostics' deviant neglect of the practice of mutual love by referring to the Lord's promulgation of a commandment (1 Jn 2:8), his total understanding of love is that it is a necessary concomitant of union with God.

## THE LOVE COMMANDMENT

In his commentary on 1 Jn 2:7–8, Bultmann not only suggests that this pair of verses has been added to a source by the redactor of the epistle but that the use of "commandment" in the singular is a reference to a logion of the Lord.[52] Undoubtedly the use of "commandment" in 1 Jn 2:7 has a referential function, but that function should not obscure the even more important fact that "commandment" is a particularly significant Johannine concept. Indeed the Johannine corpus[53] has the highest preponderance of use of "commandment" (*entolē*) and its cognate verb, "to command" (*entellesthai*) in the entire New Testament.[54] In John's Gospel the term is used once to denote a legal commandment or order issued by the Sanhedrin (11:57). Apart from that singular reference, the term is used either of the charge or mission given to Jesus by the Father (10:18; 12:49, 50; 14:31) or the commandment given by Jesus to his disciples (13:34; 14:15, 21; 15:10, 12).[55] In this latter sense, the terminology is restricted to the farewell discourses, where, indeed, it seems to have an imperative force.[56] It is questionable, however, whether it is the imperative force which predominates in the use of the terminology when it is applied to the "commandment" of the Father to the Son. In those passages, "commandment" seems rather to indicate the will of the Father directing the Son to the work of salvation and indicating to Him the means by which the salvation of men should be accomplished.[57] From this perspective, "commandment" seems to have a universal rather than a specific sense, and a salvific rather than an imperative sense. This suggests that the Johannine use of "commandment" has some similarity with the LXX in which "commandment" (entolē) is used as an expression for the will of God.

If, then, we look to the Old Testament in the hopes that it will shed some light on the Johannine notion of "commandment" we find that it is principally to the Deuteronomic literature that we must look.[58] Indeed, "the whole spirit of Deuteronomy is expressed by the term, 'commandment'."[59] "Commandment" is a relational term which can be understood only within the convenantal context. The "commandments" are the covenant obligations imposed by Yahweh and undertaken by Israel. Specifically one can look to the Decalogue as a synopsis of these obligations. They represent the material content of the covenant prescriptions. Yet the formal sense of the "commandments" is something other than the material (ethical) content of the ten commandments.

The entolē of the Septuagintal version of Dt corresponds to the Hebrew miswa, both terms having the basic sense of "command." The emphasis lies on the fact of being commanded. There is, thus, a relational element and a personal quality inherent in the connotation of the term. This personal quality means that the commandment derives from moral authority, rather than from forceful constraint or arbitrary demand. In most instances of the use of entolē in Dt, the commandment is of divine origin. Thus entolē generally indicates God's will. The stress is on the Lawgiver who would lay claim to the service of man in order that man be united to Himself. The commandment is parallel to God's instruction (nomos, "the law") and thus is, at least in some sense, a revelation of God Himself.[60] Thus the commandment is a convenantal reality,[61] a sign of Israel's special relationship with Yahweh. In context, therefore, the commandment is not only an expression of the divine will but is also, as Spicq notes,[62] both an instruction and a salvation device. The first and fundamental content of *entolē*, taken in its singular Deuteronomic sense, is the imperative of love.[63] All the other commandments depend on love. To love[64] is to keep God's commandments.[65] Finally, and most significantly, "the *entolē* . . . becomes a mode of the presence of God to His people and an evidence of the dynamic and active quality of this presence."[66]

This Deuteronomic concept of commandment appears to have provided the model for the Johannine concept. In the first instance, the Johannine concept has an all-embracing sense which is linked to the history of salvation. This is particularly evident in those passages which speak of the commandment which the Father has given to Jesus. The material content of the "commandment" is Jesus' death (10:18)[67] or his revelation (12:49, 50). Thus the "commandment" has to do with the Father's will directing the revelatory and salvific mission of Jesus: "the Father who sent me has himself given me commandment what to say and what to speak. And I know that his commandment is eternal life" (12:49b–50a). Since the context raises the issue of the authority of Jesus' revelatory message and since the author invokes the "poverty principle"[68] in response, it is clear that the commandment concept is one which includes its obligatory force. The idea of commandment as precept to be fulfilled by Jesus is likewise present in 15:10: "I have kept my Father's commandments and abide in his love." In this case John speaks of commandments, in the plural, as he always does[69] when commandment is the object of the verb *tērein* (to keep).

A link to the history of salvation is no less present when the evangelist writes of the commandment which Jesus gives to his disciples. The constant reference to the Passion, the comparison between Jesus and the disciples, and the situation of the love commandment within the farewell discourses provide the history of salvation framework for the love commandment. Indeed the situation of the love commandment within the farewell discourses provides another positive point of comparison between the Johannine and the Deuteronomic notions of commandment. Dt is one of the oldest examples of the farewell discourse genre. In its entirety it is presented as the address of the departing Moses to the nation of Israel.[70] There Moses is the mediator of the covenant and the lawgiver; now Jesus appears as the mediator of the covenant and the lawgiver.[71] In both cases the binding force of the precept is inherent in the notion of the commandment which is given.

Yet the commandment is not simply a precept to be obeyed. The new commandment is a commandment which Jesus gives to his disciples.[72] It is the gift of the departing Jesus. The use of the verb *didonai*[73] by the evangelist serves to place the new commandment among the great realities of divine salvation with which John employs the powerful verb "to give": the Spirit (3:34; 14:16), the bread of life (6:11, 27, 31, 32 (2x), 33, 34, 37, 39, 51, 52, 65), the living water (4:10, 14, 15), peace (14:27), eternal life (10:28; 17:2), glory (17:22, 24), the power to become children of God (1:12) and the word of God (17:8, 14). These are the "gifts of God" (4:10) which Jesus gives to his own. The new commandment is no less a gift. It is the legacy which Jesus gives to those whom he is about to leave.

That legacy is not only commandment to be kept; it is also revelation to be treasured. Already in Dt, "commandment" had the sense of divine revelation and instruction. That sense is preserved in Jn's use of commandment which appears predominantly in a passage which serves as an instruction to the disciples by Jesus as to the meaning of his departure. The revelatory nature[74] of the Johannine commandment is highlighted by the parallelism between "word" and "commandment" in 14:21, 23. Jesus' commandment is the word which he entrusts to his disciples. It makes known to them God's plan for them.

In Dt, the commandment was also a mode of God's active and dynamic presence. In this respect it can be suggested that the love commandment is the modality of Jesus' presence[75] with his disciples after his departure. Jesus' glorification involves his separation from his disciples and their attendant distress. The farewell discourses seek to express the meaning of his departure. In 13:34–35 it appears that the solution to the problem of Jesus' absence is the presence of love. Mutual love is the new mode of Jesus' presence among his disciples.[76] His presence constitutes the moral demand.

## THE NEW COMMANDMENT

The love commandment is called a "new commandment" (*entolē kainē*) in Jn 13:34. Otherwise the commandments which Jesus addressed to his disciples are called "my commandments," with the pronomial adjective *emē* as in 14:15; 15:10, or the pronoun *mou* as in 14:21; 15:12. Outside of Jn 13:34, Jn employs the adjective *kainos* but once, i.e. in reference to the "new tomb" in which the body of Jesus was placed.[77] The love commandment appears elsewhere in the NT,[78] but is not called a new commandment except in 1 Jn 2:7–8 and 2 Jn 5. In a real sense, the love commandment is not a new commandment at all, as even the author of 1 Jn must admit.[79] Not only does the love commandment go back to Jesus but it was an integral part of the Torah[80] to such an extent that rabbinic legend ascribes to R. Hillel the summation of the entire Torah in the golden rule.[81]

Given this situation, one must ask why and in what sense did the Johannine school[82] interpret the love commandment as a new commandment. The designation is certainly somewhat unusual and warrants reflection. Reflection is not absent from the writings on John. As a matter of fact, commentators on the Fourth Gospel are rather inclined to devote considerable attention to the expression. Thus Ceslaus Spicq indicates no less than eight reasons why the Johannine love commandment is styled a "new commandment."[83] (1) The new commandment places mutual love among the specific elements of the new economy of salvation, the new covenant replacing the old. (2) The innovation in the commandment is that love is given an unequaled place and made the object of a fundamental and quasi-unique precept. (3) In relation to Lev 19:18, love has a new object, determined by ties of faith, not blood ("one another" rather than "your neighbor"). (4) In reference to the Sermon on the Mount's love of enemies, the Lord at the Last Supper asked for reciprocal love which will constitute the Church as a society of loving and loved men. (5) The great innovation is the nature and mode of the new love insofar as the disciples' love is rooted in Christ. (6) Mutual love is not an additional rule of conduct nor is there given a new reason for loving; rather, love is gift as well as precept. (7) The mode and activity of love are changed insofar as praying and doing good give way to self-sacrifice, a love for the other which is greater than one's love for oneself.[84] (8) The love commandment constitutes the Church as truly as does the Eucharist in that the Eucharist is a memorial of his going, and love a sign of his presence.

While an extensive enumerated list is somewhat overwhelming there is something to be said for each of the reflections offered by Spicq.[85] It would appear, nevertheless, that the most fundamental reason for calling the love commandment a "new commandment" is that it is the commandment for the final times. The dualism of the Johannine *Welt-anschauung* is apparent in the Gospel, and is quite explicit in the very context in which the author of 1 Jn explains the new commandment.[86] There it appears that the love commandment is the commandment which obtains among those who exist in the light, whereas it is not kept by those who walk in the darkness. In the epistles as in the Gospel, Johannine dualism is often expressed by antithetical images. This is in keeping with the realized eschatology[87] of the Johannine school. The Synoptists' espousal of consequent eschatology, on the other hand, generally provides for a contrast between the present age and the age to come. Within this perspective the realities of the age-to-come are often called "new."[88] In effect, "new" is equivalent to "eschatological" or "of the final times." The Johannine school has retained this sense of "new" when it speaks of the "new commandment." In Jn, however, the love commandment is not new from a temporal perspective; it is new only from the qualitative point of view. The love commandment as exposed by Jn derives its newness, i.e. its characteristic uniqueness, from the new eschatological world which Jesus brings.[89]

In its specifically Johannine interpretation,[90] the love commandment is new because it is an eschatological commandment but it is eschatological because it is a gift of the Johannine Jesus. At root then the Johannine love commandment is a new commandment because of its reference to Jesus. Yet John does not consider the love commandment a "new" commandment because he is citing a traditional Jesuanic logion (which, of course, he does); rather, the commandment is new because it is the final challenge and gift of the departing Jesus for his own. It is a reality of the post-resurrection era; it pertains to the times dominated by the apparent absence of the glorified Jesus. In this sense it is a rule for the new eschatological community. Yet it is more than a rule since it is Jesus' gift to the community of light created by the gift of his presence. Thus, with Schnackenburg, one can understand the commandment as new in the light of John's profound understanding of discipleship.[91] Thus, too, with Lazure we can understand the commandment as new because it is qualified by "as I have loved you."[92] The absent-present Jesus and the disciples are the poles of the relationship which constitutes the newness of the Johannine love commandment.

The Johannine love commandment is "new," then, insofar as it is specifically Christian.[93] But is it new with the more or less explicit specificity of the new covenant so that the gift of presence which it

entails is properly qualified as the Johannine analogue to the institution
of the Eucharist?[94] There are, in fact, substantial reasons for consider-
ing Jn 15:1-8 as a Eucharistic text,[95] but it is in Jn 13 rather than Jn
15 that the love commandment is styled a "new commandment." The
symbolic action (Jn 13:1-12) which serves as a prelude to that portion
of the farewell discourse which presently contains the new commandment does not, however, appear to have a sacramental reference clearly
in view.[96] Thus it would be difficult to argue for a specifically Eucharistic sense of the Johannine love commandment.[97] This opinion is all
the more probable in that Jn does not cite the new covenant formula
of Jer in reference to the new commandment as do the Synoptists in
their respective narrations of the institution of the Eucharist.

On the other hand, there are sufficient parallels between the literary form and content of Dt and the literary form and content of Jn
13-17 to suggest a Deuteronomic model for the latter. In this case, the
new commandment would indeed be a reality of the new covenant,
even though Jn does not formally describe it as such. Indeed it is not
only *a* reality of the new covenant; it is *the* reality of the new covenant[98] insofar as all the commandments are reduced to one[99] by the Johannine Jesus. Thus without citing the *berith*-formula itself and without
making reference to Jer's new covenant, Jn is able to establish the love
commandment as the covenantal stipulation *par excellence* of the new
covenant[100] and to indicate that the bond of union between the Father
and the new people of God is constituted by the fulfillment of that
obligation in covenant of which Jesus is the mediator.


## *AS I HAVE LOVED YOU*


It is, in fact, the Christological reference which constitutes the
essential novelty of the Johannine new commandment.[101] John has inserted the love commandment in a literary framework which interprets
it within the context of Jesus' great saving presence-absence, his glorification and return to the Father. Indeed, by his repetition of the "as
I have loved you" formula in 13:34[102] John has drawn emphatic attention to the singular importance of the Christological reference. Hence
the crucial question for the interpreter becomes that of the significance
of this Christological reference. What is the meaning of "as I have loved
you," stated and emphasized again?[103] What precisely is the sense of

the *kathōs* in the expression? Does it mean "as" or "because"? Is Jesus' love for his own the exemplar, the motivation, the foundation, or the source of the disciples' love for one another?

To respond disjunctively is effectively to sap the Johannine formulation of the love commandment of its unique strength. When John writes that the disciples are to love "as I have loved you," he implies that Jesus is at once[104] the model, the reason, the ground, and the mediator of the disciples' love for one another. Thus we must look to various levels of meaning in the expression "as I have loved you" rather than opt for one or another meaning to the exclusion of all others.

Certainly one ought not to set aside, as readily as does Bultmann,[105] the fact that Jesus' love for his disciples is the model of their love for one another. In the present redaction of the text, the footwashing scene (Jn 13:1–20) is clearly presented as an example of Jesus' love for his disciples. It is situated within the context of Jesus' love for his disciples unto the end (v. 1) and terminates with a discussion on the exemplary character of Jesus' action (vv. 13–20).[106] Within that discussion Jesus' action is presented as "an example that you also should do" (v. 15). The parallelism between v. 15, "For I have given you an example, that you also should do as I have done to you,"[107] and v. 34, "A new commandment I give to you, that you love one another, even as I have loved you," is, moreover, such to link the commandment with John's exposition of the exemplary gesture.[108] The gesture not only situates the commandment within the perspective of Jesus' Passion-glorification but serves notice that the fulfillment of the commandment is effected in loving service.[109] Thus Cerfaux noted that the footwashing is "the example, the symbol, and the commandment of brotherly love."[110]

When John returns to his exposition of the love commandment in 15:12–17, "love" (*agapē*) serves as the catch-word to link vv. 12 and 13 together. Thus, the love with which Jesus lays down his life for his friends (v. 13)[111] is implicitly proposed as a model for the disciples' love for one another.[112] Indeed the particularism with which the significance of the Passion is formulated in v. 13 — lay down his life "for his friends" (*hina tis tēn psuchēn autou thē huper tōn philōn autou*) — is consistent with the particularism of the object of the love commandment and the particularism of that love for his own (13:1) which serves as the springboard for John's reflection on the significance of the Passion. From the love of Jesus manifest in his passion, one can point to the intensity and extent of the love which ought to be characteristic of Jesus' disciples.

In effect, Jesus' laying down his life for his friends is not only an example of great love; it ultimately constitutes the love of the brethren as Christian love.[113]

Thus it would seem not only legitimate but exegetically imperative to speak of an ethics of imitation[114] with respect to the Johannine formulation of the love commandment. The ethics of imitation is not foreign to Johannine thought. The soteriological-Christological saying of Jn 12:24 is also followed (v. 25) by a call to imitation.[115] Thus, and with respect to the love commandment, Jesus' love for his disciples serves as the norm of fraternal love. More specifically Jesus' love for his own is normative with respect to its object, its intensity, and its quality as loving service.

The ethics of imitation proposed in 13:34 is grounded in the salvific act that Jesus is to accomplish as he departs from his disciples. The Passion-glorification of Jesus inaugurates the time for the fulfillment of the love commandment and serves as the basis for the obligatory force of the commandment.[116] Because Jesus has loved his own and that unto his hour, the disciples must love one another. In this sense the memory of Jesus' love for his own should serve as a motivating force, urging the disciples to love one another. The disciples must love one another not only "as" Jesus loved them (the ethics of imitation) but "because" Jesus loved them (the motivation for brotherly love).

As with most covenant motifs, it is the memory of a divine favor in the past which creates future covenantal obligations. It is the memory of what Jesus is for the disciples which allows for the Johannine insertion of the love commandment in the farewell discourses. It is as the one who is about to accomplish that for which he has been sent, that Jesus can command the disciples to love one another. Indeed, as has already been suggested, the love commandment is no arbitrary decree of some despot but the legacy of the departing Lord. The very use of the word *entolē* suggests that the person of the Lawgiver is of importance for the obligatory force of the commandment. In no case is the commandment to be separated from the one who commands; but in the case of 13:34 the circumstances of the command give its fulfillment an urgency which it would not otherwise have. Thus fidelity to the memory of Jesus who loved them unto the end moves[117] the disciples to love one another.

To move the discussion one step further, we must agree with Bultmann that the *kathōs* of v. 34 expresses the integral connection between the "love one another" and Jesus' love which they have experienced.[118] One can then speak of Jesus' love as the foundation of the disciples' mutual love.[119] The disciples' love for one another is grounded in the love of Jesus in the sense that the disciples' love for one another is the fulfillment of the purpose of Jesus' love. The love which the disciples have for one another continues the love which Christ has for them. Jesus loves them in order that they might love one another.[120] His love culminates in their love,[121] one for the other. His love is the enabling force of their love. As Bultmann writes: "The imperative is itself a gift, and this it can be because it receives its significance and its possibility of realization from the past, experienced as the love of the Revealer: *kathōs ēgapēsa humas.*"[122] The commandment itself is the gift of Jesus and the possibility of its own realization.[123]

At the deepest level, however, the *kathōs* of 13:34 overcomes the extrinsicism of the commandment. What the departing Jesus leaves to his disciples is not so much an order, but his presence in another mode. The love of the disciples for one another has its ontological root in the love of Christ which in turn is the love of God for them. It is, in fact, characteristic of Johannine theology to get back to the very foundation of the salvific realities.[124] Thus John, alone among the evangelists, offers a profound theological interpretation of love, an interpretation that is appropriately called "metaphysical."[125] Brotherly love means that the loving disciples participate in the very life of God.[126]

To grasp the realities toward which the Gospel is pointing, we must begin with the love of the Father for Jesus.[127] Twice (Jn 3:35; 5:20) John notes that the Father's love for the Son is the source of all that the Son has. It is because of the Father's love that the Son has all things (3:35); because of that same love the Son is able to do the works of the Father (5:20). In effect, the mission of the Son results from the Father's love. In fulfilling his mission, the Son abides in the Father's love (15:10). The *menein en* formula of Jn 15:10 underscores the reciprocal immanence of the Son and the Father. The Son, by fulfilling his mission, has kept the Father's commandments. Thus the Son abides in the Father and the Father in Him.

Yet the very love of the Father for the Son is the exemplar of the love[128] which Jesus extends to his disciples (15:9). The relationship is such that de Dinechin speaks of the *Analogatum Princeps* of similarity.[129] The Son's relationship with his disciples is like the relationship which the Father has with Him. The Father's love for the Son is thus the paradigm of the Son's love for his disciples: "As the Father has loved me, so have I loved you *(kagō humas ēgapēsa)*" (15:9). There is similarity, but there is no extrinsicism because the Son abides in the Father's love. Thus one can say that the Son loves his disciples with that love with which he is loved.[130]

When now Jesus commands his disciples to love one another, it appears that the love which he has for the disciples is the *tertium quid*, the mediating link, between the Father's love and the disciples' love for one another. Were one to combine, more immediately than the evangelist has done, vv. 9 and 12 of Jn 15, the text would read: "As the Father has loved me, so have I loved you; as I have loved you, so you love one another." In effect this means that the disciples are also the recipients of the Father's love, through the mediation of Jesus' love for them. This the evangelist states explicitly in the Priestly Prayer: "Thou hast sent me and hast loved them even as thou hast loved me" (17:23). That love does not remain extrinsic to the disciples since the Father's love with which the disciples are loved is in them: "that the love with which thou hast loved me may be in them" (17:26).

Although the evangelist does not make use of the powerful *menein en* formula to speak of the disciples' being in the Father's love, he does so when he reflects on the love which the disciples have for one another: "abide in my love. If you keep my commandments, you will abide in my love, just as I have kept my Father's commandments and abide in his love" (15:9c–10). The commandment above all which the disciples are to keep is the love commandment which follows almost immediately (15:12). It is clear that to "abide in my love" is the same as to "abide in me and I in you."[131] Thus the reciprocal immanence of Christ and the disciples is the existential situation of those disciples who truly love one another as Jesus has loved them. Such reciprocity is not a reward for keeping the love commandment.[132] Rather the love commandment is gift. Here, as so often in the Fourth Gospel, the Giver abides in the gift which He gives.[133]

Thus within the broad context of Jesus' mission, understood both in terms of commandment and of Jesus' participation in the life of the Father, falls the love commandment in its specifically Johannine formulation. The disciples' love for one another is caught up in a series of participatory relationships[134] in which we can discern two main motifs. On the one hand there is the Father's command to the Son bearing upon the totality of the Son's mission, and the command of the Son to his disciples at the hour of fulfillment of that mission. In a real sense, the mission of the Son is fulfilled in the love commandment. On the other hand, there is the Father's love for Jesus, Jesus' mediating love for the disciples, and the disciples' love for one another. The love of the disciples for one another has its true source in the love of God as Father.[135] In a very real sense, then, there is reciprocal intimacy between the Father and Jesus, between Jesus and his disciples, and between the Father and the disciples because of the reality of love.[136]

## LOVE ONE ANOTHER

Now the significance of "love one another" (*hina apagate allēlous*) as the content[137] of Jesus' new commandment comes to the full. The evangelist has sought to interpret the meaning of Jesus' glorification-return to the Father. To do so, he has employed the genre of the farewell discourse. The genre which he has chosen requires that the Departing One have something to say about the relationships which ought to obtain among those whom he is about to leave. Departure is not the moment for universal legislation; rather, it is the moment for memory and family spirit. Thus John's Jesus speaks of mutual love rather than of love of enemy[138] or love of neighbor[139] precisely because he is presented as giving instructions to his own as he is about to leave them: they are to be one among themselves even as he is one with them.

Yet it is not only the choice of literary genre which has dictated the particularism of the Johannine formulation of the love command-ment. The Johannine dualism,[140] so apparent in the exposition of the love commandment in 1 Jn 2 but also present in the farewell discourse, especially in its second part, has also contributed to a shaping of the apparently restrictive object of the love commandment in its Johannine formulation.[141] In Jesus the final times have arrived for those who are his disciples; they indeed belong to the light, and not to the darkness. The eschatological salvation of the future[142] is made present in the love of the community.[143] In effect, the love commandment in Jn is particularistic in its formulation because it is a reflection on the Church in the situation of Jesus' absence-presence. In somewhat similar fashion,

but without the depth of theological reflection present in John's formulation of the love commandment, even the love commandment of
the Old Testament was rather particularistic in its formulation. "Love
thy neighbor as thyself" (Lev 19:18) speaks more of love among the
Israelites than it speaks of a universal love. Yet this prescription is not
so restrictive as it is a covenant stipulation bearing upon the relationships which ought to obtain among those who are covenanted with
God and with one another. The love commandment of John is also a
covenant reality—the way of those who belong to the new covenant,
abiding in the Father through the mediation of Jesus' love.

   If the literary genre adopted in Jn 13–16, Johannine dualism, and
the covenant connotation of the love commandment in Jn prompt a
formulation of the commandment in terms of "brotherly love," one
can speak of the sectarian character of John's formulation of the love
commandment. It is sectarian in the sense that it is a reflection on the
Johannine church against a dualistic background, but it is not sectarian
if that means that hatred for those outside of the brotherhood is the
necessary concomitant of those who belong to the brotherhood. Oftentimes the dualism of the Fourth Gospel has prompted a comparison
between it and the Qumran writings.[144] Both speak of love within the
community.[145] Indeed it would appear that brotherly love is the binding force of the members of the sect according to the views of the
Qumran sectarians. Thus some commentators suggest that John's exposition of the love commandment is similar to that of Qumran's.[146]
But the parting of the ways comes with the realization that John's love
commandment never explicitly challenges the disciples to hate those
who do not belong to the brotherhood.[147] His reflection simply bears
upon the relationships which ought to obtain among the disciples themselves.[148]

   Indeed in 13:35 John appears to have defined discipleship in terms
of "love for one another."[149] The gift-commandment of brotherly love
forms Jesus' followers into a community and provides that community
with its identity before the world.[150] Since the community is constituted by Jesus' love, the mutual love which it evidences before the world
is its mark of recognition and its sign of credibility.[151] The community
is composed of those to whom the gift of the love commandment is
given. As love is a concrete expression of the life of God in the world,
those who receive the gift of the love commandment are those who
are begotten of God.[152] John joins love and faith together.[153] As those

who believe are begotten of God, so those who love are begotten of God. It is to the children of God that the love commandment is given. Thus it is most appropriate that the proclamation of the love command-ment in its Johannine formulation formed a traditional part of the bap-tismal catechesis within Johannine circles.

The love which is given and which constitutes believers as mem-bers of the faith community is, however, not a static reality. Love must produce its fruits. In fact, Jn 15:9–17, with its theme of love, is re-ally an interpretation of the idea of bearing fruit which is found in the parable of the vine and the branches.[154] A life of love must be the nor-mal occupation of the disciple. To love is the way which the disciple has to do righteousness.[155] His loving is the visible manifestation of the fact that he is the child of God. Thus love is more than a command-ment for the disciple. It is his way of life, his mandate.[156]

Thus it is the ecclesial situation of the Johannine community which has prompted the seemingly restrictive formulation[157] of the new com-mandment of love, but it is the Christological gift inherent in that com-mandment which yields its richness. To separate the Johannine formu-lation of the love commandment, "that you love one another," from its Johannine context, "a new commandment I give to you . . . even as I have loved you, that you also love one another," is to misrepresent Johannine thought. Yet it is only by means of such an exegetically un-warranted separation that one can arrive at the conclusion that John intended to restrict the scope of application of the traditional (i.e. Syn-optic) logion on love.[158]

The Johannine love commandment is not so much a precept as it is a gift. It does not so much imply a dictate from above as a pres-ence from within. Looked at as one of the salvific gifts which Jesus gives to his own, the love commandment is indeed for those whom he has chosen and to whom Jesus gives the gifts of salvation. The sal-vific gifts are given to those who are his disciples, for it is among and with them that Jesus abides. Thus Jesus' love for his disciples, as the revelation of the Father's love, is made present in the love which they have for one another. It is this pregnant theological reflection which constitutes the new commandment as an expression of that Revelation which the Revealer has come to make known. It is the reality of this participatory love which is Jesus' abiding in them, that is significant for all men, past and present:[159] "By this all men will know that you are my disciples, if you have love for one another" (Jn 13:35).

## NOTES

1. Rudolf Schnackenburg, *The Moral Teaching of the New Testament* (New York–London, 1964), pp. 328–329.

2. Ernst Käsemann, *The Testament of Jesus. A Study of John in the Light of Chapter 17* (Philadelphia, 1968), p. 65.

3. Raymond E. Brown, *The Gospel According to John (xiii–xxi)*, AB 29A (Garden City, 1970), p. 681.

4. It is commonly noted that the Gospel of John, unlike the Synoptics (Mk 12:28–34 and par.), unlike 1 Jn as well (1 Jn 4:10, 20 [2x], 21; 5:2), does not refer to God as the direct object of the disciples' love. Cf., for example, André Feuillet, "La morale chrétienne d'après saint Jean," *Esprit et Vie* 83 (1973), 665–670, pp. 669–670; K. Ottoson, "The Love of God in St. John Chrysostom's Commentary on the Fourth Gospel," *Church Quarterly Review* 166 (1965), 315–323, p. 317. The problematic entailed by John's omission of God as the object of love will not be my concern in the present article.

5. Stauffer, for example, comments: "It is not love for one's fellow man which Jesus proclaimed, with which the Johannine corpus is concerned: it is the love of the Christian brother and fellow-believer." Even C. H. Dodd noted that "Probably . . . the early church narrowed the concept of neighbour until it was equivalent to church member." Cf. E. Stauffer, *Die Botschaft Jesu* (Bern–Munich, 1959), p. 47; C. H. Dodd, *Gospel and Law* (Cambridge, 1951), p. 42.

6. Ludwig Berg has relegated, in effect, this discussion to a relatively secondary place by stressing that the emphasis of the love commandment is on the spontaneity of love, "that man should *be loving*," rather than on the object of love, "that man should love *someone*." He finds a confirmation of his opinion in the exemplarity of God's love. Cf. L. Berg, "Das neutestamentliche Liebesgebot-Prinzip der Sittlichkeit," *Trier Theologische Zeitschrift* 83 (1974), 129–145, esp. pp. 134–136.

7. Cf. Jn 15:12.

8. Among the characteristic traits of the farewell discourse found in Jn are the use of direct style ("I-you") and the characteristic expression, "little children" (Jn 13:33. Cf. T. Gad 4:1–2; 6:1; T. Rub. 1:3, 4:5; T. Iss 5:1, 6:1). Cf. Noël Lazure, "Louange au Fils de l'homme et commandement nouveau. Jn 13, 31–33a. 34–35," *Assemblées du Seigneur* 26 (1973), 73–80, p. 74. For a brief exposition of the literary genre, one might consult R. E. Brown, *o.c.,* pp. 597–603.

9. Cf. John F. Randall, *The Theme of Unity in John XVII:20–23* (Louvain, 1962), pp. 63–83.

10. André Feuillet, "The Structure of First John. Comparison with the Fourth Gospel. The Pattern of Christian Life," *Biblical Theology Bulletin* 3 (1973), 194–216.

11. For some general considerations on Johannine "love" vocabulary, cf. Ceslaus Spicq. *Agape in the New Testament*, vol. 3 (St. Louis, 1966).

12. The usage of the formula to compare the relationship between Jesus and

his disciples with that among the disciples is restricted to Jn 13:15, 34; 15:12; 17:14, 16. De Dinechin considers this to be a third (of four) type of *Kathōs*-relationship, which he calls "*agape* as similitude." Cf. Olivier de Dinechin, "ΚΑΘΩΣ: La similitude dans l'évangile selon saint Jean," *Recherches de Science Religieuse* 58 (1970), 195–236, pp. 208–209.

13. Cf. J. M. Reese, "Literary Structure of Jn 13:31–14:31; 16:5–6, 16–33," *CBQ* 34 (1972), 321–331, p. 321.

14. Thus, in various ways, A. Merx, P. Gaechter, C. H. Dodd, C. K. Barrett, A. Wikenhauser, R. Schnackenburg, M. E. Boismard, etc. A brief discussion of the issue is offered by R. E. Brown, *o.c.*, pp. 582–586. George Johnston divides Jn 13–16 into three speeches, 13:31–14:31, 15:1–16:4a, 16:4b–33, without, however, accepting a duplicate version theory. Cf. George Johnston, *The Spirit-Paraclete in the Gospel of John*, SNTSMS, 12 (Cambridge, 1970), pp. 72, 168.

15. Cf. Heinrich Zimmermann, "Struktur und Aussageabsicht der johanneischen Abschiedsreden (Jo 13–17)," *Bibel und Leben* 8 (1967), 279–290. Zimmermann (p. 289) even cites the change of locale, indicated at Jn 14:31, as support for his theory.

16. Cf. Jurgen Becker, "Die Abschiedsreden Jesu in Johannesevangelium," *ZNW* 616 (1970), 215–246, p. 218.

17. Cf. J. Becker, *art. cit.*, p. 220. Becker cites Heimüller, Wellhausen, Hirsch, and Richter.

18. Cf. J. M. Reese, *art. cit.*

19. Cf. J. M. Reese, *art. cit.*, pp. 323–324. Schnackenburg agrees that vv. 34–35 are a redactional insertion. In favor of his opinion he cites seven arguments including the link between vv. 33 and 36 and the fact that Jn 14 does not dwell on the love commandment. See R. Schnackenburg, *Das Johannesevangelium 3. Kommentar zu Kap. 13–21*, HTKNT 4/3 (Freiburg, 1975), p. 59. Bultmann suggests that vv. 34–35 are the evangelist's insertion into his "revelation discourse" source. See R. Bultmann, *The Gospel According to John* (Oxford, 1971), pp. 523–524. Heinz Becker, however allows for the trace of sources in 13:31–38 but concludes that the pericope is largely the composition of the Evangelist. See H. Becker, *Die Reden des Johannesevangeliums und der Stil der gnostichen Offenbarungsrede*, FRLANT, 50 (Göttingen, 1956), p. 94.

20. Cf. N. Lazure, "Louange," p. 73.

21. J. M. Reese, *art. cit.*, p. 323.

22. G. Reim, "Probleme der Abschiedsreden," *Biblische Zeitschrift* 20 (1976), 117–122, p. 117.

23. Cf. John L. Boyle, "The Last Discourse (Jn 13, 31–16, 33) and Prayer (Jn 17): Some Observations on Their Unity and Development," *Biblica* 56 (1975), 210–222.

24. In these five chapters (Jn 13–17) John has gathered together his version of material which the Synoptics have dispersed throughout. We might cite the mission logia (Mk 6:7–11 and par.), the instruction on life in the Christian community (Mk 9:35–40), the warning about persecution and the promise of divine assistance (Mk 13:9–13), the prediction of glory (Mk 13:26–27), the prediction of Judas' be-

trayal, Peter's denial, and the disciples' scattering (Mk 14:18-21, 26-31). Lagrange was in fact so impressed by some of these parallels that he considered Jn 15:1-17 to be the Johannine parallel of the Synoptics' mission discourse. We should also note the presence of the "Truly, truly, I say to you" formula—a formula which Lindars has identified as generally indicating a traditional logion. Cf. Jn 13:16, 20, 21; 14:12; 16:20, 23 (with "you" in the plural); Jn 13:38 (with "you" in the singular). Cf. M.-J. Lagrange, *Saint Jean. Études bibliques*, 6th ed. (Paris, 1936), p. 399; B. Lindars, *The Gospel of John, New Century Bible* (London, 1972), p. 48.

25. Cf. Francis J. Moloney, *The Johannine Son of Man*. Biblioteca de scienze religiose, 14 (Rome, 1976), p. 195. Cf. p. 199.

26. Cf. R. Bultmann, *The Gospel*, p. 525, n. 2; R. E. Brown, *o.c.*, p. 607; O. de Dinechin, *art. cit.*, p. 212.

27. Cf. R. Thysman, "L'Éthique de l'Imitation du Christ dans le Nouveau Testament. Situation, notations et variations du thème," *ETL* 42 (1966), 138-175, pp. 173-174. Thysman speaks of the salvific deeds as grounding "imitation ethics."

28. Cf. Lucien Cerfaux, "La charité fraternelle et le retour du Christ (Jo., XIII, 33-38)," *ETL* 24 (1948), 321-332, rp. in *Recueil Lucien Cerfaux* II, 27-40, cf. p. 37; R. Percival Brown, *entolē kainē* (St. John 13, 38), *Theology* 26 (1933), 184-193, pp. 184-185, 193; Jack Seynaeve, "La 'Charité' chrétienne est-elle dépassée?" *Revue du Clergé Africain* 27 (1972), 389-413, pp. 393, 399.

29. Cf. Georg Richter, *Die Fusswaschung im Johannesevangelium. Geschichte ihrer Deutung. Biblische Untersuchungen*, 1 (Regensburg, 1967), pp. 252-259. Cf. J. D. G. Dunn, "The Washing of the Disciples' Feet in John 13:1-20," *ZNTW* 61 (1970), 247-252.

30. Cf. Piet van Boxel, "Glaube und Liebe. Die Aktualität des johanneischen Jüngermodells," *Geist und Leben* 48 (1975), 18-28, p. 25.

31. On the other hand, Dibelius argued that it was vv. 13-15 which do not fit well into the context. The linchpin of his thesis was that v. 13 offered an example of "heroic" love which is not otherwise characteristic of the thought of the Fourth Evangelist. Cf. Martin Dibelius, "Joh 15, 13. Eine Studie zum Traditionsproblem des Johannesevangeliums," in *Festgabe für Adolf Deissmann zum Geburtstag 7 November 1927* (Tübingen, 1927), pp. 168-186.

32. Cf. P. van Boxel, *loc. cit.*

33. I cannot now consider the interrelationship among the five books in the Johannine corpus (Jn, 1, 2, 3 Jn, Rv) in full detail. As a working hypothesis, I would only suggest that the five books emanate from the same, somewhat closed, circle of Christians. Thus I find it useful to speak, as does Culpepper, of "the Johannine school." Nevertheless I am inclined to the view that no two of the writings which directly concern the present essay—Jn, 1 Jn, 2 Jn—derive from the same hand. Notwithstanding my acceptance of this view, and without therefore implying common authorship, it seems useful to maintain the traditional designation "John" as an indiscriminate signum to identify the authors of the respective texts. Cf. R. Alan Cul-

pepper, *The Johannine School. An Evaluation of the Johannine-school Hypothesis based on an Investigation of the nature of Ancient Schools,* SBL Dissertation Series, 26 (Missoula, 1975).

34. Cf. David L. Mealand, "The Language of Mystical Union in the Johannine Writings," *Downside Review* 95 (1977), 19–34, p. 32.

35. Thus, Matthew Vellanickal. Cf. *The Divine Sonship of Christians in the Johannine Writings,* AB 72 (Rome, 1978), p. 234. Rudolf Schnackenburg speaks only of "the beginning of their Christian life" whereas Bultmann speaks of "the point within history in which the Christian proclamation was received by the believers." Cf. R. Schnackenburg, *Die Johannesbriefe,* HTKNT 13/3, 2ⁿᵈ ed. (Freiburg, 1963), p. 111; R. Bultmann, *The Johannine Epistles, Hermaneia* (Philadelphia, 1973), pp. 27, 111. For a similar opinion, cf. Johannes Schneider, *Die Briefe des Jakobus, Petrus, Judas und Johannes. Die katholische Briefe, NTD,* 10, 9ᵗʰ ed. (Göttingen, 1961), p. 150.

36. Cf. 1 Jn 2:7, 18, 24; 3:11; 4:3.

37. Cf. J. Schneider, *o.c.,* p. 191; R. Schnackenburg, *Die Briefe,* p. 311 (both in reference to 2 Jn 5. Cf. also H. Conzelmann, "'Was von Anfang war,'" *Neutestamentliche Studien für Rudolf Bultmann BZNW* 21 (Berlin, 1954), 194–202, esp. pp. 195–199; V. Furnish, *The Love Command in the New Testament* (Nashville–New York, 1972), p. 152. This opinion is also offered by Alphonse Humbert. Cf. A. Humbert, "L'observance des commandements dans les écrits johanniques," pp. 187–219 in *Studia Moralia,* 1 (Rome, 1963), p. 206.

38. Cf. A. E. Brooke who writes that "the real force of the expression is to heighten the contrast of the 'newer' teaching which places knowledge higher than love." A. E. Brooke, *The Johannine Epistles, ICC* (Edinburgh, 1912), p. 35. Commenting on 2 Jn 5, Schnackenburg notes that the love commandment is formulated not only to insist on brotherly love but also to underscore the link with older tradition. Cf. R. Schnackenburg, *Die Briefe,* p. 311. Cf. also R. Bultmann, *The Johannine Epistles,* p. 27; J. Schneider, *o.c.,* p. 150.

39. In this respect Balz, Brooke, and others note that the Jesuanic commandment is also the commandment of God. Cf. Horst Balz, *Die katholische Briefe, NTD* 10, 11ᵗʰ ed., (Göttingen), p. 170; A. E. Brooke, *o.c.,* p. 35.

40. Cf. Marinus de Jonge, *De Brieven van Johannes. De Prediking van Het Nieuw Testament* (Nijkerk, 1968), p. 82.

41. *Ibid.*

42. Cf. the *palin* ("yet" [RSV], literally "again") in 1 Jn 2:8.

43. Bultmann's comment is apropos. He writes: "*Alēthēs* therefore does not mean 'true' in the sense of 'correct', but characterizes the 'new commandment' as something verifying itself as real. That it verifies itself as real in the congregation is also said in 3:14." R. Bultmann, *o.c.,* p. 27, n. 20.

44. Cf. H. Balz, *o.c.,* p. 171; R. Schnackenburg, *Die Johannesbriefe,* pp. 111–112; R. Bultmann, *The Johannine Epistles,* p. 27.

45. Cf. J. Becker, *art. cit.*

46. Cf. R. Schnackenburg, *Die Johannesbriefe*, p. 111; David L. Mealand, *art. cit.*, p. 32. Vellanickal writes, "*agapē* in Jn becomes an objective reality, a form of existence, a concrete expression of the life of God in this world." Cf. M. Vellanickal, *o.c.*, p. 314.

47. Cf. J. Schneider, *o.c.*, p. 151.

48. We must note the practicality of the love commandment's demand. Mutual love is a matter of exercise, practice, action. Thus Schnackenburg, contrary to Brooke (p. 177) takes the *hina* clause of 2 Jn 5 as dependent on *erōtō* ("beg") rather than on *entolēn* ("commandment"). In effect the text should be understood as follows: "And now, lady, not as writing you a new commandment, but the one we have had from the beginning, I beg you to love one another." The practical aspect of the love ethic is also emphasized in 2 Jn 6, linked externally to v. 5 by the catchword "love" (*agapē*). To love one another is to "follow" (*peripatein*) his commandments. The author uses *peripatein* (literally, "to walk"), the verb traditionally used of behavior in Jewish and Christian writings. Stress on the reality of love is also strongly emphasized at 1 Jn 4:7–10. Cf. R. Schnackenburg, *Die Johannesbriefe*, pp. 311–312; M. de Jonge, *o.c.*, pp. 246–247.

49. Cf. A. Feuillet, "The Structure."

50. M. Vellanickal, *o.c.*, p. 303.

51. Cf. Heinrich Schlier, "Die Bruderliebe nach dem Evangelium und den Briefen des Johannes," in *Mélanges Béda Rigaux*, ed. by A. Descamps and A. de Halleux (Gembloux, 1970), 235–245, p. 243.

52. Cf. R. Bultmann, *The Johannine Epistles*, p. 27.

53. The Book of Revelation offers an exception to the otherwise Johannine predilection for "commandment."

54. Cf. Noël Lazure, *Les valeurs morales de la théologie johannique (Évangiles et Épîtres), Études bibliques* (Paris, 1965), p. 31. *Entolē* ('commandment') appears eleven times in Jn (10:18; 11:57; 12:49, 50; 13:34; 14:15, 21, 31; 15:10 [2x], 12), fourteen times in 1 Jn (2:3, 4, 7 [3x], 8; 3:22, 23 [2x], 24; 4:21; 5:2, 3 [2x]), and four times in 2 Jn (2 Jn 4, 5, 6 [2x]). It also appears in Rev 12:17; 14:12. *Entellesthai* ('to command') appears only in Jn 8:5; 14:31; 15:14, 17. It appears some twelve other times in the NT, including five times in Mt.

55. Cf. William Hendricksen, *New Testament Commentary. Exposition of the Gospel According to John*, vol. 2 (Grand Rapids, 1954), p. 252.

56. Cf. C. Spicq, *Agapē*, 3, p. 49; *Théologie morale du Nouveau Testament*, 2. *Études bibliques* (Paris, 1965), pp. 507–509.

57. Cf. N. Lazure, *Les valeurs morales*, p. 144.

58. Cf. Matthew J. O'Connell, "The Concept of Commandment in the Old Testament." *Theological Studies* 21 (1960), 351–403, esp. pp. 351, 369.

59. J. van der Ploeg, "Studies in Hebrew Law." *CBQ* 12 (1950), 248–259, 416–427, p. 258.

60. With van Boxel, we can note the similarity between "words" and "com-

mandments" (Ex 20:1; Dt 5:5, 22). Cf. P. van Boxel, *art. cit.*, p. 26. Something similar is to be found within the Johannine corpus (1 Jn 2:4–5). Cf. N. Lazure, *Les valeurs morales*, p. 138; H. Schlier, *art. cit.*, p. 241.

61. Thus O'Connell describes the commandment of Dt as "the creative and redemptive pattern, revealed by God, for Israel's existence as His holy people." M. J. O'Connell, *art. cit.*, p. 372.

62. Cf. C. Spicq, *Agape*, 3, p. 49.

63. Cf. M. O'Connell, *art. cit.*, p. 394; A. Lacomara, "Deuteronomy and the Farewell Discourse (Jn 13:31–16:33)," *CBQ* 36 (1974), 65–84, pp. 73–74; William L. Moran, "The Ancient Near Eastern Background of the Love of God in Deuteronomy," *CBQ* 25 (1963), 77–87, p. 78.

64. A specific formulation of the commandment of brotherly love is not found in Dt, as it is in Lv 19:18. G. E. Wright considers this to be an accidental phenomenon insofar as "the motive of brotherly love is so basic and prominent in the exposition of the law." Cf. G. E. Wright, *Deuteronomy. Interpreter's Bible*, 2 (New York, 1953), p. 401.

65. Cf. Dt 10:12, 11:1, 22; 19:9.

66. M. J. O'Connell, *art. cit.*, p. 394. Cf. pp. 382–383.

67. Here the RSV renders *entolē* as charge.

68. Cf. David M. Stanley, "Believe the Works," *The Way* 4 (1978), 272–286, p. 281.

69. Jn 14:15, 21; 15:10 (twice). These are, in fact, the only passages in the Gospel in which the plural is used. 2 Jn uses the plural seven times (2:3, 4; 3:22, 24; 5:2, 3 [twice]), five times with the verb *tērein*. Lazure claims that the distinction between the singular and the plural should be maintained. The singular has reference to a specific precept, whereas the plural refers to the total will of God. Cf. N. Lazure, *Les valeurs morales*, pp. 126–127.

70. Cf. Dt 1:1; 32:45; 33:1. Cf. A. Lacomara, "Deuteronomy," p. 84.

71. Cf. A. Lacomara, who writes: "Jesus is the first-person subject of the 'I-thou' form of address and hence, like Moses in Dt, he is not a mere herald of the law, he is a lawgiver: '*I* give you a new commandment' (Jn 13:34; cf. 14:15, 15:12, 14). In the OT it is only in Dt that we find a parallel to this presentation of the law in the person of the mediator." A. Lacomara, *art. cit.*, p. 67; A. Humbert, *art. cit.*, p. 202.

72. Bernard has gone beyond the evidence of the text in asserting apropos Jn 13:34 that, "He claimed to 'give commandments,' and so claimed to be equal to God." Cf. J. H. Bernard, *A Critical and Exegetical Commentary on the Gospel of St. John, ICC* (Edinburgh, 1929), p. 326.

73. Cf. A. Vanhoye, "L'œuvre du Christ, don du Père," *Recherches de Science Religieuse* 48 (1960), 387–391.

74. Cf. N. Lazure, *Les valeurs morales*, pp. 130–131. That the commandment is Jesus' revelatory word is also indicated in 1 Jn where we find a parallelism between

Jesus' commandments and his word in 2:4–5 and where the love commandment is styled "the message" (*aggelia*) in 3:11.

75. While noting that Jn has no symbol for love, P. S. Naumann has shown that in Jn "love is the presence of Christ," Cf. P. S. Naumann, "The presence of Love in John's Gospel," *Worship* 39 (1965), 369–371. Cf. also C. Spicq, *Agape*, p. 54.

76. While the verb *didonai* occurs some eight times in Jn 17, it is relatively rarely used in the farewell discourses. However it does serve to indicate that peace (14:27), the Spirit (14:16), and the "new commandment" (13:34) are Jesus' gift to his disciples. Certainly the gift of the Spirit is the answer to Jesus' absence; it is the new mode of his active presence. Something similar can also be said of the new commandment.

77. Cf. Jn 19:41.

78. Cf. Mk 12:31 and par.

79. Cf. 1 Jn 2:7–8 and *supra*, pp. 108.

80. Lv 19:18.

81. *Mishnah*, Ab 1:12.

82. That the love commandment is called a "new commandment" in Jn 13:34, 1 Jn 2:7–8, and 2 Jn 5 would seem to indicate that the epithet is common to the Johannine school. That the author of 1 Jn who wants to stress the relative antiquity of the love commandment nevertheless feels constrained to call the love commandment a "new commandment" would seem to indicate that the designation enjoyed the force of normative tradition within the Johannine school. Thus it is difficult to agree with the contention of Alphonse Humbert and Noël Lazure that the "new commandment" designation of Jn 13:34 indicates a literary dependence on 1 Jn 2:7–8. An argument in favor of the Humbert-Lazure position might be that vv. 34–35 are a relatively late addition in the redaction of Jn 13. However vv. 7–8 would also seem to warrant the judgment that they too are a traditional element inserted by a redactor into material taken from a source (thus, Bultmann). In any event 1 Jn seems to have been composed after Jn, in which case it is more likely that 1 Jn 2:7–8 and 2 Jn 5 depend on Jn 13:34–35 than vice versa. Cf. A. Humbert, *art. cit.*, pp. 205–206; O. Prunet, *La morale chrétienne d'après les écrits johanniques* (Paris, 1957), p. 106; N. Lazure, *Les valeurs morales*, p. 229; R. Bultmann, *The Johannine Epistles*, p. 27.

83. Cf. C. Spicq, *Agape*, pp. 53–54.

84. Cf. also, E. C. Hoskyns, *o.c.*, p. 450; R. Schnackenburg, *Moral Teaching*, p. 324.

85. Surprisingly Joseph Bonsirven gives two reasons why "new" is an appropriate qualification of the Johannine love commandment. In the first instance he cites the universal extension of the commandment. Cf. J. Bonsirven, *Épîtres de saint Jean* (Paris, 1935), p. 116.

86. 1 Jn 2:7–11.

87. The purpose of the present article allows me this generalization, à la C. H. Dodd, despite the consequent eschatology of Jn 5:25–29, etc.

88. New wineskins (Mt 9:17; Mk 2:22); new things (Mt 13:52); new covenant (Mt 26:28; Mk 14:24; Lk 22:20); new teaching (Mk 1:27); new cloth (Mk 2:21); new wine (Mt 2:22; Lk 5:38); new garment (Lk 5:36 [3x]). Cf. Mt 26:29; Mk 14:25.

89. Cf. Roy A. Harrisville, *The Concept of Newness in the New Testament* (Minneapolis, 1960), p. 93; R. Bultmann, *The Gospel*, pp. 526, 527; L. Cerfaux, *art. cit.*, pp. 38–39; V. Furnish, *o.c.*, pp. 138, 151, etc. Bultmann writes, with characteristic and correct conciseness: "Jesus' command of love is 'new' even when it has been long-known, because it is the law of the eschatological community, for which the attribute 'new' denotes not an historical characteristic but its essential nature" (p. 527). Cf. E. Käsemann, *o.c.*, pp. 67–70. Among other reflections, Käsemann states that "brotherly love is heavenly solidarity directed towards individual Christians" (p. 70).

90. The Synoptic formulation of the love commandment, i.e., as the great or first commandment(s), from among the 613 of the Torah is not endowed with the same eschatological qualification as is the Johannine formulation in which the commandment is given as Jesus' legacy to his disciples at the moment of his departure. Thus the Synoptists' love commandment could not be properly described as a "new commandment." Nonetheless Cerfaux has correctly exploited Mt 25:34–45 as an indication that charity is the normal occupation of the Christian who is waiting for the Parousia, i.e., who is in a state of eschatological anticipation. Cf. L. Cerfaux, *art. cit.*, p. 32.

91. Cf. R. Schnackenburg, *Moral Teaching*, p. 325.

92. Cf. N. Lazure, *Les valeurs morales*, p. 230.

93. Cf. L. Cerfaux, *art. cit.*, p. 38; N. Lazure, *Les valeurs morales*, p. 230; J. Seynaeve, *art. cit.*, p. 395; S. Cipriani, "Dio e amore. La dottrina della carità in San Giovanni," *Scuola Cattolica* 94 (1966), 214–231, p. 221.

94. Cf. Alfred Loisy, *Le Quatrième Évangile*. (Paris, 1903), p. 736; G. H. C. Macgregor, *The Gospel of John, MNTC* (London, 1928), p. 283.

95. Cf., for example, B. Sandvic, "Joh. 15 als Abendmahlstext," *Theologische Zeitschrift* 23 (1967), 323–328; R. E. Brown, *The Gospel*, pp. 672–674; D. J. Hawkins, "Orthodoxy and Heresy in John 10:1–21 and 15:1–17," *Evangelical Quarterly* 47 (1975), 208–213, p. 212.

96. Cf. J. D. G. Dunn, *art. cit.*; Georg Richter, "Die Fusswaschung Joh 13, 1–20," *Münchener Theologischer Zeitschrift* 16 (1965), 13–26.

97. In effect, the main arguments for the Eucharistic interpretation of the Johannine new comandment seem to be its placement within the farewell discourse and its connotation as Christ's presence. These arguments seem weak and unnecessary to me, especially in view of John's treatment of the profound significance of the Eucharist in Jn 6. Thus I would take issue with the position modestly suggested by Furnish (*The Love Command*, pp. 138–139), and advanced by R. Percival Brown (*art. cit.*, pp. 190–191), and André Feuillet (*Le mystère de l'amour divin dans la théologie johannique. Études bibliques* (Paris, 1972), p. 98).

98. Thus Raymond Brown writes: "The newness of the commandment of love is really related to the theme of covenant at the Last Supper—the "new commandment" of John xiii 34 is the basic stipulation of the 'new Covenant' of Luke xxii 20." R. E. Brown, *The Gospel According to John (xiii–xxi), AB* 29A, p. 614.

99. Cf. A. Loisy, *o.c.,* p. 769; J. H. Bernard, *o.c.,* pp. 485–486; E. C. Hoskyns, *The Fourth Gospel,* 2nd ed. (London, 1947), p. 450; A. Feuillet, "La morale chrétienne d'après saint Jean," *Esprit et vie* 83 (1973) 665–670, p. 669; "Le Temps de l'Église" p. 68; P. van Boxel, *art. cit.,* p. 27; R. Schnackenburg, *Das Johannesevangelium,* p. 123; *Econtra,* V. Furnish, *o.c.,* p. 137. Cf. A. E. Brooke, *The Johannine Epistles,* p. 177.

100. Cf. J. L. Boyle, *art. cit.,* pp. 210–211; A. Feuillet, *Le Mystère,* p. 88.

101. Cf. R. Schnackenburg, *Das Johannesevangelium,* 3, pp. 59–60.

102. Cf. Jn 15:12.

103. With R. P. Brown we can note that a "sub-final clause introduced by *hina* to define the content of a command or a request is extraordinarily frequent in the NT." The second *hina* clause reaffirms and amplifies the first, with which it is coordinated. Cf. R. P. Brown, *art. cit.,* p. 189; L. Morris, *The Gospel According to John, NICNT* (Grand Rapids, 1971), p. 633, n. 73.

104. Fully a half-century ago, Macgregor already wrote that, "Jesus' love is to be at once the source and measure of theirs." Cf. G. H. C. Macgregor, *o.c.,* p. 289. De Dinechin also points to a fuller understanding of the *kathōs* formula by citing the "three dimensions: logical, chronological, and unifying" of the relationship. Cf. O. de Dinechin, *art. cit.,* p. 210. Brown notes that "For John *kathōs* is not only comparative but also causative or constitutive, meaning 'inasmuch as.'" Cf. R. E. Brown, *The Gospel,* p. 663.

105. Cf. R. Bultmann, *The Gospel,* p. 525. Undoubtedly Bultmann's rejection of the interpretations of Loisy and Schumann, the former suggesting that Jesus' love offers a model for the intensity of the disciples' love and the latter suggesting that Jesus' love offers a model for the manner of the disciples' love, owes to his exegetical apriori. An existential analysis of the text does not leave room for an exemplary role to be accorded to the love of the historical Jesus.

106. It must be granted that there is considerable discussion as to the relationship between Jn 13:1–12 and 13–20. Substantial opinion holds that vv. 13–20 are a later addition to the tradition. As such they serve to add a paraenetic reflection to a tradition which is essentially Christological and soteriological in emphasis. Cf. M. E. Boismard, "Le lavement des pieds," *Revue biblique* 71 (1964), 5–24; G. Richter, "Die Fusswaschung Joh 13, 1–12," pp. 301–320; "Die Deutung des Kreuzetodes Jesu in der Leidensgeschichte des Johannesevangeliums (Jo 13–19)," *Bibel und Leben* 9 (1968), 21–36; J. D. G. Dunn, "The Washing of the Disciples' Feet." On the other hand, Alfons Weiser has argued vigorously against Richter's position. He holds that basically the verses have been inserted into the narrative by the evangelist himself. Cf. A. Weiser, "Joh 13, 12–20—Zufügung eines späteren Herausgabers?" *Biblische Zeitschrift* 12 (1968), 252–257.

107. Apropos 13:15, Victor Furnish comments: "Jesus has provided not just an ideal model or pattern to be imitated. His action becomes 'exemplary' insofar as his disciples themselves have been served by his love." V. Furnish, *The Love Command*, pp. 136–137.

108. Thus de Dinechin classifies the saying of 13:15 along with those found in 13:34 and 15:12 within the third type of similitude found in Jn, i.e., "*agapē* as similitude." Cf. O. de Dinechin, *art. cit.*, p. 208.

109. Even Bultmann and Käsemann underscore service as the content of the love commandment in Jn. Cf. R. Bultmann, *The Gospel*, p. 526; E. Käsemann, *o.c.*, pp. 61–62.

110. L. Cerfaux, *art. cit.*, p. 37, Cf. R. Schnackenburg, *o.c.*, p. 324; A. Feuillet, "La morale chrétienne," pp. 667, 670; J. Seynaeve, *art. cit.*, p. 393.

111. The command may in fact be formulated according to some well-known proverb. Cf. Plato, *Symposium* 179B (Brown); Aristotle, *Nicomachaen Ethics* IX, 8; 1119C, 18–20 (Feuillet); Tyrt. 6:1ff (Bultmann).

112. Cf. R. E. Brown, *The Gospel*, p. 682.

113. Cf. D. J. Hawkins, *art. cit.*, p. 213; R. Schnackenburg, *Das Johannes-evangelium*, p. 124.

114. Cf. A. Feuillet, *ibid.*; R. Thysman, *art. cit.*, p. 172; J. Seynaeve, *art. cit.*, p. 399; A. Lacomara, *art. cit.*, pp. 76–77; and A. Loisy, *o.c.*, p. 736. Nevertheless Hendriksen remarks that "the love of Christ cannot *in every sense* be a pattern of our love toward one another." W. Hendriksen, *o.c.*, p. 305.

115. Cf. A. Weiser, *art. cit.*, pp. 254–255.

116. Cf. R. Thysman, *art. cit.*, pp. 172–173; A. Plummer, *The Gospel according to St. John* (Cambridge, 1882), *ad loc.* Jack Seynaeve comments that this Johannine love commandment derives its entire motivation from a christological fact—charity manifested by Christ himself. Cf. J. Seynaeve, *art. cit.*, p. 396.

117. Cf. N. Lazure, *Les valeurs morales*, p. 220.

118. Cf. R. Bultmann, *The Gospel*, p. 525. In somewhat similar vein, Lacomara writes: "The love that is to be expressed in mutual charity is nothing less than the love that found supreme expression on the cross. It is because of this love, and according to the measure of this love, that the disciples are to love one another, the *kathōs* of 13:34 and 15:12 signifying both 'because' and 'as.' Because the Passion, the foundation of this law is new and, strictly, unparalleled, the law of charity is not a repetition of a former stipulation, but the enunciation of a new code by which the new community is to be bound together and united to Jesus." Cf. A. Lacomara, *art. cit.*, p. 77. Similarly H. van den Bussche, *Le Discours d' Adieu de Jésus* (Tournai, 1959), p. 58.

119. Bultmann often speaks of the "foundational" (*begründend*) sense of *kathōs*. Cf. R. Bultmann, *The Gospel*, pp. 527–528, and *passim*. Indeed, he states that, "The only thing that is specifically Christian is the grounding of the command and, in line with this, its realization." *The Gospel*, p. 542, n. 4. Cf. also H. Schlier,

"Die Bruderliebe," p. 238, n. 1, p. 244; and R. Schnackenburg, *Das Johannesevangelium*, p. 60.

    120. Cf. R. Bultmann, *The Gospel*, p. 525.

    121. Cf. L. Cerfaux, *art. cit.*, p. 37; O. de Dinechin, *art. cit.*, p. 209.

    122. R. Bultmann, *The Gospel*, p. 525. Cf. H. Schlier, *art. cit.*, pp. 239–240.

    123. Cf. R. Schnackenburg, *Das Johannesevangelium*, p. 60.

    124. Cf. L. Cerfaux, *art. cit.*, p. 38.

    125. Already Martin Dibelius had spoken of the double nature of *agapē* in Jn: its popular aspect and the "metaphysical" conception. Cf. M. Dibelius, "Joh 15, 13"; also A. Feuillet, "Le Temps de l'Église," pp. 69–70; *Le mystère*, pp. 20, 84. Cipriani has, however, taken issue with Dibelius' "metaphysical" interpretation. Cf. S. Cipriani, *art. cit.*, p. 218. A weakness of Dibelius' position was, in fact, his separation of the ethical from the ontic dimensions of the love commandment and finding only the latter to be characteristic of Jn. These two aspects compenetrate one another.

    126. With somewhat more precision than a strict interpretation of the text warrants, Feuillet has even written that "the Christian life has become like a reflection of the Trinitarian relations." Cf. A. Feuillet, "La morale chrétienne d'après saint Jean," p. 666. Cf. also A. Feuillet, *Le mystère*, p. 58; "Un cas privilégié de pluralisme doctrinal: La conception différente de l'agapē chez saint Paul et saint Jean," *Esprit et Vie* 82 (1972), 497–509, p. 501.

    127. Cf. H. Schlier, *art. cit.*, pp. 235–239. Cf. also R. Schnackenburg, "Excurs 10. Die Liebe als Wesenseigentümlichkeit Gottes," in *Die Johannesbriefe*, pp. 206–213.

    128. Jn 15:9. Cf. A. Humbert, *art. cit.*, p. 204.

    129. Cf. O. de Dinechin, *art. cit.*, pp. 198–199.

    130. Cf. Jürgen Heise, who comments: "The love of the Son for his own is grounded in the love of the Father for the Son (cf. 3:25). In the love of the Son the Father's love has been revealed to the world." Cf. J. Heise, *Bleiben. Menein in den Johanneischen Schriften*. Hermeneutische Untersuchungen zur Theologie, 9 (Tübingen, 1967), p. 89.

    131. Jn 15:4. Cf. J. Heise, *o.c.*, p. 90.

    132. Cf. J. Heise, *o.c.*, p. 90

    133. With Brown and Feuillet one can cite the influence of Wisdom motifs. Divine *Sophia* abides in men and makes them God's friends. Cf. R. E. Brown, *The Gospel*, pp. 682–683; A. Feuillet, *Le mystère*, pp. 42–43.

    134. Cf. A. Humbert, *art. cit.*, pp. 188, 215; O. Prunet, *o.c.*, p. 99.

    135. Cf. J. L. Boyle, *art. cit.*, p. 218. Prunet distinguishes this "theological" sense from eschatological and the ecclesiastical sense of the love commandment. Cf. O. Prunet, *La morale chrétienne d'après les écrits johanniques*, Paris, 1957, p. 98.

    136. Cf. O. de Dinechin, *art. cit.*, pp. 214–215; H. Schlier, *art. cit.*, p. 241. The point is well emphasized by David L. Mealand, who writes: "It is because God has known his own from the beginning, and has revealed himself to them in his Son, that they in turn know and trust him. But above all it is in the dynamic of *agapē*

that the mutuality consists. Dodd expresses this very well when he speaks of indwelling as due to the love which is 'the very life and activity of God.'" Cf. D. L. Mealand, *art. cit.*, p. 31 with reference to C. H. Dodd, *The Interpretation of the Fourth Gospel* (London, 1952), p. 196.

137. The *hina* clause is to be taken epexegetically so that "love one another" constitutes the commandment. Cf. R. E. Brown, *The Gospel*, p. 607; R. Schnackenburg, *Das Johannesevangelium*, p. 60. Bultmann comments: "And in so far as the content of the *entolē* is *hina agapatē allēlous*, the care for oneself is changed into a care for one's neighbour." Cf. R. Bultmann, *The Gospel*, p. 525. Cf. 2 Jn 5 where the *hina* clause, *pace* Brooke (*o.c.*, p. 173), relates to *erōtō*. Cf. R. Schnackenburg, *Die Johannesbriefe*, pp. 311–312.

138. Cf. Mt 5:43 (44–48). Cf. Lk 6:27–28, 32–36.

139. Mk 12:31 and par.

140. Cf. N. Lazure, *Les valeurs morales*, p. 232.

141. In this respect it is to be noted that Jesus' love is also directed to "his own." Cf. Jn 15:9. The Father's love is, however, directed to the world. Cf. Jn 3:16.

142. Cf. Jn 14:2.

143. Cf. J. Becker, *art. cit.*, pp. 230, 232; O. Prunet, *o.c.*, p. 106.

144. Cf. James Charlesworth, "A Critical Comparison of the Dualism in 1 QS 3:13–4:26 and the 'Dualism' Contained in the Gospel of John," *NTS* 15 (1968–1969), 389–418.

145. Cf. QS 1:9–11 and 2:24–25; 5:4, 24–26; 6:25–27; 7:4–9; 8:2; 10:17–18; 11:1–12; CD 6:20; 7:2–3; 13:18.

146. For example, Lucetta Mowry who has written: "To be sure, the evangelist hesitates to press his exclusion to an attitude of hatred for outsiders, but by implication he approaches the Qumran point of view." L. Mowry, *The Dead Sea Scrolls and the Early Church* (Chicago, 1962), p. 30. Cf. E. Käsemann, p. 59. Still more nuanced is the view of Leon Morris: But we should not without further ado assume that the attitudes of Qumran and of John are the same, or even basically similar. . . . Nevertheless it is of interest that the Qumran exhortations to brotherly love should be more nearly paralleled in John than in other parts of the New Testament. L. Morris, *Studies in the Fourth Gospel* (Grand Rapids, 1969), pp. 338–339. In a similar vein, cf. R. E. Brown, "The Qumran Scrolls and the Johannine Gospel and Epistles." CBQ 17 (1955), 403–419, 559–574, pp. 561–564.

147. Cf. F. C. Fensham, "Love in the Writings of Qumran and John," *Neotestamentica* 6 (1972), 67–77, esp. pp. 69, 75.

148. It is surprising, therefore, that Schnackenburg speaks, in context, of the universality of Christian love in contrast to the particularism of Judaism. Cf. R. Schnackenburg, *Die Johannesbriefe*, p. 111.

149. In v. 35 John uses one of his descriptive definitions. Cf 16:30; 1 Jn 2:3, 5; 3:16, 19, 24; 4:9, 13; 5:2, in each of which is found a following *hoti* clause. Cf. R. Bultmann, *The Gospel*, pp. 525, n. 1; 539.

150. Cf. V. Furnish, *The Love Command*, p. 139; R. E. Brown, *The Gospel*, p. 613; P. van Boxel, *art. cit.*, p. 23; C. Spicq, *Théologie morale*, pp. 493, 506. The latter speaks of the "institutional law of the Church" and the "constitution of the Church."

151. Cf. N. Lazure, *Les valeurs morales*, p. 229; S. Cipriani, *art. cit.*, p. 229; A. Feuillet, "Le temps de l'Église," p. 69.

152. Cf. 1 Jn 2:29–3:10. Cf. M. Vellanickal, *The Divine Sonship*, pp. 295, 313–314.

153. Cf. R. Schnackenburg, *Moral Teaching*, p. 325; H. Schlier, *art. cit.*, pp. 240–241; R. Bultmann, *The Gospel*, p. 529. Bultmann considers Jn 15:1–17 to be a commentary on 13:34–35. He notes that, "The exposition of the command of love as the essential element in the constancy of faith makes it clear that faith and love form a unity; i.e. that the faith of which it can be said *kathōs ēgapēsa humas*, is authentic only when it leads to *agapan allēlous.*

154. Cf. R. E. Brown, *The Gospel*, p. 680; R. Schnackenburg, *Das Johannesevangelium*, p. 127.

155. Cf. M. Vellanickal, *The Divine Sonship*, p. 295; A. Humbert, *art. cit.*, p. 209; H. Schlier, *art. cit.*, p. 244.

156. Cf. N. Lazure, *Les valeurs morales*, pp. 144–145; "Louange," p. 79.

157. Cf. M. Vellanickal, *The Divine Sonship*, p. 299.

158. A more accurate reflection on the limited scope of the Johannine formulation of the love commandment is offered by Feuillet who writes of "a privileged case of doctrinal pluralism," Cf. A. Feuillet, "Un cas privilégié."

159. Abbot already called attention to the frequent use of the present subjunctive in the farewell discourse(s): the precept extends to all future generations. Cf. C. A. Abbott, *Johannine Vocabulary Diatesserica*, 4 (London, 1905), p. 2529. From another point of view, a similar point is made by N. Lazure (*Les valeurs morales*, pp. 216–217).

# 6

## Paul's First Reflections on Love

IN AN ANALYSIS which has been cited several times over since its publication in 1951,[1] the late C. H. Dodd distinguished four motifs which characterize the paraenesis of the early Christian church. An eschatological orientation, its reference to the Body of Christ, the theme of discipleship, and the primacy of love are the qualities which give a Christian character to the moral exhortation attested by the pages of the New Testament.

It is certain that Paul's letters witness to the preeminent place accorded to love by early Christian preachers. Indeed, more than sixty percent of the New Testament occurrences of the word "love," ἀγάπη, are to be found within the Pauline corpus.[2] Paul uses the verb "to love," ἀγαπᾶν, more frequently than do the three Synoptists together and only slightly less frequently than does the author of the Fourth Gospel.[3] This linguistic evidence confirms one's initial impression that Paul must have been one who preached about love, even if it was the evangelist John who has provided us with the essential elements for our theological reflection on love.

Nevertheless when studies are made of Paul's ideas on love, reference is all too readily made to the great epistles. In his first letter to the Corinthians we find the great paean on love (1 Cor 13). In his letter to the Romans, Paul wrote that "God's love has been poured into our hearts through the Holy Spirit which has been given to us" (Rom 5:5). In Gal 5:22 love is cited as the first of the fruits of the Spirit. Such reflections are certainly significant. Yet they belong to a later stage in the development of Paul's thought. Paul's thought had matured considerably before he wrote the great epistles. It was shaped by countless efforts of evangelization; it was refined in the crucible of his controversy with the Judaizers.

Perhaps, then, it might prove interesting to look at the earliest of Paul's letters, his first to the Thessalonians, in order to see how he first began to speak about love to those whom he had evangelized. Such an examination of Paul's earliest reflections on love seems to be all the more warranted in that an image of Paul the preacher appears to emerge from the words of his first letter to a degree not found in his later correspondence.

In this earliest letter, and from the merely statistical point of view, we find that Paul employs the noun "love," ἀγάπη, five times (1:3; 3:6; 3:12; 5:8; 5:13), the verb "to love," ἀγαπᾶν, twice (1:4; 4:9) and the adjective "beloved," ἀγαπητός, once (2:8). Thus some mention of love is to be found in each of the chapters of Paul's first epistle. Such a statement cannot be made about any of the other letters in the Pauline corpus with the exception of Phlm, which has but one chapter, and the deutero-Pauline 2 Thess, Eph and Col.

It is, of course, well known that Paul's missionary preaching was largely inspired by the type of preaching that took place in the Jewish synagogues of the diaspora.[4] Already prior to Paul, love had acquired an important place in the moral vocabulary of Judaism.[5] Thus the letter to Aristeas, an anonymous Jewish document written shortly before Paul's conversion to Christianity, reports the following conversation: "The king spoke kindly to him and then asked the next, 'What is it that resembles beauty in value?' And he said, 'Piety, for it is the pre-eminent form of beauty, and its power lies in love, which is the gift of God. This you have already acquired and with it all the blessings of life." (Aristeas, 259).

Accordingly, a number of scholars, ranging from A. Brieger (1925)[6] to Béda Rigaux (1959)[7] and Willi Marxsen (1979),[8] have come to the conclusion that the faith-hope-love triad which is commonly associated with Paul by reason of the oft-quoted 1 Cor 13:13 is, in fact, a pre-Pauline formula which the apostle has borrowed from an earlier tradition. Subsequently Paul made of this triad a touchstone of his own moral exhortation. Thus the faith-hope-love formula lies beneath the epistolary development found in Rom 5:1–5, Gal 5:5–6 and Col 1:4–5. In Paul's first letter to the Thessalonians, the triad occurs twice, namely at 1 Thess 1:3 and 1 Thess 5:8. The fact that in the latter passage Paul is making use of Is 59:17 which identifies only two pieces of armor, the breast plate and the helmet, in its description of the divine panoply but that Paul nevertheless incorporates faith, hope, and love, all three, into his accommodation of the prophetic text serves as an indication that the "Pauline formula" is indeed pre-Pauline.[9]

## FAITH, LOVE, AND HOPE

In faith, hope, and love Paul has found an adequate description of the Christian life.[10] Together these three terms epitomize the way in which the reception of the Gospel shapes the life of the individual as well as that of the Christian community. In 1 Thessalonians, as in his later letters, Paul always places faith in the initial position when he uses the traditional triadic formula to describe the condition of the Christians to whom he is writing. This is as it should be since the first manifestation of one's Christian condition is that one has received the word of God "as what it really is, the word of God, which is at work in you believers" (1 Thess 2:13). Faith is the new mode of existence of the Christian. Yet faith, as Paul says in his letter to the Galatians "works through love" (Gal 5:6). Thus Paul associates faith with love, not only in the triadic formula found in 1 Thess 1:3 and 5:8, but also in 1 Thess 3:6 where Paul cites the report about the faith and love of the Thessalonian Christians which he has received from Timothy as "good news."

In 1 Thess 3:6, Paul does not write about hope because it is precisely with respect to hope that Paul must address his remarks as he corresponds with the Thessalonians. Their problem is the ill-founded grief which they experienced as they saw some of their brethren die before the Parousia of the Lord takes place.[11] It is this problem which forms the burden of Paul's discourse in 1 Thess. His response to the problem leads Paul to focus upon that hope which is directed to the Parousia of the Lord. Thus Paul reserves the place of emphasis, the third member of the triad, for hope when he writes of faith, love and hope in 1 Thess 1:3 and 5:8. When the problem within the community is that of disunity, as it was at Corinth, Paul places love in the emphatic position as he uses the traditional faith, hope, and formula to describe the Christian life (1 Cor 13:13; cf. Rom 5:1-5; Gal 5:5-6). Where the problem is anxiety caused by the delay of the Parousia, as it was at Thessalonica, Paul uses his faith-love-hope formula in such a way as to underscore the importance of hope (1 Thess 1:3; 5:8; cf. Col 1:4-5). No matter what the real situation of his addresses is, however, Paul always mentions faith in the first place.

For Paul love would seem to be the normal condition of the Christian.[12] Paul expects to find love in a Christian community. So, having been reassured by Timothy as to the faith and love of the Thessalonian Christians,[13] Paul could write to them in this fashion: "concerning love of the brethren you have no need to have any one write to you, for you yourselves have been taught by God to love one another" (1 Thess 4:9). Just as we are self-taught to do many things, the Thessalonians are "God-taught" to love one another. We need not think specifically of a particular revelation of God to the Thessalonian community, nor of the Christian baptismal catechesis,[15] nor of the exposition of the biblical texts on love (esp. Lev 19:18), nor of the tradition of Jesus' words on love, in order to appreciate the kernel of Paul's message. In the totality of their Christian experience, the Christians of Thessalonica have learned a lesson which comes from God, namely that they are to love one another.

Such a realization suggests that for Paul God Himself is somehow the ground of that love[16] which is characteristic of the life of the Christian believer. In the first of his letters, Paul's thought has not yet reached that stage of clarity which was later his as he emphatically told the communities of Rome and Galatia that love is the gift of the Spirit of God (Rom 5:5; Gal 5:6). Yet even now in his first literary reflections on love, Paul seems to suggest that love is a gift of God. The presence of love among his Thessalonian Christians serves as a motivation of his prayer of thanksgiving (1:3), as if he were aware that love is one of God's gifts. The increase of love is the subject of Paul's prayer of petition (3:11–13), as if he knew that God alone was the source of love's strength. This emerging awareness seems to have been with Paul as he writes: "since we belong to the day, let us be sober, and put on the breastplate of faith and love, and for a helmet the hope of salvation" (5:8). The words are taken from Isaiah[17] who describes God clothing himself with armor. Even though the Christians of Thessalonica are exhorted to put on faith, love, and hope, Paul's underlying suggestion may well be that it is ultimately God himself who clothes his faithful children with the breastplate of faith and love.

## THE CHRISTIAN CONDITION

For Paul, this love which comes from God is not a merely peripheral addition to Christian existence. It is not a virtue which can be exercised on occasion.[18] Rather love is characteristic of the Christian life itself. It denotes the eschatological mode of existence which is of the essense of the Christian condition. Love is a reality of the final times, to which Christians belong by reason of their baptism and their sharing in the eschatological reality of the Christ event.

In the opening section of the final chapter of his first letter to the Thessalonians, Paul repeatedly emphasizes the eschatological condition of the Christian.[19] The poles of his reflection are light and darkness,[20] day and night, alertness and drunkenness,[21] God's salvation and God's wrath. It is the first member of each of these dichotomous expressions which characterize the Christian who is eschatologically situated. Because their situation is that of the final times, Paul can urge his addressees to put on faith and love, as well as hope.

The eschatological quality of that love which characterizes Christian existence is no less underscored by Paul when he relates the labor of love to the steadfastness of hope (1:3) and tells those who listen to the reading of his letter that their existence in faith, love, and hope is one which situates them before "our God and Father." The Christian existence is one which is maintained under the watchful eye of the Father.[22] Yet love is directed to the Parousia of the Lord Jesus Christ since love is the condition of the true Christian who is to be found "unblamable, in holiness before our God and Father, at the coming of our Lord Jesus with all his saints" (3:13).

That God's gift of love qualifies the essentially eschatological condition of the Christian does not mean that love is easy. The eschatological times are times of affliction (3:4). The use of the metaphor of armor in 5:8 suggests that the life of love is something of a struggle. Paul's thoughts in this regard are most explicit when he gives thanks to God for what has taken place among the Thessalonians, their "labor of love" (1:3). The expression is a powerful one. From Paul's use of the word "labor" elsewhere in the epistles,[23] we know that labor denotes some very concrete and practical initiatives. Such initiatives are demanding. They involve pain and difficulty. They require effort. Yet real "labor" is not in vain.[24] It will attain its effect and reap its reward.

Given this connotation of the term "labor," it is apparent that what Paul has come to appreciate in the life of his Thessalonian Christians is that which we might describe as an active love. The love of the Thessalonians for which Paul gives thanks to God is one which pours itself out in concrete expressions of love. It is a love which demands effort and perseverance on the part of those who recognize the true nature of their eschatological condition. It is a love which cannot be in vain because it is a love which expresses itself in Christian service.

## FRATERNAL LOVE, AND BEYOND

The love of the Thessalonian Christians is one which goes beyond their love of Paul himself (3:6) to embrace the entire community. The love of the Thessalonian Christians is a love for one another (3:12; 4:9) which Paul does not hesitate to call "fraternal love," φιλαδελφία. Paul speaks of "fraternal love" in only one other passage of his letters, namely Rom 12:10, but the phraseology is quite apropos in 1 Thess 4. To Paul, who wrote in an era which was not as sensitive to the basic equality between men and women as is ours, the Christian community is a brotherhood.[25] Frequently he addressed the Christians of Thessalonica as "brethren." In fact, this nomenclature seems to be almost Paul's favorite form of address to them (cf. 1 Thess 1:4; 2:1, 9, 14, 17; 3:7; 4:1, 6, 10, 13; 5:1, 4, 12, 14, 25, 26, 27).

It is the fraternal love which exists among the Thessalonian Christians which welds them into a single community. Their love for one another is a fact of their Christian existence. Thus, even though Paul prays that their love for one another might increase and abound (3:12) he must acknowledge that the Christian existence of those to whom he is writing is such that his writing about fraternal love might seem somewhat superfluous (4:9).

Nevertheless even as Paul commends the fraternal love of the Thessalonian Christians, he acknowledges that fraternal love binds the Christians of Thessalonica to other Christian communities. The fraternal love which Christians have for one another is not, nor can it be, a love which is closed in on itself. It is a dynamic reality which binds those who have experienced the Father's love into a love relationship which is ever open and outreaching. If Paul finds the love of the Christians of Thessalonica commendable in itself, and if he judges it to be a worthy object of his prayer,[26] it is not because fraternal love within the Christian community is in any sense exclusive. Rather it is that true love must exist within the community if it is to exist as a Christian community.

Fraternal love must bind the members of the Christian community together so that they might be bound in love to other Christian communities,[27] indeed so that they might be bound in love to all men.

Fraternal love within the community is a first instance of Christian love and a necessary expression of that truly Christian love which reaches out to all.[28] The power of Christian love is not centripetal; rather it is centrifugal. It is not introverted; it is all-inclusive. Thus Paul prays not only that the Christians of Thessalonica love one another; he also prays that they love all.[29]

In his prayer Paul alludes to one of the distinctive aspects of his own teaching on love, which resonates with the traditional Christian teaching on love. It is not limited to other Christians; rather it is extended to all individuals and all peoples. Without saying so, Paul probably intends his addressees to understand that their love for one another must be so open as to embrace even their enemies.[30] Such openness distinguishes Christian love from the narrowness of a restrictive "brotherly love" which attains only to those with whom one stands in physical, social, or religious relationship. Indeed, it may be the open and dynamic quality of the love which he preached that led Paul to avoid speaking of "brotherly love." The term is apropos, but so easily misconstrued!

Paul returns to the topic of Christian love in the final exhortations of his letter when he challenges the Thessalonians to "always seek to do good to one another and to all" (5:15). The object of the exhortation is virtually equivalent to the object of the prayer which was Paul's in 3:12. Exhortation and prayer alike show that the object of Christian love is not only the members of the community. Love is to be directed "to one another and to all." There is no love which "is for all" unless it is concretized in love for "one another."

Some of the ways in which Christian love can be expressed are spelled out in Rom 12, a chapter in which Paul emphasizes the fact that truly Christian love positively embraces those outside the community. In 1 Thess, Paul simply exhorts the Thessalonians to seek to do good to one another and all. In fact, this rendering of Paul's Greek text offers a meaningful specification of his words by adding the infinitive, "to do," to the translation. A more literal translation would be "seek good for one another and for all."[31] Christian love is a dynamic reality, but it is not consistent with a Pelagian outlook. Sometimes the most loving thing to do is to do nothing at all. To seek another's good often includes allowing those who are loved to do for themselves. Indeed, to seek the good of the beloved frequently means that one only contributes to the atmosphere or situation in which the beloved truly experiences what is good for him, her, or them.

With his final exhortations, Paul also singles out certain members of the community as worthy love objects. These are the leaders of the community "who labor among you and are over you in the Lord and admonish you" (5:12). Paul exhorts the Thessalonians to "esteem them very highly in love" (v. 13).[32] Although his words may not mean much more than "show your appreciation to your leaders," the motivation for such appreciation as is cited by Paul is noteworthy. The leaders of the community are to be treated with love because of their work. Perhaps Paul has deliberately singled out the leaders of the community as an object for his exhortation to love, and perhaps he has cited their work within the community as a reason for this love, because the ministry of the leaders of the Christian community includes the task of admonition. Few like to be corrected. The true Christian, however, responds to correction with love.

## A COMMUNITY WHICH IS LOVED

Although Paul is not a residential leader of the community at Thessalonica, he had evangelized them and never lost his father's concern for them (2:11). Indeed, Paul could say of those to whom he was writing that they "had become very dear to us" (2:8), literally that "they had become beloved" (ἀγαπητοὶ). The verbal adjective means "worthy of love," "loveable," "someone who is held in affection and regarded with interest." The description is particularly appropriate to typify the relationship which exists between a father and his children. It is so used in the Synoptics' baptismal scene, where Jesus is presented as "my beloved Son" by the heavenly voice of the Father (Mk 1:11 and par.). Paul has a father's affection for the Christians at Thessalonica.[33] He shares with them not only the religious instruction which consists of the Gospel of God but also his very self (2:8). As a father he has given himself to his children.

Indeed Paul's love for the Christians of Thessalonica was such that he could cite his love for them as an example of the love which they ought to have for one another and for all. Paul prays: "May the Lord make you increase and abound in love to one another and to all men, as we do to you" (3:12). To paraphrase Paul's prayer in language that might be more familiar to us, we might say, "I pray to God that you love one another . . . as I love you." A father's love burns with the desire that it be shared in a measure that has no limits.

The recipients of Paul's paternal love, the Thessalonian Christians, are "beloved by God" (1:4). It is not only human affection and mutual service which bind them together. They are called into being as a community by the God who loves them. Paul's words recall a description found on the Rosetta Stone, of those who were "beloved by Ptah."[34] The Christians of Thessalonica are not, however, the beloved of some local deity. They are beloved by the God to whom the Bible bears witness as the One who loves Israel. The prophet proclaimed God's love for his people (Jer 11:15). The psalmist celebrated Yahweh's love for Israel (Ps 60:5; 108:6; 127:2). Now Paul proclaims that the Christians at Thessalonica are the beloved of God.

Paul's words resound with connotations of salvation history. As Israel and God's servants, Moses (Sir 45:1) and Solomon (Neh 13:26), had been beloved in the past, now it is the Christian community which is the privileged object of God's love. The community of Thessalonian Christians, drawn largely from among the pagans (cf. 1 Thess 1:9), now takes its place as a community beloved by God. The Thessalonian Christians are the object of God's election. Indeed, when Paul describes the Christians of Thessalonica as "beloved of God" he is virtually interpreting the idea of election. To be chosen by God is to be loved by the Father.

Paul's choice of the perfect participial form of the verb is significant. It shows the permanency of God's love.[35] His love for the Christian community is not a reality of the past so much as it is a reality which constitutes the present. This present is the eschatological time of salvation, in which God shows his love by sharing his word (1:5; 2:13), his Gospel, with those whom he loves. Manifesting his love in this fashion, God reveals himself not only as "our God" but also as "our Father" (1:3).[36] He loves his children with that love which only a Divine Father can have.

## NOTES

1. C. H. Dodd, *Gospel and Law* (New York, 1951), pp. 24–25.

2. See C. Spicq, *Agape in the New Testament*. Vol. 2: *Agape in the Epistles of St. Paul* (St. Louis, 1965), p. 103.

3. Ibid., p. 15.

4. A studied analysis of Paul's use of motifs from the Hellenistic Jewish missionary sermon has been done by C. Bussmann, in *Themen der paulinischen Mission-*

*spredigt auf dem Hintergrund des spätjüdisch-hellenistischen Missions-literatur* (Bern, 1971), pp. 38–56. Shorter reflections on this aspect of Paul's preaching can be found in G. Bornkamm, "Faith and Reason in Paul," in *Early Christian Experience* (New Testament Library) (London, 1969), 29–46, pp. 32–33; and J. Munck, "1 Thess i. 9–10 and the Missionary Preaching of Paul: Textual Exegesis and Hermeneutic Reflections," in *New Testament Studies* 9 (1962–63), 95–110, pp. 101–102.

 5. See R. Joly, *Le vocabulaire chrétien de l'amour est-il original? "Philein" et "agapein" dans le grec antique* (Brussels, 1968).

 6. A Brieger, *Die urchrisliche Trias Glaube-Liebe-Hoffnung* (Heidelberg, 1925), pp. 65–69, 82, 126ff., 137–138, 161–165.

 7. B. Rigaux, "Vocabulaire chrétien antérieur à la première épître aux Thessaloniciens," in J. Coppens *et al.* (eds.), *Sacra Pagina II* (Gembloux, 1959), 380–89, p. 387. Rigaux suggests that the triad may have been patterned after Old Testament triads, such as that found in Num 6:24–26.

 8. W. Marxsen, *Der erste Brief an die Thessalonicher* (Zurich, 1979), p. 25.

 9. In his monumental work, *Agape. Die Liebe als Grundmotiv der neutestamentlichen Theologie* (Dusseldorf, 1951), p. 106, n. 2, Viktor Warnack cites E. J. Bicknell, E. B. Allo, J. Sickenberger, A. von Harnack, R. Schütz and M. Dibelius as other proponents of the pre-Pauline origin of the triad. He adds his personal endorsement to this view.

 10. See R. F. Collins "The Faith of the Thessalonians," *Studies on the First Letter to the Thessalonians* BETL 66 (Louvain, 1984), 209–229, pp. 212–13.

 11. The literature on this topic is quite abundant. A good introduction into the matter is provided by F. Laub, *Eschatologische Verkündigung und Lebensgestaltung nach Paulus* (Biblische Untersuchungen, 10, Munich, 1973), pp. 123–28. After the original publication (without notes) of this article in 1981, I. Howard Marshall published his commentary on Paul's first letter to the Thessalonians in which he surveys five different ways in which modern commentators attempt to understand the grief of the Thessalonians. See I. H. Marshall, *1 and 2 Thessalonians* (Grand Rapids, 1983), pp. 120–122.

 12. See C. Spicq "La Charité fraternelle selon 1 Th 4:9," in *Mélanges bibliques rédigés en l'honneur de André Robert* (Paris, 1956), pp. 508–09.

 13. 1 Thess 3:6.

 14. The term Θεοδίδακτοι occurs only here in New Testament; in extant literature older than the New Testament there is only one known use of the term. See O. Merk, *Handeln aus Glauben* (Marburger theologische Studien, 5), (Marburg, 1968), p. 51.

 15. Spicq does, however, think of baptismal catechesis as that to which Paul is making reference to the Thessalonians being "God-taught." See C. Spicq, *art. cit.*, p. 510; *op. cit.*, p. 18.

 16. See 1 Thess 1:4.

 17. Is 59:17; cf. Wis 5:18; Eph 6:14–17.

18. Love is, according to Spicq, the first requirement of the Christian vocation. See C. Spicq, *art. cit.*, p. 508.

19. 1 Thess 5:5–10. In the German language literature, this eschatological condition of the Christian is frequently cited as *eschatologische Existenz*.

20. On the importance and significance of this theme in Paul, see L. R. Stachowiak, "Die Antithese Licht-Finsternis — Eine Thema der paulinischen Paränese," in *Theologische Quartalschrift* 143 (1963) 385–425.

21. Valuable reflections on this theme, particularly as it appears in 1 Thess 5, are to be found in E. Lövestam, "Spiritual Wakefulness in the New Testament," in *Lunds Universitets Arsskrift*, N. F. 1, Bd. 55, Nr. 3, (Lund, 1963), pp. 45–58.

22. See D. Buzy, "Première épître aux Thessaloniciens," in L. Piroi and A. Clamer (eds.), *La Sainte Bible*, 12, (Paris, 1951), 129–170, p. 138.

23. 1 Cor 3:8; 15:58; 2 Cor 6:5; 10:15; 11:23, 27; Gal 6:17; 1 Thess 2:9; 3:5.

24. Cf. 1 Thess 3:5 (comp. 2:1).

25. See H. Schürmann, "Gemeinde als Bruderschaft," in *Ursprung und Gestalt. Erörterungen und Besinnungen zum Neuen Testament. Kommentare and Beiträge zum Alten und Neuen Testament* (Dusseldorf, 1970), pp. 61–73.

26. 1 Thess 3:12.

27. See esp. 1 Thess 4:9–10. For reflections on this pair of verses, see not only the commentaries, but also C. Spicq, *op. cit.*, pp. 16–19; F. Laub, *op. cit.*, pp. 68–69.

28. 1 Thess 3:12. The Greek text of this verse does not include the noun "men," found in the RSV translation, but not in the NAB and NEB. JB reads "the whole human race."

29. Ibid.

30. Love for one's enemies is a theme found in the Q tradition and taken over by Matthew and Luke in the Sermon on the Mount/Plain (Mt 5:44; par. Lk 6:27). Comp. Rom 12:14.

31. The Greek of 1 Thess 5:15b is ἀλλὰ πάντοτε τὸ ἀγαθὸν διώκετε καὶ εἰς ἀλλήλους καὶ εἰς πάντας; the RSV translation, "always seek to do good to one another and to all," and the NEB translation, "always aim at doing the best you can for each other and for all men," preserve the dynamic character of Paul's exhortation by incorporating the notion of doing in the translation. The NAB translates the verse more literally, "always seek one another's good and, for that matter, the good of all," but in such a way as to overshadow the dynamic character of the exhortation. (The NAB also adds into the translation "for that matter," for which there is no expression in Paul's Greek text).

32. See C. Spicq, *op. cit.*, pp. 116–19.

33. The paternal imagery of 1 Thess 2:11 is parallel in expression and in thought to the maternal imagery of 2:7. On the paternal metaphor in this section of 1 Thess see especially P. Gutierrez, *La paternité spirituelle selon saint Paul* (Paris, 1968), pp. 87–117.

34. See B. Rigaux, *op. cit.*, p. 371. Rigaux makes reference to W. Dittenberger, *Orientis graeci inscriptiones selectae* (Leipzig, 1902–05), 1, 90, 4.

35. See C. Spicq, *op. cit.*, p. 16, who writes: "ēgapēmenoi, 'beloved', is one of the most authentic descriptions of the faithful. Its perfect participial form shows the immovable permanence of the love of God. Christians are forever the privileged objects of the Father's love."

36. On God as Father in 1 Thess, see R. F. Collins "The Theology of Paul's First Letter to the Thessalonians," *Studies,* 230–252, pp. 232–34.

PART FOUR

# The Bible and Sexuality

# 7

# Human Sexuality
# in the Jewish Scriptures

RECENT YEARS HAVE SEEN the appearance in print of a veritable spate of articles which have sought either to comment upon the ministerial role of women according to the epistles of the Pauline corpus or to counter the charge that Paul the apostle was a misogynist. For the most part, this literature has been the exegete's response to or, perhaps, even participation in the women's liberation movement. On the other hand, there has been a remarkable dearth of literature devoted to reflection on human sexuality from the standpoint of a biblically-nourished Christian faith.[1] This lack of scholarly publication on the topic is all the more notable within the Roman Catholic tradition insofar as the Fathers of Vatican Council II called for an exposition of moral theology "more thoroughly nourished by scriptural teaching."[2] Despite this exhortation, recent Roman documents on sexual ethics and on the ministry of women in the Church have been strongly criticized precisely because they, so it is said, have not been sufficiently nourished by biblical reflection. It is not the intention of the present article to provide a commentary upon either of these Roman documents. Nor does the scope of the present article provide for the thorough analysis and reflection on the pertinent biblical texts which the study of human sexuality truly warrants. The intention pursued in the present article remains somewhat modest. It is to provide an overview of some of the basic insights on human sexuality, as well as on some of the specific responses to issues of sexual responsibility by men of Jewish and Christian faith whose testimony has been preserved for us in the pages of the sacred Scriptures of both Testaments.

## THE OLD TESTAMENT

*The Context*

The distinctiveness of insight into the significance of human sexuality conveyed by both the Old and the New Testaments cannot be gleaned apart from a consideration of the contexts in which the views of Jews and Christians were formed. The Near Eastern context within which the traditions presently contained in the Old Testament developed was religiously oriented. Within such a context, as in every religiously oriented society, sexuality and its expression in the marital relationship were valorized from a religious point of view. The instrument of such valorization was the myth, expressed in both oral and ritual form. By means of myths, the ancients projected their experience into the sphere of the gods. The myths, thus constituted, served a purpose which was at once paradigmatic and functional. The stories about the gods reflected man's nature as he saw it and his experience as he lived it. The resultant patterns of divine behavior became archetypes of human nature and society, of which man's nature and his activity were but poor reflections. Accordingly, the myths which expressed something of the sexual activity of the gods both articulated for the ancient man the meaning of his sexuality and sexual experience and authenticated the role of sexuality in that human society which lived by its myths.

In the Ugaritic and Babylonian cultures, there existed myths which centered upon the fertility aspect of sexuality. According to these myths, the earth became fertile by means of a union between male heaven and female earth. As the earth becomes fertile because of the rain which falls upon it, the ancient myth narrated the story of the father-god (personification of a storm) who impregnates the mother-goddess (the personification of the earth).

Another group of myths focused upon the love-passion aspect of sexuality. In these myths, the conduct of the goddess represents the sexual attraction by which man is seduced by a woman. According to the Babylonian myth, Ishtar, the Babylonian Venus, seduced Tammouz and others. The Gilgamesh epic, often cited by scholars because of its interesting analogies with Gen 2–3, tells both the tale of Enkiddu who falls to the wiles of a seductive goddess and the tale of Gilgamesh himself who spurns the advances of Ishtar by reminding her of her multiple affairs.

Sexuality's destructive capacity receives expression in still other myths. The Ras Shamra tablets tell the story of the Canaanite goddess Anath who has Aqhat destroyed when he refuses to yield to her seduction, who dismembers Mot, the personification of the rain, and who even threatens El, the supreme god of the pantheon.

Another group of myths tells the story of marriages between the gods, the *hieros gamos*. These myths are not concerned with the union between a father-god and a mother-goddess, rather they celebrate the giving in marriage of a daughter to someone's son. For example, the Ugaritic texts speak of the marriage of Nikkal with the moon god.

While it is clear that these myths articulate the meaning of human sexuality, with its passion and its power to destroy, its fertility and its celebration in marriage, it is important for us to realize that it is generally not the same members of the pantheon who appear in the different types of myths which focus upon the different aspects of human sexuality. Fertility, passion, destruction, and marriage are not synthetically united in one single overarching myth; rather each element is valorized in a distinct series of myths with its own characters from the heavenly pantheon. This indicates not only the polyvalence of human sexuality, but also a fragmentary view of human sexuality among the members of the ancient Near-Eastern society. The essential aspects of human sexuality were dissociated from one another in order to receive a mythical elucidation.

As the different values in human sexuality received verbal articulation in the myth, so they received dramatic expression in the cultic myth. To the *mythos* corresponded the *dromenon*. Its rites were a dramatic reproduction of divine actions. By participating in these rites, the individual associated himself with the actions of the gods and thus benefited from their actions. Sympathetic participation in the cultic myths was, therefore, not only a matter of valorizing a human experience; it was also a means of assuring divine benevolence upon human activity. Consequently, when the various aspects of the human sexual experience are dramatized and valorized by sympathetic participation in cultic myths, the sexual rites must be seen as much more than promiscuous sexual license under the guise of religious experience. Participation in mythical rites of a sexual nature was both an attempt to render meaningful the awesome experience of human sexuality and to assure that the experience of human sexuality would be blessed by the gods.

*Fertility Myth*

Throughout the Ancient Near East, particularly in Mesopotamia and Syria, the fertility myth was of special importance.[3] At the basis of the myth was the belief that the earth's annual fertility cycle was an annual renewal of creation—in effect, the earth was produced once again each year. This annual cycle was a production of life from death insofar as it was necessary for the fertility god to die. Fertility itself resulted from the union of a male god and his consort, a female goddess. The Canaanite fertility god, Aleyan Baal,[4] often appears in the Bible. According to the Canaanite myth, the fertility god creates by winning a victory over his chaotic enemies, and then being sexually united to his consort. In fact, the fertility myth received dramatic expression in the fertility rites of various agrarian societies. For example, during the celebration of the Babylonian New Year's festival, fertility was dramatized by means of the sexual union between the king and a temple prostitute, in effect a priestess chosen for the occasion. In similar fashion, a fertility-celebrating ritual orgy took place in Canaan. By means of sympathetic participation in the deities' sexual union, the fertility of the land was assured.

This form of cultic myth, the fertility myth, ought to be distinguished from the celebration of other cultic myths which gave expression to other values of human sexuality. As in the myth itself, so in the cult there was a dissociation of the various values inherent in human sexuality. Thus, the institution of sacred prostitution dramatized the attraction of the love goddess. In a general way, this was true even of the cults celebrated in the high places of Canaan, even though the syncretistic character of Canaanite worship occasioned some confluence among the myths and their attendant cults. Yet, it ought not to be thought that the high places of Canaan were the scene of unlimited sexual encounters, as if sexual promiscuity were the order of the day. Rather, we are dealing with a cult which had its own norms. Within this perspective, it may be well to abandon "prostitution" as the appropriate designation for the activities which occurred in the high places,[5] and speak rather of ritual intercourse. The "evil" of this cult, against which the prophets so strongly inveighed, was not so much its sexual aberration as its worship of a deity other than Yahweh.

## Characteristics of Sexuality in Myth

In any event, the context in which the biblical tradition on sexuality occurred was that of a pre-scientific world which valorized human sexuality by means of myth. Two characteristics of that understanding of human sexuality stand out. First of all, there was a fragmentation of the different values in the human sexual experience insofar as these values were elucidated by means of myths in which different divine characters appeared. Human sexuality was not seen as an integrated reality. In a sense, the Greeks also had a fragmented view of human sexuality. The oft-quoted statement of the Pseudo-Demosthenes bespeaks this fragmentation from the standpoint of the male who has need of different women to fulfill different (sexual) needs in his life: "We have harlots for our pleasure, concubines for daily physical use, wives to bring up legitimate children and to be faithful stewards in household matters."[6] Secondly, human sexuality was experienced as something mysterious. For man, sexuality was almost an alien reality. Its power had to be appropriated by means of participation in a cultic myth. As the earth received its fertility by means of a ritual dramatization of sexual union among the gods, so the woman's ability to attract a male, as well as her ability to conceive, were "actualized" through her participation in the rites of the high places. On the other hand, a number of ancient taboos, as well as practices designed to ward off the influence of demonic powers, indicated the ancients' understanding of the human sexual experience as an extra-human reality.

## Development of Biblical Traditions of Sexuality

It was within such a context, in which sexuality was considered to be an extrahuman reality and in which sexuality was valorized in a fragmented fashion, that the biblical tradition developed. Within Israel Yahwistic monotheism was the basic context within which the ancient Israelites lived and understood their sexuality. The very fact that Yahweh was the only God of Israel (Dt 6:4) meant that the Israelite faith did not admit the existence of any goddess-consort. In effect, Yahwistic monotheism meant that myths were not an apt means for articulating the values inherent in the human sexual experience. Yahweh is alone in his divinity; there is no mother-goddess, no lover-goddess, no wife-goddess. The absence of myths meant that cultic myths by means of which man could appropriate to himself the sexual powers of the deities were foreign to the monolatry of authentic Yahweism. Thus, sacred prostitutes, both male and female, were banned from Israel (Dt 23:17–18). The magical rite of bestiality (Ex 22:19) was to be eschewed.

Israel's faith in Yahweh as its God was never totally pure. A lapse into syncretism meant that occasionally myths and cultic rites of a sexual nature were introduced into Israel. In the fifth century, the Jews of Elephantine knew of a divine trinity in which Anath, the consort of Baal, enjoyed a similar relationship with Yahweh. After the schism of 926, sacred prostitutes were found in the land (1 Kg 14:24); women were even to be found in the temple of Jerusalem at the time of Josiah's reform. Typical of the tendency to lapse into syncretism was the erection of the golden calf at the time of the Exodus (Ex 32). Not surprisingly, the calf was endowed with some of the characteristics of the Canaanite Baal; its cult included orgiastic elements. The introduction of these myths into Israel were clearly deviations in the faith of a people who acknowledged Yahweh as their sole God and Lord (Dt 5:6).

A second result of Yahwistic monotheism, even in its more primitive henotheistic form, was that Israel did not admit of the dissociation of cult and morals. The single God who was worshipped in cult was the God to whom man owed his allegiance in daily life. Among the peoples of the ancient Near East, Israel was alone in not separating religion and morals. According to the vision of Yahwistic faith, the moral life was itself a form of religious worship. The utilization of the model of the Hittite *berith* enabled Israel to combine in a single listing of covenant stipulations obligations to Yahweh God and obligations to one's fellow Israelite. Thus both worship and morality were seen from a single perspective. To the prophets of Israel belongs the credit for railing against a baneful separation of the two domains.

The consequences of this aspect of the unique relationship between Israel and its God were that the human sexual experience could not be seen as an alien experience. It was not to be separated from the other aspects of secular life. There was neither need for nor the possibility of man's appropriating the powers inherent in a divine sexual *ekstasis* unto himself. In short, the secularization of human sexuality was a consequence of Yahwistic monotheism. In this respect it might be well noted that Israel was unique among the ancient peoples in not ascribing immorality to the deity. Its cult was singular in that it did not consist of immoral practices — practices prescribed in ordinary life, but proscribed in cult. Such a fragmentation of life's experiences was impossible within the faith vision of a people who admitted but one Lord of heaven and earth.

## THE VISION

Within this context of Yahwistic monotheism, the meaning of the human sexual experience had to be elucidated. An ancient attempt to do so is contained within the Yahwist's story of the creation of the woman (Gen 2:4b–24). This tradition, committed to writing in the tenth century B.C., antedates the written form of the Priestly author's creation narrative by some three centuries or so. The Yahwist's account reflects still more ancient traditions and is influenced by Israel's Wisdom tradition. The account must be seen in a tandem relationship with the account of the primordial sin (Gen 3). Above all, the Yahwist's creation story must be recognized as an etiological narrative: the strength of the sexual attraction is to be accounted for by the manner in which Yahweh made the first woman and placed her in relationship to the first man.

### Valorization of Sexuality

The climax of the first part of the Yahwist's diptych is his account of the meaning of human sexuality. The author focused his attention on the origin of the sexes in order to give to sexuality a valorization different from that which it received in the Canaanite myths. In his account he does not stress the position of man and woman in the world as did the later Priestly narrative, rather he lays the emphasis on the mutual relationship of man and wife within the household. The account is unique in the annals of Near Eastern literature in that the account treats woman as the complement and equal of man. The theological perspective is that of a beneficent God who cares for man by providing for him a garden for pleasure, animals for service, and woman for companionship. In this sense, the narrative is anthropocentric. Yet it is clear from Gen 2:18 that man was not created by Yahweh in order to live a solitary existence. For man, solitude and loneliness are tantamount to helplessness. Yahweh would not leave his creation in a condition which was "not good." His creature was intended — hence the importance of the "deliberation" pictured in v. 18 — as a social being. Human sociability can be realized only in a relationship with a being "like unto himself" (kenegdo). The terminology contains the notion of similarity as well as that of supplementation. Indeed, the idea that man is whole only in his complementarity with another being who is like unto himself seems to be the thrust of the entire narrative.

### Man and Woman

Several traits in the account point to the accuracy of Speiser's comment on v. 18 to the effect that "the traditional 'helpmate for him' is adequate, but subject to confusion. . . . The Hebrew complement means literally 'alongside him,' i.e. 'corresponding to him.'"[7] Such correspondence to man cannot be found among those who are subservient to him, the animals named by Adam. Both the man and the one who is complementary to him are superior to the inhabitants of the animal world. The detail of Adam's rib points to the singleness of life in which primordial man and woman are joined. In Sumerian, the sign IT signifies both "life" and "rib," prompting the use of the rib as a symbol of the life force. The man and the woman share a common life. Similar thoughts, otherwise expressed, are contained in the man's encomium: "That at last is bone of my bones and flesh of my flesh; she shall be called Woman because she was taken out of Man." Three times the woman is referred to as z'oth.[8] Thus the Yahwist notes that the woman is different from those other beings among the man sought for a helper fit for himself. It was only to her that the man could speak of his flesh and his bone, a common Old Testament expression to designate that another was as close as one's own body. Finally, the bit of popular, but incorrect, etymology contained in v. 23b shows that the woman and the man are similar in kind.

### Origin of the Sexes

The Yahwist's creation narrative quite obviously merits a fuller exegetical treatment than we are able to accord it in the present article.

However, these few remarks are hopefully sufficient to make it clear that the Yahwist's account is not so much an account of the creation of man as it is an account of the origin of the sexes.[9] His narrative underscores the idea that the sexual distinction is willed by Yahweh, that man is sociable by nature, that woman is similar to man, and that the sexes are complementary to each other. The underlying idea is that sexuality finds its meaning not in the appropriation of divine creative powers, but in human sociality.

V. 24 contains a proverbial reflection which the Yahwistic redactor offers in place of a more primitive epithalamion. An introductory "therefore" ('al-ken) makes it clear that there is but one fact that really needs explanation: namely, the extremely powerful drive of the sexes to one another. By destiny man and woman belong to one another. This belonging is not appropriately expressed in a merely transitory sexual encounter, such as might occur in the high places, rather it is expressed in the cleaving of the man to his wife. This sexual differentiation finds its significance in a permanent relationship between a man and a woman. Cleaving implies a devotion and an unshakeable faith between humans; it connotes a permanent attraction which transcends genital union to which, nonetheless, it gives meaning. There can be no mistaking the author's intention. He concludes his narrative by interpreting the divinely-ordered sexual differentiation and the sexual drive within the perspective of a permanent social union between man and woman. His perspective is neither that of sexuality ordained unto fertility nor that of sexuality as an ultra-human reality. Rather, human sexuality is an eminently human reality whose meaning is that of human wholeness.

*Shame and Sexuality*

After his final reflection on the meaning of human sexuality, the Yahwist introduces Gen 2:25 as the hinge which joins the two parts of his diptych. The unabashed nakedness of the man and his wife looks to the nakedness to which the man and Yahweh make reference in Gen 3:10–11. Shameless sexuality was divinely ordered; shameful sexuality is the result of sin.[10] Such is part of the contrast which the Yahwist would set before his readers in the two parts of his narrative. In each account, the woman appears as the principal figure. A reflection on human sexuality appears to be a leitmotif on the entire narrative. There is no justification for interpreting the tree as the "tree of sexual consciousness" or for interpreting the ban on the "forbidden fruit" as a ban on sexual intercourse. Nevertheless, the account of the sin in Gen 3 is replete with distinctly sexual overtones: the serpent, the nakedness, the verb "to know," etc. The presence of sexual motifs is to be acknowledged.[11] The introduction of such sexual themes is, however, not to be explained on the grounds that the Yahwist considered some form of unchastity to be the first sin. Rather, sexual motifs are present because the Yahwist wanted to demonstrate that sin was a rejection of the sovereignty of Yahweh. In his day the rejection of Yahweh's Lordship and Yahwistic monotheism concretely took the form of participation in the sexual rites of the Canaanite fertility cults. As sin in the Yahwist's experience was a participation in sexual devotion to a Canaanite Baal, so his description of the primordial sin was cast in sexual terms.

*Curses*

This reflection means that we ought not to see the Yahwist's narrative of the Fall as having merely, or even principally, a sexual significance. Indeed, the author has broadened his perspective beyond that of the merely sexual by the addition of the curse of the man in Gen 3: 17–19. Nevertheless, there are some sexual motifs in the narrative which the purpose of the present article prompts us to exploit. In the judgment of condemnation which Yahweh pronounces against the woman there is an implicit polemic against Canaanite fertility rites.[12] The logion derives from an initiation formula whose solemn pronouncement ought to ensure abundant progeny for the woman.[13] By introducing the notion of pain into the formula and indicating that it is pain rather than children that is to be multiplied, the Yahwist has effectively transformed a formula of blessing into a curse. The second part of the condemnation appears to be an affirmation that it is not a Canaanite Baal who is lord over the woman, but her husband. In similar fashion, the cursing of the serpent, as well as the cursing of the field, may well be part of an anti-Canaanite polemic.

The curse speaks of the pain of child bearing and the woman's submission to her husband. This double condition, in fact, characterizes the situation of woman such as the Yahwist knew it. It briefly describes the sexual experience of woman such as it was lived in fact. This existential description stands in sharp contrast to the author's vision of that oneness of partnership which Yahweh intended when he created man as a sexual being. In effect, the Yahwist's account in Gen 3 presents a description of the perversion of the sexual life from its primitive integrity. The relationship between man and woman which ideally was to have been a deep and permanent union in mutual love has now given way to the domination of man over woman and the passionate attachment of woman to man. The Yahwist attributes this perversion of human sexuality to man's rejection of Yahweh's Lordship. The Yahwist shares with the sage (Wis 13) the notion that sin embodies its own punishment: i.e. the perversion of the good order of creation intended by God. The notion will be taken up again by the Apostle Paul in Rom 1. In a word, the existential situation of the human sexual experience is not as it ought to be. Such is the common affirmation of the Yahwist, the wise man, and the apostle.

## Priestly Interpretation of the Origin of the Sexes

Some three centuries or so after the Yahwist documented his tradition, the Priestly author gave literary expression to the six-day story of creation (Gen 1:1–2:4a). At the apex of Yahweh's creative activity stands the creation of man and woman, set apart from the other works of creation by means of the divine reflection in v. 26. In some ways, the account can be viewed as a corrective of the Yahwist's tale of the origin of the sexes, insofar as the earlier account might be construed to suggest the inferiority of woman on the grounds that she was created out of and after man.[14] The Priestly author reflects that the creation of man is, in fact, a creation of male and female: "So God created man in his own image, in the image of God he created him; male and female he created them" (Gen 1:27).

A polemic intent can be discerned in the formulation of this statement. In a somewhat lapidary statement, the Priestly author warns his readers against assuming that the creation of man was originally that of an androgynous man. Von Rad accurately comments: "By God's will man was not created alone but designated for the 'thou' of the other sex. The idea of man, according to P, finds its full meaning not in the male alone, but in man and woman."[15] The simple statement affirms that woman by nature is neither fallen nor incomplete. There is no need for her to abandon her femininity to pursue masculinity as if the fullness of the humanum was to be found in masculinity alone.

Polemic intent might also be discerned in the Priestly author's narrative insofar as Yahweh is not represented as a sexual being. That Yahweh is described in anthropomorphic, though not in sexual, terms is significant in that the representation of the gods in the literature and graphic arts contemporary with the biblical accounts normally picture the gods as male and/or female. The absence of any allusion to divine bisexuality not only serves to underscore the idea that the author is subtly countering the notion of an androgynous primal man similar to the deity, but also reinforces the idea that the similarity between the male-female and God is to be found in the operational[16] rather than in the physical realm. The silence about Yahweh's sexuality is all the more noteworthy in that contemporary Canaanite myths usually described the creation event as the result of divine fertility achieved through some form of sexual relationship.[17] That this silence is more than merely circumstantial clearly appears when consideration is given to the fact that at the time when the Priestly account was put in writing the use of the image of marriage to describe the relationship between Israel and Yahweh was already current. The Priestly author's message is clear: sexuality is of the human realm.[18] That the whole man exists as male and female is according to the very plan of the Creator. From the very beginning of human existence, man was male and female.

In effect man[19] is sexual because God intended him so, not because God himself is sexual. This means that the relationship between man and God is to be found in the operational rather than in the physical realm. The relationship is summed up in the author's words, "in our image, after our likeness" (Gen 1:26). Although Westermann held that the double expression qualifies only the creative activity as such, most commentators would agree with Von Rad that the be is to be taken as a be essentiae[20] so that the total expression means "let us make man as our image and likeness." Each of the terms has a meaning of its own, so that the combined expression may be seen as an example of hendiadys. Since "image" (selem) normally denotes an actual plastic work, the imagery recalls that of the sovereign emblem which sovereigns would use to claim dominion over their property. Yahweh, in effect, claims dominion over the heavens and earth which he has wrested from chaos by implanting his standard upon the earth. The sign of his dominion is, however, his likeness (demut). Without accepting Cohen's contention that likeness introduces the notion of lineage into the text,[21] it can be affirmed that the term conveys, in somewhat abstract fashion, the idea that the image is similar to Yahweh. In other words, like God, man is a personal being.[22] That man, male and female, has been created in God's image and likeness renders man capable of receiving a task from God, i.e. capable of being God's vicegerent over creation. The task, to dominate the earth, does not belong to the definition of God's image; rather it is its consequence.[23] It is this resultant task which occupies the focus of the author's attention.

The imagery, then, is in the task, not in the sexual differences between male and female. Indeed, the fact that the prophets had so strongly opposed the fertility rites makes it highly unlikely that the Priestly author wished to bring his image of God anthropology into relationship with the sexual differences between men and women.[24] Nevertheless, it is as sexually differentiated that man has received his task. Human sexuality is at once rendered a secular reality and ennobled. The human task is not entrusted to the male, but to sexually differentiated humanity whose wholeness is to be found in the complementarity of the sexes. The idea of "man" finds its fullness not in a male, but in male and female. As Emile Brunner has said, "That is the immense double statement, of a lapidary simplicity, so simple indeed that we hardly realize that with it a vast world of myth and Gnostic speculation, of cynicism and asceticism, of the deification of sexuality and fear of sex completely disappears."[25]

*Complementarity*

This essential complementarity is affirmed as being "very good" (Gen 1:31). Although essentially a reality of the secular order, human sexuality is a sacral value by reason of the blessing which God pronounces upon the sexed humanity which He has created. The word of blessing effectively removes the procreative ability from the notion of God's image and ensures the fertility which results from the male-female relationship. Progeny is a gift from God, the fruit of his blessing. Progeny are conceived because of the divine power which has been transferred to man. Man does not have to appropriate that power unto himself. Thus progeny are a real vocation. The blessing also indicates that fertility is the purpose of the sexual distinction, albeit not the exclusive purpose of the distinction.[26] Thus, the blessing of Gen 1:28 has effectively separated fertility-oriented sexuality from man's being created in the divine image, has removed fertility from valorization in fertility rites, and has likewise proclaimed that fertility is a secular reality. As such it belongs to the sacral order because all that is of the saeculum is of God's sacrum.

In short, the creation stories of Gen 1 and Gen 2 offer a biblical view of human sexuality as it ought to be. Sexuality is the work of the Creator, and as such it is very good. Sexual differentiation belongs to the primal plan of the Creator. Human fullness is to be found in the male and female complementarity. Sexuality essentially belongs to the human order. Sexuality is ordered to sociality and to procreation. Male and female are not inferior to one another — rather they are similar to one another and share equally in the task which the Creator has entrusted to mankind.

## Vision and Reality

There is, however, distance between the vision and the reality. The second part of the Yahwist's diptych describes the reality and attributes the distanciation to the sin of male and female. The consequence of sin is that the relationship between male and female is profoundly disturbed. As the Yahwist's creation story focused upon the creation of woman, so does his story of the primal sin. Nevertheless, it must be noted that both male and female were involved in that sin; moreover, the shame resulting from sin should not be considered as the awakening of the sexual instinct, rather shame must be considered insofar as both male and female experience their own degradation as a result of sin. In this sin-induced state of degradation, the woman is afflicted in her fertility and in her relationship to man. The Yahwist has apparently reworked a fertility blessing in vogue in the Canaanite cults to affirm that the woman's bearing of progeny is a matter of multiplied sorrows. Similarly, instead of the loving union which ought to have existed between male and female, the woman experiences a profound desire for the man in whom she does not find complementarity, but humiliating domination. The male will be the master of the female, not only in social and domestic life, but also, and especially, in the sexual life.

## Sexuality: Good in itself

In these two mythical descriptions of the origin of man, it is not affirmed that human sexuality is meaningful only with respect to marriage. The goodness of sexuality owes to the Creator's act itself. Man exists as sexually differentiated by reason of the creative will, a sexual differentiation which allows man to receive the divine blessing that man increase and multiply. Thus the Priestly author's narrative should not be so narrowly interpreted, as if human sexuality found its meaning only with respect to marriage and/or procreation.[27] Similarly, the Yahwist's tale is that sexuality is unto sociality. Yet, he is able to affirm that it is because man has been created sexually as male and female that the marital relationship is explicable. It is the very fashion in which Yahweh created man as sexually differentiated that leads man to leave his own family in order to attach himself to the family of his wife.

## Canticle of Canticles

That human sexuality belongs to the secular order and is good in itself can also be gleaned from the presence in the Old Testament of the Canticle of Canticles. Scholars have long puzzled over the nature of this book which seems to have so little, if anything, to do with religious instruction. Consequently, many commentators, particularly among the Fathers and contemporary exegetes of the French school, have tended to see in Ct an extended allegory on the relationship between Yahweh and Israel. This type of allegorical interpretation paid due deference to the religious nature of the Bible. An argument in its favor was the allegorical use of conjugal love to symbolize the covenant union between Yahweh and Israel in the book of Hosea. Nevertheless, current exegetical interpretation has generally abandoned such an allegorical interpretation of the Canticle of Canticles. Similarly, exegetes are no longer inclined to interpret the canticle as if it were a drama or an expurgated remnant of one or another fertility cult ritual. Rather, a gradual consensus is emerging to the effect that Ct deals with love songs which simply extol love between the sexes.[28] Indeed, it is most commonly suggested today that Ct is a collection of love songs, perhaps incomplete, put together as a song-cycle composed for a wedding celebration of some seven days duration, a custom that still exists among some Palestinian and Syrian Arabs.[29]

The songs are frankly sensuous. The imagery is erotic. The metaphors of Ct 4:1–7 and 7:1–3 accentuate, rather than couch, the lover's joyful contemplation of the body of his beloved. The warmth, the sensuousness, the playfulness, and the fantasy of the sexual experience pervade the entire book. The search passages in the songs recall the sexual fantasy of a young girl who dreams of the joys of sexual love.[30] The content of the book is so obviously sexual, yet so tender and human, that the reader must agree that Murphy's contention that "the primary meaning of the Song would then have to do with human sexual love — the experience of it, its delights, its fidelity and its power."[31]

Although Ct is blatantly sexual and sensuous, it is not vulgar in the least. Its description of sexual revery and sexual pleasure are couched in the most human and tender of terms. An occasional euphemism and, perhaps, the deletion of some of the most erotic songs in the collection moderate somewhat the merely physical rapture of which the song sings. The description of the bride as "a garden locked, a fountain sealed" (Ct 4:12) bespeaks the value of chastity to one who savors the sensuous joy of his beloved's kiss (Ct 4:11). Yet, in not one of the songs contained in the present collection is there the slightest suggestion that human sexuality is anything less than an aspect of the humanum, a gift of God for man to enjoy.

It is under this respect that the presence of Ct in the Bible alongside the instruction of the Torah, the prayers of the Psalmist, and the oracles of the Prophets is to be understood. It is for this reason that tradition could gather this collection of songs under the rubric of "the most beautiful canticle," thereby inferring that the collection was the chef d'oeuvre among the 1,005 songs traditionally ascribed to King Solomon (1 Kg 4:32). It is from the vantage point of this consideration that we can understand why Akiba, the second century martyr-rabbi of the school of Hillel, could say of Ct that "all the world is not as worthy as the day on which the Song of Songs was given to Israel, for all the writings are holy, but the Song of Songs is the Holy of Holies."[32] The collection simply celebrates the apex of God's very good creation, male and female in the reality of their sexual attraction for one another.

Indeed, the sages of Israel were able to extol the goodness of the creation in a way that Westerns, who slip into an implicit and ungodly dualism which dissociates the sacred from the secular, are generally unable to do. Thus Qoheleth is able to speak of the joys of eating and drinking which are "from the hand of God" (Eccl 2:24).[33] In similar fashion, the wisdom preserved in the book of Proverbs can speak with mysterious wonder of "the way of a man with a maiden" (Prv 30:19) and of the affectionate infatuation of the young groom for his bride

(Prv 5: 18–19). Because the God of Israel was the Creator and Lord of all, nothing which belonged to his creation was less than his gift to be enjoyed. Thus, human sexuality with its mysterious attraction, its sensuous physicality, its joyful pleasure, its memories, and its dreams could only be counted among the good things that God has made.

To affirm the goodness of human sexuality in all its dimensions is not to affirm that human sexuality lies beyond the sphere of human responsibility nor is it beyond the pale of that over which man has dominion as God's vicegerent. Human sexuality was indeed a dimension of human experience which fell within the parameters of Yahweh's hegemony and the covenant relationship. The presence of "Thou shalt not commit adultery" within the covenant clauses of the Decalogue (Ex 20: 14; Dt 5: 18) served as a clear reminder that the fashion in which man lived his sexuality was not independent of his relationship to Yahweh, the God of his people.[34] Similarly, the different outcomes of the encounter between Joseph and Potiphar's wife (Gen 39) and that between David and Bathsheba (2 Sam 11) indicate well that human sexuality is not an awesome force over which man has no control. These stories, told so often in Jewish tradition, clearly proclaim that man is responsible[35] for the way in which he uses his sexuality, that God-given gift over which he exercises dominion in Yahweh's name and by Yahweh's power.

## SOME PARTICULARS

The Bible clearly attests to the extent of that responsibility by means of the ancient myths which it continued to convey orally and eventually set down in writing, the legendary tales of the patriarchs, judges, and kings, the judgments of the prophets, and the laws incorporated into the Book. These are too numerous to treat in a study as limited as is the present essay. Yet, surely something must be said since the laws which developed and the tales which were narrated speak of man's responsibility for the good gift of sexuality which Yahweh had given to him. Nevertheless, some hesitation must be expressed, since a necessarily brief treatment is inevitably overly-simplified; moreover, a cursory overview runs the risk of separating ancient Israel's sexual attitudes and ethic from its basic attitudes and ethic. To do so would be to do violence to the understanding of human sexuality had by the ancient Israelites. For them, human sexuality was not especially problematic among the various dimensions of the human experience and patterns of social conduct. Sexual offenses were not treated as a category apart. They were sins like every other sin.[36] No clearer attestation of this can be had than the fact that the apodictic ban on adultery stands among the precepts of the Decalogue rather than at the beginning of the Commandments.

## Sexual Morality

The sexual morality of ancient Israel was more concerned with morality than it was with sex. Indeed, social realities, economic factors, cultic purity, and procreation were among the most powerful factors in the development of Israel's sexual ethic. These factors were even more significant in the shaping of the sexual ethic than any specific understanding of human sexuality as such.

Consistent with the vision expressed in the early chapters of Genesis and the songs of the Canticle of Canticles was a generally positive attitude towards human sexuality. Prudery was virtually unknown. Menstruation (Lv 15: 19–24; 18: 19; 20: 18), the foreskin (1 Sm 18: 25, 27), and the sexual organs (Ex 20: 26; 28: 42; Lv 18: 6; Dt 25: 11) were spoken of quite openly. Despite this openness in dealing with sexual realities, the biblical authors occasionally employed a variety of euphemisms. Thus, "to uncover her nakedness"[37] and "to know"[38] were frequently used to denote sexual intercourse. The Prophets would employ one or another periphrasis from time to time.[39] Yet on the whole, the biblical texts evidence a frankness in dealing with sexual realities. This frankness reflects the Bible's radical demythologization of sexuality.

Nakedness was, nevertheless, not common among the Israelites, pace Ct 5: 3. They shared with many other ancient Semites the notion that nakedness was shameful. It was a sign of humiliation and degradation. To be stripped naked was a shameful punishment. Prisoners of war were exposed to nakedness (Is 20: 2–4). The vengeance of the Lord is likened to the stripping of a virgin whose nakedness would be displayed to all (Is 47: 3). According to a custom mentioned frequently in the prophets, but not explicitly attested in the Torah, a woman guilty of adultery was stripped naked and exposed to the gaze of all in the pillory.[40]

The Song of Solomon sings of that mutuality and reciprocity

which are essential to an authentically human sexual experience. These personal qualities were important for the ancient Israelites. Jacob's love for Rachel and Tobit's for Sarah are legendary. The fidelity of a covenanted marriage was so highly valued that restrictions were developed so that a wife would not be too easily abandoned by her spouse. Proverbs exhorted man not to despise the wife of his youth. Even the two versions of the Decalogue show the emerging awareness of woman as something other than man's chattel. Whereas the earlier version (Ex 20: 17) had cited woman among man's possessions, the later version (Dt 5: 21) singled her out from among the household goods and devoted an independent precept to the wife.[41]

## Sexual Ethic: Marriage and Family

Perhaps the vision of equality and partnership offered in the first pages of Genesis does not represent the existential ethos of ancient Israel. Nevertheless, the values of relationship, fidelity, and the dignity of women were truly a part of Israel's existence. Despite the appreciation of these values, it is clear that Israel's sexual ethic was largely shaped by the social reality of marriage and family. Despite Deuteronomy's surprisingly positive attitude toward women, women were clearly subordinate in their position. A woman's husband was the *baal* (Gen 18:12), i.e. possessor or lord; she was the *be'ulat ba'al* (Dt 22:22), i.e. that which is possessed. The language of the day, "to marry" for the male and "to be given in marriage" for the female bespeaks the woman's social inferiority. The extent of the husband's "lordship" over his wife is evident in the tales of the patriarchs using their wives entrance into the harem as a means of ensuring their own safety.[42] Only as a mother was a woman properly appreciated; thus the barren woman would mourn her infertility (Gen 30:1; Jg 11:37) or pray that the Lord take away her shame (1 Sm 1:10–11).

The ancient Israelite social system was one in which marriage[43] was generally endogamous: i.e., men preferred to marry within the clan. Thus Jacob was twice married to a daughter of Laban, his mother's brother (Gen 28:1–2; 29:12, 19). Inversely, one of the obstacles to the proposed marriage between Dina and Sichem was that the latter belonged to an uncircumcised clan (Gen 34:14). Still more sharply attested than endogamy was polygamy.[44] The wives and concubines of the patriarchs and other leaders of Israel are well known. Polygamy was not without its difficulties, however. Rivalry and jealousy were easily present (Gen 16:3–6). When practiced by kings, polygamy was a means of cementing political alliances (2 Sm 5:13–16; 1 Kg 11:1–3). The marital union of the Israelite king with a non-Israelite included its own danger, viz., that the worship of a heathen deity be introduced into the royal house of Israel. Hence, the disdain with which Solomon's marriages were regarded and the development of the royal law of Dt 17:17: "He shall not multiply wives for himself, lest his heart turn away." Nevertheless, polygamy was essentially ambivalent. While attesting to a man's wealth and assuring the importance of his progeny, polygamy also assured that there would be fewer unattached women. In practice, polygamy served the purposes of the male; in origin, it served the purposes of the female insofar as it once seemed better that every nubile woman be in some sort of fixed relationship to a man.[45]

### Incest and Adultery

Within the social context of the extended family, Israel's law shared with those of its neighbors two virtually exceptionless taboos. The one was the prohibition of incest, the other, the ban on adultery. The distinguishing of social roles within the extended family was extremely important. Hence, the significance of the taboo against incest. Indeed, in Israel, the laws against incest (Lv 18:6–16; Dt 27:20, 23) were so severe that even the offspring of incestuous unions were banned from the assembly of the Lord down to the tenth generation (Dt 23:2). Despite the severity of the ban, the prophets continued to cry out against the incest of Israel (Am 2:7).

The ban on adultery received its clearest formulation in the precept of the Decalogue (Ex 20:14; Dt 5:18). However, a double standard was operative.[46] A married man was not considered to have committed adultery if he had sexual intercourse with an unbetrothed maiden (Dt 22:28–29), a harlot, or a slave girl. Anytime a married woman had sexual intercourse with a man other than her husband she was considered an adulteress and could be subjected to the ordeal for suspected adultery (Nm 5:11–31).[47] The reason for the double standard was clear enough. Since the wife was the exclusive possession of her husband (the "chattel motif"), her sexual union with another man was essentially an affront to her husband. Thus, a man could sin by adultery only against the marriage of another man; whereas, a wife sinned by adultery against her own marriage. This same principle was operative in ancient Roman law. In any event, the prohibition of adultery was not unmixed with factors deriving from economy and the importance of procreation as formative influences upon Israel's sexual ethic. A wife's infidelity rendered impossible determination of the paternity of the children she bore. Illegitimate children were not only an economic burden for the putative father; they also implied that part of the family's patrimony was, in a sense, being alienated. It would be passed on to someone who did not truly belong to the blood line.

If economic factors were a significant factor in the restriction (and extension) of polygamy, as well as in the ban on adultery as far as a married woman was concerned, economic factors appear to have had a major influence on the development of other aspects of Israel's sexual ethos. It is not as if one ought to think that specific elements of Israel's sexual code were formed solely by economic factors. Rather, economic factors were one of the many elements that had a role to play. In most circumstances, the economic factors were mixed with others, remaining, nonetheless, a significant factor in the development of Israel's sexual ethic.

Thus, the payment of the *mohar* (Gen 34:12; Dt 22:29) was a significant element in Israel's sexual ethic. This "bride's price" was agreed upon and paid to the father of the bride at the time of the betrothal. To some degree the payment of the *mohar* is another indication of the relative inferiority of women in ancient Israel. There is a price to be paid for a bride. She is a possession to be bought.[48] In this same degree, the payment of the *mohar* reinforces the chattel motif insofar as wives are concerned. However, the *mohar* also reimbursed the father of the bride for the support which he had given to the maiden up until the time of her marriage. However, the paid *mohar* also prompted a husband's faithful commitment to his wife, insofar as he had an economic interest in the stability of his marriage. Finally, the *mohar* was a means of support for the wife in the eventuality that she should be divorced by her husband. Thus, an element in the development of Israel's male-female ethos which was primarily economic served to reinforce the value of fidelity in marriage, as well as the dignity of the female (by ensuring her livelihood after divorce).

*Factors in Israel's Sexual Ethics*

In the final analysis, however, the two principal factors in the development of Israel's sexual ethic were its concern for cultic purity[49] and its valorization of procreation. A curious injunction which seems to have both of these concerns at its origins is the prohibition of the wife seizing "the private parts" of a man when fighting with her husband (Dt 25:11). Insofar as this is not a protest against the practice of mutilation in the service of some deity,[50] the ban points to Israel's abhorrence of deformed sex organs (cf. Dt 23:1). Those who were sexually blemished, whether man or animal, were simply not acceptable to God. Thus males with crushed testicles should "not enter the assembly of the Lord" and priests were forbidden to function as such should they become maimed (Lv 21:20). On the other hand, as Stephen Sapp suggests, it may well be that "the importance of progeny to a man is so great that absolute priority is given to the protection of the organs that permit him to reproduce."[51]

*Bestiality*

The two motifs are also present in the laws against bestiality (Ex 22:19; Lv 18:23; 20:15–16; Dt 27:21) and homosexuality (Lv 18:22; 20:13). The prohibition of bestiality, a capital crime (Ex 22:19), was specifically incumbent upon females, as well as upon males (Lv 18:23). For man to give expression to his/her sexuality in sexual commerce with an animal is to go contrary to Israel's primitive understanding of human sexuality. Human sexuality is unto sociality. Man cannot find a helper fit for him among the animals (Gen 2:20). Beyond that, however, sexual union with beasts is a form of sexual commerce that cannot possibly lead to procreation. Finally, it is not unlikely, and Lv 18:23–30 suggests that such was indeed the case, that bestiality was associated with some Canaanite fertility rites.[52] Thus, the first commandment of the Decalogue implicitly prohibited bestiality insofar as the latter was a remnant of a cult other than that of Yahweh himself.

*Homosexuality*

Homosexual[53] activity is just as severely condemned in the biblical tradition as is bestiality. Current exegetical opinion generally holds to the view that the crime committed by the visitors to Sodom (Gen 19) is not that of homosexuality, but that of the violation of hospitality and rape. This interpretation finds its strongest argument in the parallel narrative of Jg 19 in which a female concubine suffers a fate at the hands of violent visitors similar to that of the servant of Gen 19. A supporting argument is to be found in the fact that the ancient biblical tradition, while frequently making mention of the abomination of Sodom, never explicitly links this to homosexual activity *per se*.

On the other hand, the etiological narrative of Gen 9:20–28, while proclaiming the subservience of Canaan to Israel, might also be an indication of Israel's abhorrence of homosexuality.[54] It is because the real reference is to the exposure of the sexual organs and a sexual offense, that the immodesty of Ham is distinguished sharply from the carefulness of his brothers. Von Rad has suggested that the Yahwist has bowdlerized his tradition, suppressing something more repulsive than a description of Ham merely seeing his father's sexual organs.[55] Most probably the narrative followed the lines found in the Egyptian epic, *The Contendings of Horus and Seth*.[56] If so, the more primitive tradition would have told of Ham's attempt to dominate all mankind by committing a homosexual act upon his father. Such a thought was so abhorrent to Israel that the very mention of it was expurgated from the narrative by the Yahwist. Nevertheless, the question remains as to why homosexuality was so abhorrent to Israel. The issue needs to be raised all the more insofar as lesbianism is not similarly condemned by Israel's biblical tradition. For males the precept is clear and its violation severe: "If a man lies with a male as with a woman, both of them have committed an abomination; they shall be put to death; their blood is upon them" (Lv 20:13).

The mention that homosexuality is an "abomination" (*to'ebah*) provides some key as to the reason why it was eschewed in Israel. Normally "abomination" is used by biblical authors with respect to practices and objects that were loathful for religious reasons. Homosexuality, therefore, might well be an abomination to Israel because of its association with pagan fertility rites. In fact, Dt 23:17 suggests that male prostitutes were as alien to Israel's existence as were female hierodules. Homosexual union between the Israelite and a male prostitute could be none other than an attempt to appropriate the fertility powers of the priest (the *kadesh* of Dt 23:17). Yet the biblical tradition is sharply opposed to this manner of trying to appropriate fertility. In a word, the law clearly shows that homosexuality is less condemnable as a sexual offense than it is as an act of idolatry and an inappropriate attempt to gain sexual power. Undoubtedly cultic grounds for Israel's abhorrence of homosexuality were reinforced by the universal awareness that homosexual activity is frequently a means of degrading another and ensuring their subjugation. Within Israel such degradation-subjugation was foreign to the dignity of the Israelite male whose belonging to the covenanted people was signified by the mark of circumcision which he bore in his flesh.

As the prohibition of homosexuality is to be fundamentally understood as a prohibition to participate in Canaanite fertility rites,[57] so what ambiguous evidence as is available points to the condemnation of sexual union with a prostitute only insofar as these prostitutes are involved in the cult of the fertility deities. Thus, John McKenzie writes that "It is remarkable that the entire Old Testament never manages a clear and unambiguous moral condemnation of prostitution."[58] What is clear is that the legal material of the Torah condemned ritual-intercourse (Dt 23:17–18), that the prophets condemned harlotry, and that several of the collected proverbs[59] in the canonical book of the same name vigorously condemned prostitution. What is not clear is whether the legal material is directed against sacred prostitution as such, or against certain forms of ritual intercourse; whether the prophets distinguished between ritual intercourse as it took place in the high places of Canaan (and "harlotry" as a metaphorical designation of Israel's infidelity) and simple intercourse with an ordinary prostitute; and whether the sages tended to identify secular prostitution with practices of ritual intercourse.[60] Thus McKenzie's declaration would seem to be a valid assessment of the available data.

## Fornication

Although there are frequent Old Testament references to harlots, none seem to clearly identify them as a sinful class. Still less does the Old Testament contain any clear condemnation of what would today be called fornication,[61] even though it rather strongly condemns sexual intercourse with a betrothed virgin by someone other than her intended (Dt 22:23–27). The texts likewise indicate that a man who has intercourse with an unmarried virgin must pay the bride-price and marry her, unless her father objects (Ex 22:16–17).

Two other traditions of the Old Testament ought to be cited briefly as we note the abhorrence with which the Israelites viewed participation in the Canaanite fertility rites, viz., the enigmatic "marriage" of the sons of God with the daughters of men (Gen 6:1–4) and the celerated [62] iniquity in honor of the Baal of Peor (Nm 25:6–9). The mythical tale of the sexual union of the sons of God with the daughters of men is difficult to interpret. The sons of God have been variously identified with angels, the powerful of the earth, the Sethites, and pious men. The sexual perversion to which the text makes reference has been interpreted as wild licentiousness or polygamy. However, there seems to be but insufficient grounds for such interpretations. More probable is the opinion which would contrast Gen 6:1–4 with Gen 5:1–3.[63] As long as procreation took place within the purview of the divine command (Gen 5:1–3; 9:1–7), man was acting according to his having been created in the image and likeness of God. When man violated the divine order, then an intolerable situation was created in which Yahweh was constrained to punish the perpetrators of the violation of his command. Concretely the passage seems to imply that primal sin can be described in terms of participation in the fertility rites. Those who are the devotees of the gods (the sons of God) went into the houses of temple prostitution to lie with the daughters of men who had been impressed into cultic prostitution.

At Beth Baal Peor, Phinehas killed in *flagrante delicto* a Midianite princess and a Simeonite who was engaged with her in an act of ritual intercourse. The sexual rite was apparently designed as an act of exorcism to ward off some pestilence or other. By way of commentary, Mendenhall notes that "It is hardly possible to conceive of a more heinous crime than the murder of a princess in a temple (or sacred precinct of some sort) engaged in a sacred ritual which was supposed to remove a most serious divine scourge from the entire community."[64] The act was so audacious as to mean war (Nm 31). In fact, Phinehas' action was unprecedented. No biblical narrative suggests that persons were put to death for violations of the covenant prior to this time. Phinehas thus represents the "transition from covenant to law; from the enforcement by Yahweh to the enforcement by human action."[65] His action set the legal precedent for the imposition of the death penalty on those who would transgress the Yahwistic covenant by participation in the sympathetic activity of ritual intercourse.

### Procreation

No less important in the development of Israel's sexual ethic was the value of progeny. Procreation is normally a significant factor in the

development of any culture's sexual ethic and ethos. Within Israel procreation was particularly valued insofar as large Israelite families were
considered to be the fulfillment of the promise made to Abraham (Gen
15:5). The large family was a particularly important aspect of *shalom,*
the covenant blessing *par excellence.* In later times, procreation as a shaping force in Israel's sexual ethic included the element of the possibility
of giving birth to the Messiah. Underlying these aspects of the value
of procreation particular to Israel is the general fact that in all cultures
marriage is related to children and that procreation is universally a particularly significant value in the shaping of a sexual ethic.

Already we have noted that sterility was so considered as a disvalue that the unmarried woman of biblical times bewailed her virginity, and the sterile woman beseeched the Lord that she might bear a
child. In the rabbinic era, Gen 1:28 was considered to be one of the
613 precepts of the law.[66] Indeed, it was so significant a commandment
that its violation, even the mere fact of not having children, was considered legitimate grounds for divorce in first century Palestine. As a
study of the value of procreation would necessitate a study of marriage
and the family, aspects of Israel's social life upon which we can but touch,
we would simply cite one or another ancient tale which bespeak the
value of procreation in the formation of a sexual ethic and indicate two
institutions which attest to the overriding importance of progeny as
a determinative force in Israel's sexual ethos.

The Genesis narratives contain two rather strange stories of women
who went to great lengths in order to bear children. Loosed from their
tribe and believing themselves to be the last people on earth, the two
daughters of Lot were concerned with the future of the race.[67] Resolutely they adopted the only measures that appeared available to them.
Even though their action constituted a serious violation of the universal
taboo on incest, the daughters of Lot got their father drunk and conceived by him (Gen 19:30-38). Undoubtedly the tale bespeaks the ancient belief that alcoholic ecstasy and sexual powers are somehow related. More pointedly, it declares that procreation is more important
than the observance of the ancient and universal prohibition of incest.

Equally pointed is the Yahwist's story of Tamar (Gen 38).[68] In
the development of his narrative, the Yahwist has been able to put forward two of his favorite theological ideas, namely, the role which women
have to play in the history of salvation and the pre-eminence of the tribe
of Judah from which David descended. The passage bears upon Tamar's

barren marriage to Er, the eldest of the sons of Judah. Subsequent to Er's premature death, it fell to Onan, his brother, to raise up children for the deceased. "But Onan knew that the offspring would not be his; so when he went in to his brother's wife he spilled the semen on the ground, lest he should give offspring to his brother" (Gen 38:9). Because of this sin, Onan was slain by Yahweh. It is now generally acknowledged that Onan's sin was not masturbation, nor was it the merely physical wasting of seed.[69] Rather, Onan sinned because he refused to perform the levirate duty to impregnate his brother's widow.

After the death of Onan, it fell to Shelah, the third of Judah's sons, to impregnate the unfortunate Tamar. Anxious for the life of his son, Judah delayed the marriage (Gen 38:11). Disguising herself as a prostitute, the crafty Tamar seduced her father-in-law and conceived by him. As is the case with the story of the daughters of Lot, the story of Tamar indicates that procreation is more significant than the observance of the ban on incest (Lv 18:15). It shows the importance of sexuality as a matter of personal relationships and fidelity to a covenant relationship with Yahweh.[70] Finally, it alludes to the levirate marriage as an institution designed to promote the value of procreation.

The institution of levirate marriage existed among the Hurrians, Hittites, Assyrians, and ancient Israelites, among whom the custom dated back to patriarchal times. Deuteronomic law, despite the proscriptions on incest found in Lv 18:16 and 20:21, not only permitted, but also commanded, a man to take to wife the widow of his brother should the latter have died without male heirs (Dt 25:5–10). One purpose of the law, especially as it originally existed, was to prevent a widow from alienating a part of the family's property by marrying outside of it.[71] Another purpose of the law was to ensure legal offspring for the deceased and thus provide for the continuance of his name. Finally, the law also provided for the otherwise homeless and head-less widow by providing a "redeemer" (*go'el*)[72] for her. Thus the institution of levirate marriage, like that of polygamy of which it may well be a special instance, was polyvalent.[73] Both institutions promoted the dignity of and provided for women insofar as they gave to a widow or an unmarried woman a significant male referent in a male-dominated society. Yet both institutions also clearly indicate the value of procreation in the determination of Israel's sexual ethos.

By way of conclusion to this rapid survey of Old Testament material dealing with human sexuality, we must note the singular importance of Yahwistic monotheism[74] in the development of an integrated attitude towards human sexuality. That attitude includes a vision as to the meaning of human sexuality. Nevertheless, there was a gap between the reality and the vision. The gap was caused by man's sin. Because sin touched man in his humanness, it also touched man in the fashion in which male and female experienced and lived their sexuality. Consequently the Law, as covenant gift, had much to say about the way in which male and female should live their sexuality. It was not only the vision of human sexuality which influenced the formation of its laws, but also social and economic concerns and the values of cultic purity and procreation. The intertestamental and rabbinic literature further specify the accepted modes of living human sexuality. Thus, this literature provides some of the background for the development of the New Testament attitude towards human sexuality.

## NOTES

1. Among the notable exceptions in English are: Joseph Blenkinsopp, *Sexuality and the Christian Tradition* (Dayton, 1969); Paul K. Jewett, *Man as Male and Female: A Study in Sexual Relationships from a Theological Point of View* (Grand Rapids, 1975); and Stephen Sapp, *Sexuality, the Bible and Science* (Philadelphia, 1977). The recently published study of a committee of the Catholic Theological Society of America on sexuality includes a significant chapter on the biblical teaching: Anthony Kosnik, *et al.*, *Human Sexuality: New Directions in American Catholic Thought* (New York, 1977), pp. 7–32.

2. *Optatam Totius*, 16.

3. Cf. John L. McKenzie, *The Two-Edged Sword* (Milwaukee, 1957), pp. 52–54; Joseph Blenkinsopp, *o.c.*, pp. 20–24.

4. His Canaanite consort, Anath, rarely appears in the Old Testament except in topographical *nomina composita*. In the place of Anath, the reader of the Old Testament most frequently encounters Ashtart, the Greek Astarte, a goddess identical in character to Anath.

5. Cf. Eugene J. Fisher, "Cultic Prostitution in the Ancient Near East? A Reassessment," *Biblical Theology Bulletin* 6:2–3 (1976), pp. 225–36.

6. Cf. A. Oepke, *guñe*, *TDNT* 1, p. 778.

7. E. A. Speiser, *Genesis*. AB, 1, p. 17.

8. Literally "this one"; respectively "this," "she," "she" in the RSV.

9. Cf. John L. McKenzie, *Myths and Realities* (Milwaukee, 1963), p. 171.

10. Cf. A. M. Dubarle, *The Biblical Doctrine of Original Sin* (London, 1964), pp. 74–76.

11. Cf. John L. McKenzie, *Myths and Realities*, pp. 171–74.

12. Cf. Jordi Mas I Antó, "La Condició proemial de Gn 1–11," *Revista Catalana de Teología* 1 (1976), 289–314, pp. 294–95.

13. Cf. Leonard Rost, "Erwägungen zu Hosea 4, 13f," in *Das Klein Credo und andere Studien zum Alten Testament* (Heidelberg, 1965), 53–64, pp. 62–63, n. 54.

14. Such an interpretation of the Yahwist's narrative of the origin of the sexes is not, in fact, and as I have indicated, its true meaning. However, the traditional notion that temporal priority implies ontological priority makes the Yahwist's narrative susceptible to such a misinterpretation.

15. Gerhard von Rad, *Genesis*. Old Testament Library, p. 58.

16. I would take issue with the position which sees the similarity between man and God in the "spiritual" nature of man. Such a position has most recently been espoused by Georges Cottier. See G. Cottier, "La conception chrétienne de la sexualité," *Nova et Vetera* 52:1 (1977), 1–21, p. 8.

17. Cf. G. N. Vollebregt, *The Bible on Marriage* (London, 1965), p. 67.

18. Stephen Sapp's comment is indeed apropos: "The crucial point is that human sexuality is presented as fundamental to what it means to be human and thus must be taken very seriously." See Stephen Sapp, "Biblical Perspectives on Human Sexuality," *Duke Divinity School Review* 41:2 (1976), 105–22, p. 108.

19. I use "man" here and in the following paragraphs in the biblical sense of *ha'adam*. May the reader permit the traditional rendering of biblical terms, and my inability to find a more adequate (pace Paul Jewett's "Man" and Katherine Sakenfeld's "humankind"), yet practical, terminology to serve as an apology for language that is admittedly sexist.

20. G. von Rad, *o.c.*, p. 56.

21. H. Hirsch Cohen, *The Drunkenness of Noah*. Judaic Studies 4 (University, AL, 1974), p. 63.

22. Charles Hauret, *Beginnings*, p. 55.

23. G. von Rad, *o.c.*, pp. 57–58.

24. While it is true that "in some sense man's sexuality participates in his image in God's creation" (S. Sapp, *art. cit.*, p. 108) and that "sexuality is not simply a mechanism for procreation which Man has in common with the animal world" (P. Jewett, *o.c.*, p. 13), Jewett's thesis that Man's sexuality is "a part of what it means to like the Creator" needs a careful exposition. It is clear that for the Priestly author there is a connection between being in God's image and the procreative capacity (cf. Gn 9:6–7). It is likewise clear that it is as sexually differentiated that man has been created in the image and likeness of God, and that the sexual differentiation has a meaning in itself: i.e., one that is antecedent to procreation. To this extent Jewett's thesis is correct.

25. Emile Brunner, *Man in Revolt*, p. 346.

26. See note 23.

27. The point is convincingly argued by Jewett in *Man as Male and Female*.

28. See, for example, Roland E. Murphy, "Form-Critical Studies in the Song of Songs," *Interpretation* 27:3 (1973), 413–22, p. 416.

29. Cf. Joseph Blenkinsopp, *o.c.*, p. 116.

30. Ibid., p. 119.

31. Roland E. Murphy, *art. cit.*, p. 422.

32. Cf. N. K. Gottwald, "Song of Songs," in *The Interpreter's Dictionary of the Bible*, 4: R–Z, p. 421.

33. Cf. Eccl 3:1–11.

34. Cf. Raymond Collins, "Los Diez Mandamientos para nuestro tiempo," *Actualidad Pastoral* 102/103 (1976–77), 195–97, p. 197.

35. Cf. Joseph Blenkinsopp, *o.c.*, p. 28.

36. Cf. Louis M. Epstein, *Sex Laws and Customs in Judaism* (New York, 1967), pp. 4–5.

37. Cf. Lv 18, for example.

38. Cf. Gn 4:1, 17, etc. It is to be noted, however, that the Hebrew *yd'* is not simply an euphemism. The Hebrew vocable has a broader range of meaning than the English verb "to know." The basic connotation of the Hebrew is "to experience." Sexual intercourse is, in fact, an experiencing of the female by the male (and vice-versa, although this reciprocal point of view is not generally present in the biblical texts). Cf. E. A. Speiser, *o.c.*, pp. 31–32.

39. Cf. Is 7:20; 36:12; Jer 13:22; Na 3:5; etc.

40. Jer 13:26–27; Ez 16:38–39; 23:10, 29, 45; Hos 2:5; Na 3:5.

41. Cf. Raymond Collins, *art. cit.*, p. 197, and "The Ten Commandments in Current Perspective," *supra* essay 2, p. 61.

42. Gn 12, 20, 24.

43. Since the present article is devoted to sexuality as such, its treatment of marriage and divorce will be restricted to the occasional use of marriage as an example of the factors which shaped Israel's sexual ethic.

44. Cf. E. G. Parrinder, *The Bible and Polygamy* (London, 1958).

45. Cf. Helmut Thielicke, *The Ethics of Sex* (New York, 1964), p. 107.

46. Cf. Raymond F. Collins. "The Ten Commandments in Current Perspective," *supra* p. 58.

47. The penalty was death by stoning (Lv 20:10; Dt 22:22–24; Ez 16:40), but there is not a single recorded instance of the death penalty being applied in the Old Testament.

48. The Hebrew verb "to wed" also has the meaning "to acquire property." Cf. Gn 20:3.

49. The concern for cultic purity not only warranted Israel's abhorrence for sexual practices associated with Canaanite rites, but also prompted a series of regulations designed to ensure ritual purity in those who approached the divinity. Normal menstruation (Lv 15:19–24; 18:19; 20:18) and nocturnal emissions (Lv 15:16; Dt 23:10–11) were a source of ritual uncleanness. Laws concerning the marriage of

priests (e.g., Lv 21:7-8), especially the high priest (Lv 21:13-15), were particularly severe.

50. Cf. S. R. Driver, *A Critical and Exegetical Commentary on Deuteronomy. ICC*, 5 (Edinburgh, 1955), p. 260.

51. Stephen Sapp, *o.c.*, p. 30.

52. Cf. ibid., pp. 31-32.

53. The use of the verb *'aheb* ("to love") in the narratives of the relationship between David and Jonathan has a political rather than a sexual connotation. Cf. J. A. Thompson, "The Significance of the verb LOVE in the David-Jonathan narratives in 1 Samuel," *Vetus Testamentum* 24:3 (1974), 334-38; Peter R. Ackroyd, "The verb love—*ahēb* in the David-Jonathan narratives—a footnote," *Vetus Testamentum* 25:2 (1975), 213-14.

54. This interpretation of the incident is offered by Steck, Winckler, von Rad, Zimmerli, etc. Rabbinic sayings in the Midrash and Talmud indicate that the text told of Noah's castration. Cohen, however, looks to Noah's drinking as an attempt to increase his procreative powers. Ham's offense, catching his father in the act of sexual intercourse, was an attempt to appropriate his father's wine-induced sexual prowess to himself. See H. H. Cohen, *o.c.*, pp. 7-33.

55. Gerhard von Rad, *o.c.*, p. 133.

56. Cf. J. Edgar Bruns, "Old Testament History and the Development of a Sexual Ethic," in *The New Morality* ed. W. Dunphy (New York, 1967), 37-81, pp. 75-76.

57. In similar fashion, and for a similar reason, transvestism is an "abomination to the Lord" (Dt 22:5). The wearing of the distinctive garments of the opposite sex was one of the customs connected with the Canaanite fertility cults. Cf. Hartman-de Fraine, "Sex," *Encyclopedic Dictionary of the Bible*, e. 2185; Cyrus Gordon, "Ugarit and Its Significance," *Arts* 9 (1974), 26-27.

58. John L. McKenzie, *A Theology of the Old Testament*, p. 204.

59. Prv 6:23-35; 7:1-27; 9:13-18.

60. Kosnik *et al.* contend (*Human Sexuality*, p. 16) that, in fact, the "Wisdom literature equated secular prostitution with practices of ritual intercourse."

61. Cf. Bruce Malina, "Does *Porneia* mean Fornication?" *Novum Testamentum* 14:1 (1972), 10-17, p. 11, n. 2.

62. Cf. Jos 22:17; Hos 9:10; Ps 106:28.

63. C. Houtman, "Het Verboden Huwelijk. Genesis 6:1-4 in haar context," *Gereformeerd Theologisch Tijdschrift* 76:2 (1976), 65-75.

64. George E. Mendenhall, *Tenth Generation: The Origins of the Biblical Tradition* (Baltimore, 1974), p. 117.

65. Ibid., p. 116.

66. Cf. Abraham H. Rabinowitz, "The 613 Commandments," *Encyclopedia Judaica*, 5, 759-83.

67. Cf. E. A. Speiser, *o.c.*, p. 145.

68. Cf. Luke a B. "Judah and Tamar," *Scripture* 17 (1965), 52–61, p. 61.

69. Thus, Holzinger, Chaine, Fletcher, Grelot, Speiser. The opinion of Gunkel and von Rad is similar, namely, that Onan sinned against family affection.

70. Cf. Stephen Sapp, *o.c.*, p. 32.

71. Buis and Leclercq note that the gesture of a spurned widow's stripping the sandal from the foot of her brother-in-law who refuses to perform the duties of levirate marriage is a symbol that the inheritance would not devolve to him. The use of the gesture thus confirms the economic motivation of levirate marriage. Cf. P. Buis and J. Leclercq, *Le Deuteronome, Sources Bibliques* (Paris, 1963), p. 165.

72. Ru 3:9, 12; 4:1, 3, 6.

73. Cf. F. Schroeder and A. van den Born, "Levirate Marriage," in *Encyclopedic Dictionary of the Bible*, ee. 1331–32; E. G. Parrinder, *o.c.*, pp. 23–27.

74. Cf. Joseph Blenkinsopp, *o.c.*, pp. 16–41.

# 8

# Human Sexuality
# in the Christian Scriptures

GIVEN THE ABUNDANCE of Old Testament material dealing with human sexuality, it appears somewhat surprising that the New Testament does not treat of human sexuality at such great lengths. This relative silence owes principally to two factors. First of all, the world of the New Testament authors is almost without exception, the world of the Old Testament. The traditions contained in the Old Testament are the word of God for the New Testament authors just as they are for Jesus himself. Thus there was no need for New Testament authors to repeat mechanically the laws of the Torah.[1] A second, and perhaps more significant, reason is that the New Testament authors shared with the Old Testament the basic view that human sexuality is a secular reality. Sexuality is simply one aspect of human existence for which man is responsible. As such human sexuality does not need specific religious valorization, neither through some form of cultic sexual *ekstasis* nor by means of a rigid asceticism. The former valorization would take human sexuality from the realm of the human, the latter would deny to human sexuality the goodness of its createdness. Thus the New Testament authors treat of human sexuality with a frankness and a matter-of-factness that it would be good for our aphrodisiac and overly-sexually-conscious society to emulate.

## JESUS: HIS CONTEXT

It is, however, apropos to note that the world into which Jesus of Nazareth was born was a world whose sexual attitudes and norms were formed not only by the written law, but also by the oral tradition handed down by the scribes of the various Jewish sects. Although our documentation is relatively late or apparently peripheral to "mainstream

Judaism," we do possess sufficient documentation to be able to determine somewhat more specifically the understanding of human sexuality in Palestine during the time of Jesus. Four points might serve as touchstones to illustrate that attitude, viz., the notion of the *Yetzer ha-ra*, ideas about marriage, the attitude toward women, and laws dealing with sexual matters. A brief word or two about each of these factors determinative of the attitude of the first century Jew toward human sexuality might be useful.

## Yetzer ha-ra *(Evil inclination)*

According to contemporary Jewish anthropology, each man was considered to have been born with the *Yetzer ha-ra*, the evil inclination. This impulse urges the adult man to all sorts of sin, especially sins of a sexual nature. The *Yetzer ha-ra* also prompts self-preservation and procreation in a man. Thus it can be mastered and put to good use. Thus some rabbis declare that the *Yetzer ha-ra* is good, indeed, very good, since without it there would be neither procreation nor marriage, and the human race would cease. Thus, "as R. Samuel ben Nahman observes: 'And behold it was very good.' This is the evil impulse! Is then the evil impulse good? Yet, were it not for the evil impulse no man would build a house, nor marry a wife, nor beget children nor engage in trade."[2]

## Marriage

Secondly, marriage was the ordinary way of life among the Jewish people of Palestine. Only among the ascetic Essenes did celibacy appear to have any value. Among other Jews it was often presumed that the celibate life was a life of sin. Indeed, it was a violation of the Law: "No man may abstain from keeping the Law 'Be fruitful and multiply', unless he already has children: according to the School of Shammai, two sons; according to the School of Hillel, a son and a daughter, for it is written, 'Male and female created He them.' The duty to be fruitful and multiply falls on the man, but not on the woman. R. Johanan B. Baroka says: Of them both it is written, 'And God blessed them and God said to them, Be fruitful and multiply.'"[3] This Mishnaic text clearly indicates that procreation was the predominant value to be sought after in marriage. Many other Mishnaic and Talmudic passages confirm the view that, for the rabbis, procreation was the purpose of marriage.

*Attitude toward Women*

Thirdly, the social and religious inferiority of woman was an accepted reality. Tradition has preserved for us an oft-quoted prayer which bespeaks this inferiority most acutely: "Blessed be Thou for not having made me a Gentile, a woman or an ignoramus." A theoretical basis for this inequality was found in the Yahwist's creation narrative; otherwise, woman's inferiority was ascribed to the sin of Eve.[4] Thus, we find that women "are said to require perfume, which a man does not require, because they were created from a putrefying bone, whereas man was formed from pure and wholesome earth."[5] Nevertheless, not every Jewish tradition accepted the status quo of the woman's inferiority as a situation which ought to exist. Thus a Talmudic saying proclaims the basic equality of man and woman before God: "The compassion of God is not as the compassion of men. The compassion of men extends to men more than to women, but not thus is the compassion of God. His compassion extends equally to all."[6] A clear affirmation of the social inferiority of women is to be found in the fact that, whereas Jewish men could divorce their wives for cause, Jewish women were not permitted to do so.[7] That some rabbis considered the instruction of women in the Torah to be something less than a waste of time is further confirmation of the disadvantaged position of women.

*Sexual Laws*

Within the thus stratified Jewish society, the oral Law complemented the prescriptions of the Bible with respect to human sexuality. Much of this oral tradition has been gathered together in the Mishnah whose division on Women (*Nashim*) includes extensive *halakoth* relating to marriage and human sexuality. We find a variety of sayings which indicate that cultic purity is a major determinant in the ethos of the time. For example, sexual intercourse with a menstruous woman is enjoined.

Chastity was highly valued in first century Judaism. The biblical injunction "Thou shalt not commit adultery" was understood to prohibit various immoral sexual activities. The virginity of a bride was highly prized. In this respect, the words of Philo are significant: "We, the descendants of the Hebrews, have excellent customs and laws. Other nations allow their young men of fourteen years of age to go to prostitutes and to other women who sell their bodies. But according to our laws, all hetairas are condemned to die. Until there can be legitimate relations, we do not have intercourse with a woman. Both parties enter marriage as virgins, and for us the purpose of marriage is not pleasure but the propagation of children."[8]


## JESUS: HIS ATTITUDE


Such, in brief, was the dominant attitude towards matters sexual in the milieu of Jesus of Nazareth. Sexual norms were largely derived from the biblical tradition with particular emphases added by the oral tradition of the rabbis. Thus, there was no need for Jesus of Nazareth to formulate a new or renewed sexual ethic. The silence of the Gospels indicates that Jesus gave neither a positive nor a particularly negative value to human sexuality. He accepted it as a reality with respect to which man must exercise responsibility. For the rest, it can be affirmed that Jesus' proclamation of the kingdom of God (Mk 1:15) somewhat colored his attitudes and teachings with respect to human sexuality.[9]


*Marriage and Divorce*


If, with Stephen Sapp, we consider Jesus' teachings about marriage and divorce the prime sources for discerning his understanding of human sexuality,[10] his contention may well be an overstatement of the case, even though the pronouncement story on divorce (Mk 10:1-12; par Mt 19:1-12) and the narrative of the Jerusalem dispute with the Sadducees on levirate marriage (Mk 12:18-27; par Mt 22:23-33; Lk 20:27-40), as well as the Q logion on divorce preserved as the Matthean third antithesis in the Sermon on the Mount (Mt 5:32) and as an isolated saying in Luke (Lk 16:18), do offer some evidence of Jesus' understanding of human sexuality.

A discussion of the Jesuanic logion on divorce, particularly in view of the Matthean modification (Mt 19:9, cf 5:32), would take us far beyond the scope of the present article. Moreover, there is already a vast literature on the topic; for us to attempt to add to it within the present undertaking would serve no useful purpose. However, the pronouncement story is particularly significant for our purposes insofar as it is a reaffirmation of the basic understanding of human sexuality contained in the Yahwistic and Priestly creation narratives. The references to Gen 1:27 (Mk 10:6; Mt 19:4) and Gen 2:24 (Mk 10:7; Mt 19:5) make it clear that the biblical perspective of the relationship between the sexes is the understanding shared by Jesus and the synoptic tradition. We must particularly note that these biblical citations are advanced not to further a notion of marriage in which procreation is the primary value, but to advance the idea that faithful relationship in marriage is the demand of the Gospel, as well as that of the Creator. The reinforcement of the demand for faithful commitment and personal relationship in marriage would, therefore, seem to be integral to Jesus' understanding of human sexuality.

Is this consistent with the view expounded in Mt 19:11-12, Matthew's addendum to the pericope on divorce?[11] So often this pair of Matthean verses have been cited in favor of the view that Jesus proposed celibacy "for the sake of the kingdom of heaven" as a way of life for his disciples. This interpretation, although traditional, is hardly adequate to the text.[12] Both the content and the context of v. 12 argue against the traditional interpretation. From the standpoint of content, the logion of Jesus (vv. 11b-12) is a response to the disciples' objection that it is better not to marry. The entire logion, therefore, must be seen as an argument that it is good to marry. Moreover, were "there are eunuchs who have made themselves eunuchs for the sake of the kingdom of heaven" to be interpreted as a text proposing celibacy, it would be the sole Gospel logion with this meaning—a fact which renders the authenticity of the logion somewhat suspect. From the standpoint of context, it must be noted that the Matthean addendum is an insert into a pre-Matthean context (cf Mk 10:1-16) on marriage and the family. Moreover, the social context of the times seems to preclude a celibacy-oriented interpretation of the logion. The generally low esteem in which eunuchs were held at the time of Jesus' ministry makes it highly unlikely that the text proposed celibacy as an ideal mode of discipleship. Were he to have done so, we would expect his singular teaching to be reflected in other Gospel passages.

When these several factors are taken into consideration and attention is paid to the content of the logion, it is clear that what Jesus is saying is that if his disciples cannot live up to the Creator-intended demands of marital fidelity then, and only then, is it better not to marry. Thus, the text reinforces the personal relationship view of marriage, rather than proposes celibacy as a more ideal way of life for the disciples of Jesus.

## Levirate Marriage

The Synoptic accounts of the Jerusalem dispute on levirate marriage, of which the Lukan form is the longest (Lk 20:27–40),[13] add further glimpses into Jesus' attitude towards marriage and sexuality. The pericope has the form of a scribal dispute which bears upon a hypothetical case, namely that of a widow who has been married seven times in keeping with the Deuteronomic prescriptions on levirate marriage. The tradition has obviously been preserved as an apology for the possibility of resurrection. The logion of Lk 20:38 is the climax of the entire pronouncement story. In passing, however, the passage indicates at least two significant dimensions of Jesus' understanding of marriage. First of all, there is an acceptance of the then current view on marriage. The language of Lk 20:35, "they neither marry nor are given in marriage," is an indication that the chattel motif in marriage was still current. Moreover, the mere fact that levirate marriage could serve as the hypothetical[14] subject of rabbinic debate shows that procreation continued to be regarded as the most significant value in marriage. Jesus does not seem to take issue with these elements of the popular understanding of marriage. His purpose is other: to proclaim the possibility and reality of the resurrection. In so doing, however, Jesus proclaims that marriage and the bearing of children are realities of the present order. In a word, he affirms the essential secularity of marriage.[15] Once again, his view is as traditional as that of the Priestly author of Gen 1.

In the passages which we have thus far examined, if only briefly, Jesus' proclamation of the kingdom has prompted an affirmation of the relativity of the secular reality of marriage with respect to the definitive establishment of the kingdom in the resurrection and has included a Gospel demand for marital fidelity. The coming of the kingdom and his announcement of it would seem to be even more important as a determinant factor in Jesus' attitude towards women. It is true that the Gospels do not explicitly affirm that the kingdom has come for women, as it has for children (Mk 10:13–16), as well as for the poor, the blind, the captives, and the oppressed (Lk 4:18). Yet, it is clear that Jesus has come for those who exist on the margin of society. The justice of the kingdom of God is realized insofar as God's reign is extended to those who exist on the fringes or beyond the pale of the righteous society. Numerous logia, several parables, and the evangelical descriptions of Jesus' conduct clearly affirm that Jesus had come for those who were alienated in one way or another.

## Jesus' Attitude toward Women

The social situation of first century Palestine in which women were, in fact, the chattel property of their husbands, and the religious situation in which women had but limited access to the temple precincts sufficiently bespeak the fact that women were generally considered inferior to men. In this respect, women were on the fringes of society. They were an alienated group within their homeland. Within this set of circumstances, Jesus' attitude towards women and his ministry to them is particularly significant.[16] That his ministry to women was a scandal is indicated not only by Simon's retort, "If this man were a prophet, he would have known who and what sort of woman this is who is touching him, for she is a sinner" (Lk 7:39) — a text that clearly indicates that the woman in question is a sinner, most likely a prostitute — but also by the disciples' amazement that Jesus was talking with a woman (Jn 4:27). His ministry to women was an element of the scandal of the coming of the kingdom.

Much could be written about Jesus' attitude towards women and his ministry to them. Typically an author might cite Jesus' cure of the woman with the flow of blood and his raising from the dead the daughter of Jairus (Mk 5:21–43 par.), his friendship with Martha and Mary (Lk 10:38–42),[17] and the women who accompanied and provided for him (Lk 8:2–3). Still more significant is the testimony of the four-fold Gospel tradition which cites women as the first witnesses to the Resurrection of Jesus (Mt 28:1–10; Mk 16:1–8; Lk 24:1–12; Jn 20:1–2, 11–18). The Gospel tradition unanimously affirms that women were the first witnesses to and heralds of the Resurrection of Jesus. Yet, the early credal formula of 1 Cor 15:3–6 omits the mention of women precisely because they were not deemed to be qualified witnesses in the society in which the earliest formulations of the Christian creed took place. First-century Palestine was a man's world, despite the ministry of Jesus of Nazareth.

Somewhat subjectively, perhaps, I would suggest that there are other elements in the Gospel accounts which are equally important as an indication of Jesus' attitude towards women. The first is the logion which concludes the Markan pericope on Jesus' family (Mk 3:31–35). Whereas the pericope is repeatedly concerned with Jesus' mother and brothers (vv. 31, 32, 33, 34), the concluding logion dramatically proclaims "Whoever does the will of God is my brother, *and sister*, and mother" (v. 35, my emphasis). A second Markan passage which appears particularly significant to me is Mk 10:11, the Markan version of the Jesuanic logion on divorce. Mark, and Mark alone, renders the saying "Whoever divorces his wife and marries another, commits adultery against her *(ep'autēn)*." Although it may well be argued that the *ep'autēn* is a Markan insertion into the tradition, the phrase is remarkably clear as an affirmation that adultery (divorce) is to be considered a personal offense against the aggrieved spouse. The personalism of the logion is far removed from the culturally dominant chattel motif. The third passage to which I would draw attention is the parable of the woman and the lost coin (Lk 15:8–10). As the central member of a trilogy, this parable is sandwiched between the traditional parable of the lost sheep (Lk 15:3–7, cf Mt 18:12–14) and the Lukan story of the prodigal son (Lk 15:11–32). The story of the lost coin is virtually unique within the Palestinian parabolic genre in that it features a woman as the heroine of the narrative. Together with the two Markan passages just cited, the parable of the lost coin indicates that, for Jesus, woman was essentially equal with man, especially with respect to the kingdom of God.

*Adultery*

Another way to come to an appreciation of the understanding of human sexuality had by Jesus and the early Gospel tradition is to examine the logia on adultery. There are three Synoptic passages with a Jesuanic logion on adultery: the citation of the seventh commandment among the precepts of the Decalogue (Mk 10:19),[18] the second antithesis in Matthew's version of the Sermon on the Mount (Mt 5:27–30), and a catalogue of vices found in Mk 7:21 (par Mt 15:19). Only the latter two passages require our immediate concern. A brief word about each will suffice.

The second Matthean antithesis, "You have heard that it was said, 'You shall not commit adultery.' but I say to you that every one who looks at a woman lustfully has already committed adultery with her in his heart." (Mt 5:27–28) is one of a series of three antitheses used by the evangelist to show that Jesus went to the heart of the matter. Jesus radicalized the demand of the Law and thus fulfilled the law and the prophets (Mt 5:17). Lohse has convincingly demonstrated that the transcending of the seventh precept of the Decalogue by means of the radicalization of its demand is without parallel in the Synoptic tradition.[19] Nevertheless, the antithesis shows traces of a pre-Matthean tradition.[20] The point of the logion is clear: it is not sufficient merely to abstain from the physical act of adultery. Chastity and fidelity to the demands of the kingdom is a matter of the heart. When a man has committed adultery in his heart, he has already turned his heart from the Lord and is, thus, no longer a faithful disciple.

The Gospel tradition is not alone in thus radicalizing the demand of the Law. In the ancient story of Ahikar, we read: "My son, lift not up thy eyes and look upon a woman that is bedizened and painted; and do not lust after her in thy heart; for if thou shouldst give her all that is in thy hands, thou findest no advantage in her; and thou wilt be guilty of sin against God."[21] Indeed, and somewhat curiously, a passage in the Babylonian Talmud declares a mental or imaginative sin of adultery to be more harmful than the actual transgression.[22] Consequently, it is not altogether certain that Jesus was the first to radicalize the Torah's ban on adultery by indicating the sinfulness of lustful desire. It is clear, however, that the Matthean Jesus is one who demands of his disciples respect for another's marriage. A married woman is an inappropriate object of sexual desire for any man to whom she is not married.

The sinfulness of adultery is likewise reaffirmed in a catalogue of vices (Mk 7:21–22, par Mt 15:19) where it is cited among 13 vices which come from the heart of a man and defile him. The Markan sin catalogue also includes fornication (*porneiai*), wickedness (*pornēriai*), and licentiousness (*aselgeia*) among the vices that defile a man. The emphasis on sexual sin is somewhat unusual within the Gospel tradition. Its explanation is to be found in the fact that the Christian tradition borrowed the catalogues of vices from the Hellenistic world whose dualism and Stoic emphasis on the virtue of apathy (*apatheia*) accorded greater importance to sins of a sexual nature than would normally be found among Christian traditions derived from a Jewish background. Since we are dealing with a list (a "catalogue" to use the language that has become traditional) for which there is no normative series of items, it is difficult to determine precisely what is meant by adultery, fornication, wickedness and licentiousness. Clearly, however, the author of Mk is making use of a tradition which affirms that adultery is not the only act of a sexual nature which ought to be considered sinful.

In the parallel Matthean text, the catalogue of vices has been reduced to seven items. It is clear that Mt has been influenced by the Decalogue in his reworking of the Markan tradition. The order of the Matthean catalogue clearly reflects the order of the so-called second table of the Decalogue. With adultery (*moichaiai*), the first evangelist makes reference to the sixth precept of the Decalogue. He has omitted the sins of thought and desire from his listing. Nevertheless, he has added fornication (*porneiai*) to adultery as a sexual offense which defiles man. In context, the sin alluded to was most probably commercial and/or cultic prostitution.[23]

That both the Markan and the Matthean passages list adultery and other sexual offenses within the catalogue of vices is a clear indication that the Synoptic tradition considers sexual sins to be merely sins among other sins. They are not isolated for particular consideration nor is any suggestion made that sexual sins are in any way the most grievous of sins. That sin can be committed in matters sexual is, nonetheless, a basic datum of the Gospels' moral teaching. This datum must be considered as we cite a final dimension which must be developed in any adequate consideration of Jesus' understanding of human sexuality—the forgiveness which he extended to those who had committed sins of a sexual nature.

*Woman in Adultery*

The Johannine story of the woman caught in the act of adultery (Jn 7:53–8:11) is undoubtedly the most striking expression of the fact that Jesus considered sexual sins merely as sins among other sins and that Jesus forgave even the sin of adultery. The Johannine dramatization is a late and inauthentic tradition. Nevertheless, the drama points to the thoroughly attested fact that Jesus extended his forgiveness to prostitutes and others who had committed offenses of a sexual nature. These are to be numbered among the sinners for whom Jesus came (Mk 2:17). The Lukan parable of the prodigal son (Lk 15:11–32) is a poignant drama of a father who forgives the repentant son and reconciles him to the household. It is a tale of divine mercy rendered to one who was a sinner. The Gospel portrayal of the prodigal's sin specifies that he "squandered his property in loose living" (*zōn asōtōs*) (Lk 15:13), a way of life which the elder brother's commentary interprets to be a matter of having "devoured your living with harlots" (*kataphagōn sou ton bion meta pornōn*) (Lk 15:30). To the extent that the righteous son's outrage at his younger brother's dissolute life is dramatically clear, the extent of the father's mercy is manifest in this story which forms the climax of the Lukan trilogy on divine forgiveness.

## Samaritan Woman

No explicit word of forgiveness is addressed to the Samaritan woman—she of the five husbands (Jn 4:18). Nevertheless, the tone of the narrative is such that her conduct must be considered reprehensible. Her forgiveness is evident in that she came to faith. Whereupon, she proclaimed the depth of Jesus' knowledge and queried whether he was the Christ (Jn 4:29). The sinful woman had become a disciple and witness.[24] No surer sign could be had of her acceptance by Jesus. In contrast to the woman who had anointed his feet with the ointment poured from the alabaster jar (Lk 7:38), Jesus did address an explicit word of forgiveness: "Your sins are forgiven" (Lk 7:48). The relationship between the Lukan narrative (Lk 7:36-50) and the parallel stories in the other Gospels (Mt 26:6-13; Mk 14:3-9; Jn 12:1-8) remains a moot question. In any event, however, the dialogue with Simon the Pharisee (Lk 7:39-47) and the authoritative utterance addressed to the woman (v. 48) make it clear that the Lukan story has a function different from the function of the parallel narratives in the other Gospels. Luke's narrative is a pronouncement story whose point is the divine forgiveness extended to a known prostitute. Just as the discourse material speaks of that forgiveness, so the narrative account dramatizes Jesus' forgiving presence to others. His very act is revelatory of the kingdom of God. In Luke's narrative account of the triangular relationship among Simon, the woman, and Jesus, the evangelist patently demonstrates that the kingdom of God is characterized by forgiveness, extended even to those who had not previously lived their sexual lives in a moral and responsible fashion.

## PAUL

When we turn our attention from the Gospels to the rest of the New Testament, it becomes immediately clear that it is on the Pauline material that we must concentrate in our quest for some insight into the New Testament understanding of human sexuality. Once again, the demands of conciseness preclude a truly adequate consideration of the pertinent material. Hence, we will focus upon some passages in the Pauline corpus and allow them to serve as an indication of the attitude towards matters sexual held by the early Church. Fortunately, the Pauline corpus, both the letters which are authentic and those which are not, offers abundant material for reflection.

## Pauline Context

The context in which this material was developed must first be considered, since the Pauline teaching can be rightly understood only within the context in which it was actually formulated. An appreciation of the appropriate context is all the more important insofar as our only source for understanding the Pauline attitude are letters which are occasional compositions. The points of view expressed are very much determined by the situation which has prompted the writing of any individual letter. Basically, the context of Paul's letters is not first century Palestine, whose ethos is dominated by the biblical tradition. Rather, Paul's general context is that of first century Hellenism whose weltanschauung predominated throughout the Mediterranean basin. There philosophy had a role in shaping the sexual ethic and attitude of the populace somewhat similar to the role had by the Bible and rabbinic tradition in first century Palestine. At the risk of glaring oversimplification, it can be said that the dominant cosmology, anthropology, and ethics were decidedly dualistic. Man was composed of a spiritual and a material principle. As such, sexuality belonged to the realm of the physical. The dominant ethical philosophy, Stoicism, looked to the imposition of a rational order (*logos*) on the material reality. That man should be so dominated by reason as to control his passions was the goal of the ethical life. Hence, apathy (*apatheia*) was a virtue to be striven for.

## Gnosticism

In the Hellenistic world in which the Gospel was preached, a form of syncretistic dualism, popularly known as Gnosticism, posed a threat to the life and belief of the early Church. Undoubtedly, the conflict with Gnosticism was one of the growing pains which nascent Christianity had to face. Its dualistic denigration of the body was hardly consistent with a positive evaluation of marriage and human sexuality. Thus there arose within the early Church certain encratite communities who eschewed marriage (1 Tm 4:3). Moreover, the denial of the value of the body led to two ethical abuses: a rigid asceticism and an open libertinism. Those who claimed that the body was intrinsically evil adopted the rigorist view. Those who looked to the body as valueless adopted an "it doesn't make any difference" attitude. Both attitudes were a denial of human responsibility with respect to matters sexual and were based on an anthropology basically inconsistent with the single view of man held by traditional Jewish-Christian anthropology. Indeed, the anthropology of Paul's earliest letters had a polemical intent. They attempted to inculcate that wholistic anthropology on the basis of which a truly Christian understanding of human sexuality can be developed.

*Imminent Parousia*

Another element of the historical context in which Paul's letters were written was the early Christian expectation of an imminent Parousia. Paul shared with other Christians the expectation that the time was short (1 Cor 7:29–31) and that the consummation would come soon (1 Thes 4:15, 17; 5:2–3; 2 Thes 2:7). Paul's eschatological expectations inevitably shaped his attitudes towards marriage and sexuality. Marriage was generally understood, i.e. within both the Hebraic and the Hellenistic cultures, as having procreation as its principal purpose. In a very real sense, an expectation of an imminent consummation rendered marriage purposeless. Moreover, the expectation of the consummation gave to Paul's ethic something of a crisis dimension. It may not have been an interim ethic as such, but it was an ethic formulated with the urgency of the impending end times.

The realities of Hellenistic dualism and the Christian expectation of an imminent Parousia are elements of no small import as part of the background of Paul's teaching on human sexuality. Beyond this, we should take into account three other factors. First, the occasional nature of Paul's letters means that, in principle, we do not have a synthetic presentation of Paul's thought. Much of what we do have is reactionary insofar as it is Paul's response to an intellectual error or a moral failing. Secondly, the material content of much of Paul's ethical teaching is borrowed. To some extent, this borrowed material, particularly when used for a polemical purpose, is reactionary. At the very least, it can be said that much of the content of Paul's ethical teaching shows a trace of Stoic influence, if not outright borrowing of Stoic material. Thirdly, Paul's basic anthropology, as well as his personal ethical tradition, is principally shaped by the Bible and its Pharisaic interpreters (Gal 1:14; Phil 3:5). Thus, we must affirm that Paul inherited the views of his (Jewish) community and allowed the biblical view of man to form his understanding of human sexuality.

Within the perspective of the historical context of the epistles and Paul's immediate concerns, we can briefly treat four aspects of Paul's understanding of human sexuality: his attitude toward human sexuality, his teaching on sexual responsibility, his view of marriage and celibacy, and his attitude toward women. Each of these aspects deserves a far more extensive treatment than the few brief lines that we can devote to them. To cover a few of the more significant elements, I shall concentrate particularly on 1 Cor 6–7 which is the clearest Pauline affirmation in matters sexual.[26]

*Human Sexuality*

First of all, Paul's understanding of human sexuality is basically that inculcated by the biblical anthropology somewhat developed in the light of Christian faith. The first letter to the Corinthians indicates that Paul's concern is with the right use of human sexuality; nowhere is there the slightest hint that human sexuality is evil. In 1 Cor 6–7 Paul clearly shows that human sexuality is a "bodily" reality. It belongs to man insofar as he is body (*sōma*). Had Paul a negative view of human sexuality he would undoubtedly have described human sexuality in terms of the flesh (*sarx*). The latter category indicates man in his proneness to sin; whereas, the description of man as body indicates man in his creatureliness, in his openness to redemption and resurrection. In 1 Cor 6, a context which deals with human sexuality, Paul develops his somatic anthropology in both a Christological and in a pneumatological fashion. With reference to Christ, he writes that "the body is . . . meant . . . for the Lord, and the Lord for the body" (1 Cor 6:13). It is sexual man who is somatically one with the Lord (1 Cor 6:15) and is called to share in the bodily resurrection. With reference to the Spirit, Paul asks rhetorically: "Do you not know that your body is a temple of the Holy Spirit within you which you have from God?" (1 Cor 6:19). There is no radical separation of the Spirit from the body. All gnosticizing doc-trines of a liberation of the Spirit are excluded as Paul noted the holi-ness of man's bodily and sexual existence.

It is this basic goodness of human sexuality as a God-given gift, now more fully understood by means of the Christian's awareness of man's existence in the Lord and in His Spirit, which underlies the Paul-ine attitude towards sexual intercourse (1 Cor 7:3–5). For the married, sexual abstinence is hardly an ideal. At best, abstinence is tolerable in the pursuit of a greater good:[27] "that you might devote yourselves to prayer" (v. 5). Even when agreed upon for the sake of prayer, sexual abstinence is tolerable only for a time. "Then come together again, lest Satan tempt you through lack of self-control" (v. 5). The concession (v. 6) of temporary abstinence is a clear indication that Paul considers human sexuality and its exercise within the marital context to be basi-cally good. Even the oft cited "It is well for a man not to touch a woman" (1 Cor 7:1b) can no longer be cited in favor of the still lingering view that Paul disparaged human sexuality. The phrase appears to be a sum-mation of an encratist position[28] with which Paul takes issue in the re-mainder of the chapter. That it is good for a man not to touch a woman is the position of Paul's opponents, not that of the Apostle.

## Sexual Responsibility

Paul's teaching on sexual responsibility derives from his biblical and Christian anthropology. This teaching is expressed with particu-lar urgency in the first letter to the Corinthians, a letter addressed to a Christian community living in the midst of a city long reputed for its sexual license. The Corinthian temple of Aphrodite, with its com-plement of one thousand temple prostitutes, is cited by all the com-mentators on the epistle. To "live like a Corinthian" is to live a life of debauchery, and a "Corinthian girl" was a popular euphemism for a prostitute. It was to Christians living in a milieu thus characterized that Paul wrote 1 Cor. To these Christians is addressed an exhortation: "Shun immorality. Every other sin which a man commits is outside the body; but the immoral man sins against his body" (1 Cor 6:18). Thus Paul condemns the conduct of the incestuous man, "of a kind not found even among pagans" (1 Cor 5:1b) and explicitly forbidden by the bib-lical tradition (Lv 18:8), and urges that he be excommunicated from the Christian community. He also takes strong issue with those who would use the libertine slogan "all things are lawful for me" (1 Cor 6: 12)[29] as the justifying rationale for indiscriminate sexual union with prostitutes (cf. 1 Cor 6: 15–16). Such a use of human sexuality is contrary to the Christian vocation and the consecration of the Christian's bodily person. Paul's somatic anthropology,[30] in which the use of "body" language (sōma) implies a relationship to the body of Christ and the Resurrection, makes sexual sin a unique sin[31] in the Pauline ethic. 1 Cor 6: 18b underscores this uniqueness quite strongly.

In 1 Cor 6, Paul also makes use of a catalogue of vices (1 Cor 6: 9–10) to inculcate a Christian attitude of sexual responsibility. This catalogue is one of the two passages[32] in the New Testament which clearly distinguish prostitution from adultery. It states that: "neither the immoral (pornoi), nor idolaters, nor adulterers (moichoi), nor sexual perverts (malachoi), nor thieves, nor the greedy, nor drunkards, nor revilers, nor robbers will inherit the kingdom of God." Elsewhere Paul uses similar catalogues with a similar purpose. When he contrasts existence in the Spirit with existence according to the flesh (Gal 5: 16–26), Paul offers examples of works of the flesh "fornication (porneia), impurity (akarthasia), licentiousness (aselgeia), idolatry, sorcery, enmity, strife, jealousy, anger, selfishness, dissension, party spirit, drunkenness, carousing, envy" (Gal 5: 19–21). Once again, we are dealing with borrowed ethical material.[33] It is difficult to determine with precision the nature of the sexual sins which are cited, namely, fornication, impurity, licentiousness, and sexual perversion. However, it is clear that adultery is not the only form of sexual immorality. It is also clear that sexual immorality is antithetical to the demands of the kingdom and the walking in the Spirit which ought to characterize the Christian's way of life.

*Marriage and Celibacy*

When we attempt to offer a brief overview of Paul's teaching on marriage and celibacy, it is to 1 Cor 7 that we must especially return. The literature on the chapter is rather extensive, and justifiably so. Suffice it, therefore, to highlight one or another aspect of Paul's teaching. The first is the Pauline affirmation that "each one has his own special gift (charisma) from God, one of one kind and one of another." (1 Cor 7: 7). Paul affirms his position that both marriage and celibacy are gifts of God. Since a charisma is essentially a gratuitous gift, it is clear that neither marriage nor celibacy constitutes the recipient in a position of greater personal holiness, nor can it be said that the recipient of one or the other gift can lay legitimate claim to a greater place of honor within the Church. The call to the married life, as well as the call to the celibate state, is a gift to be received in the openness of a faith response.

The entire chapter is dominated by Paul's expectation of the Lord's impending return and the soon-to-be-realized consummation. Consequently, Paul's view is not particularly favorable to the initiation of marriage (1 Cor 7:8, 26, 36). Rather, his point of view is that each one ought to remain in the state in which he was called to the Christian faith (1 Cor 7:20), be that married or unmarried. By reason of this perspective, one might easily get the impression that Paul views marriage as a means of abating concupiscence (1 Cor 7:2, 5, 9) or as a necessary evil. In fact, his point of view is quite the contrary. The idea that the unbelieving husband is consecrated through his wife and the unbelieving wife is consecrated through her husband (1 Cor 7:14)[34] and the implication that marriage is a vocation unto peace (1 Cor 7:15) affirm the essential goodness of marriage. So too does the future notion that the married are "in the Lord" (*en kuriō*, v. 39). Consequently, the affirmation of 1 Cor 7:38: "he who marries his betrothed does well" should not be taken as a begrudged concession; it is rather Paul's judgment on marriage in the Lord.

Nevertheless, it remains true that Paul clearly affirms that "he who refrains from marriage will do better" (1 Cor 7:38b). This affirmation is made from the standpoint of Paul's eschatological perspective: "The form of this world is passing away" (1 Cor 7:31b). Paul's option for celibacy is an option for an eschatological ethic.[35] Paul's eschatological hopes seem to have provided him with two eschatologically motivated thrusts in urging the unmarried state rather than the married state.[36] First, Paul suggests that during the penultimate time, Christians should be free to serve the Lord as he himself was (1 Cor 7:32b, 34b). Secondly, unmarried Christians would be spared anxiety about their spouses during the end-time (1 Cor 7:28b, 33, 34c). Thus Paul affirms his eschatological preference for the celibate state over the married state. The latter he affirms to be not only good, but also salvific.

### Attitude toward Women

Finally, some brief word must be said about Paul's attitude towards women. Increasingly, Paul is cited as the archetype of Christian misogynists, "the eternal enemy of Woman."[37] In contrast, Robin Scroggs' controversial[38] articles affirm that "Paul is, so far from being a chauvinist, the only certain and consistent spokesman for the liberation and equality of women in the New Testament."[39] Undoubtedly, the truth of the matter must lie somewhere between these two extreme positions. Furthermore, Paul's eschatology with its eschatological reservation, "the yet though not yet of the final times" means that each of the positions represents something of the truth with respect to Paul's attitude towards women. On the one hand, Paul seems to promote the culturally conditioned inferiority of women by means of theological arguments (1 Cor 11). On the other hand, Paul seems to affirm that with respect to Christ, there is no subordination of woman to man (Gal 3: 28). In a word, the Pauline position seems marked by ambivalence.

The impartial way in which Paul expounded the Gospel to men and women without distinction would seem to indicate his positive attitude towards women. His preaching to women means that he has abandoned his traditional rabbinic reservation with respect to women. Moreover, as W. Derek Thomas has written: "That the first candidate for baptism at Philippi was the woman Lydia points to a new status for women, a new estimate of the value and place of woman in the purpose of God."[40] Finally, the importance of persons as such, without reference to their sex, seems to have been implied in the Apostle's teaching.

## Freedom of Male and Female

No passage is more explicit in this regard than Gal 3:28: "There is neither Jew nor Greek, there is neither slave nor free, there is neither male or female (ouk eni arsen kai thēlu); for you are all one in Christ Jesus." The formula is taken from the baptismal liturgy[41] and is cited as an expression of Paul's deepest theological convictions. It hearkens back to the Priestly author's creation narrative[42] and affirms that in the eschatological community of Christ there is no advantage in being either male or female.[43] One and the other have been freed from sin, death and the law by Christ. Thus the baptismal fragment is an affirmation that both male and female share in that freedom which is a gift of Christ.

However, the text does not contain an immediate mandate for social reform. Despite the fact that Jew and Gentile are one in Christ, social and cultural differences distinguished one group from the other.

Despite the fact that there is neither slave nor freeman, Paul did not argue for the abolition of slavery. In similar fashion, though he affirmed the created and eschatological oneness of male and female, Paul did not seek to change the social situation of women.[44] Scroggs' words are apropos: "*Distinctions* between groups remain. *Values* and *roles* built upon such distinctions are destroyed. Every human being is equal before God in Christ and thus before each other."[45]

## Social Distinctions

In effect, this reflection means that Paul did not consider the place of women to be a problem. He does not really reflect on it in his epistles, except in the first letter to the Corinthians where he takes an admittedly reactionary position. That position is expressed in 1 Cor 11:2–16, a passage which offers more than an ordinary difficulty for the interpreter.[46] In response to certain practices in the Corinthian Christian community, practices which received visible expression in the presence of unveiled believers in the assembled community, Paul reverted to conventional Jewish wisdom and developed a midrash on Gen 2 in order to put women "in their place." Most likely, the practices were based on an enthusiastic pneumatism which tended to abolish all social distinctions within the Church. Paul's notions of freedom and equality were apparently so misrepresented as to imply the abolition of all sexual differences.

Paul responds that the presence of the eschaton does not abolish all sexual differences. In his response, he reflects on the order of creation, makes a mysterious reference to the angels (v. 10), and appeals to nature and the customs of the churches (vv. 14–16). While admittedly using traditional and customary arguments to affirm the social distinction between men and women, in effect an affirmation of the inferiority of woman, Paul's argumentation is not entirely anti-feminist. He affirms most clearly that woman is subordinate to man in v. 3, yet also affirms that all superordination and subordination are to be understood only in Christ, who is the norm of all subordination.[47] Moreover, Paul recognizes the Christian vocation of women. It falls to them to pray and to prophesy (v. 5) provided that they are properly attired. Indeed, the strange reference to angels is a reference to the cultic presence of angels, implicitly proclaiming the cultic function of women in the Christian assembly. Finally, Paul's affirmation that woman is the glory of man (v. 7b) is a reference to Gen 2: 18–25.[48] The reference, Feuillet maintains, does not so much place woman in an inferior and despicable position, as it constitutes an affirmation of woman's nobility. Equal to man as the image of God, she is also the glory and pride of man.[49]

## Pauline Ambiguity

Thus, Paul's thought seems to be quite ambiguous. When he stresses the equality of woman with man in Christ, he does not conclude to the social equality of women and men. When he comments on social differences, he affirms the cultural subordination of women, all the while suggesting that in Christ, woman is on a par with man. His position is really not so much that of the misogynist as it is that of the defender of the status quo. However, that status quo is of an era which is already that of the last times. The affirmation of the social inferiority of women owes to the fact that the eschaton has not fully come, it is the sexual dimension of the eschatological reservation.

## Problem Passages

Two other Pauline passages which clearly affirm the subordination of women to men are the injunctions that "women should keep silence in the churches" (1 Cor 14: 34–35) and "wives be subject to your husbands" (Col 3: 18). The easiest way to deal with these passages might well be to say that they do not belong to authentic Pauline material.[50] However, they do belong to the Pauline tradition and each of these injunctions is reaffirmed in the deutero-Pauline material. That a woman is to keep silence in church is reaffirmed in 1 Tm 2: 12, and that a wife is to be subject to her husband recurs in Eph 5: 22.[51] In these two passages, as in the passages of disputed authenticity, the position of the author is clearly reactionary. In each case the reaction is to the phenomenon of Gnostic enthusiasm within the Church. Lest Gnostic prophetesses lead the faithful astray, they are enjoined from speaking to the assembly. Wherever enthusiasm leads to a situation of unreality in which social differences are abolished,[52] a traditional household code was cited in order to remind the Church that the promise of the resurrection had not wiped out the world in which we live.

## Goodness of Sexuality

Despite this reaction, which gives the impression of a less than favorable attitude toward women, the deutero-Pauline material is not completely negative in its judgment on woman and human sexuality. The very household code which serves as an expression of the subordination of wives to husbands served the author of Ephesians as a basis for the most profound New Testament exposition of the significance of Christian marriage (Eph 5:22–33). By use of the single verb *agapan* to describe both the husband's love for his wife and Christ's love for the Church, the author of Ephesians implies that the marital love of Christian spouses participates in the love of Christ for the Church.[53] At another level, and from a somewhat different perspective, the use of the household code in this letter implies that the sexual relationship must be seen within the context of the Lordship of Christ, who unites all things in himself (Eph 1:10). That realization implies the goodness of human sexuality and the marital relationship to which it gives occasion.

Another positive aspect of the deutero-Pauline attitude towards human sexuality is its clear opposition to a rigid asceticism. 1 Tim 5:23 is almost humorous in its denial of the validity of an encratist position with respect to the enjoyments of this life. Some of these ascetics not only called for abstinence from alcoholic drink, but also called for the avoidance of marriage (1 Tim 4:3). In such circumstances the author of the Pastorals affirms that women "will be saved through childbearing" (1 Tim 2:15). Far from being a condemnation of woman to the sole function of biological motherhood, the passage is an affirmation of the dignity of motherhood, the value denied by those whose errors the author is condemning. Undoubtedly the author's insistence on the value of marriage is one of the factors which lead him to include among the qualities of the bishop that he be the husband of one wife (1 Tim 3:2).

## Conclusion

By way of conclusion to this all too hasty overview of some of the principal New Testament passages which yield information about the sexual attitudes of the New Testament Church, we must note that Paul's eschatology was probably the most singularly decisive factor which helped to shape his sexual attitudes, and those of the churches which he evangelized. Not only did Paul opt for celibacy over marriage because of his expectation of the coming times, he also had to deal with those who misunderstood his eschatological proclamation, those who took his proclamation of the new Adam and the reality of the resurrection to rationalize a blatant licentiousness or a rigid asceticism. Caught in the eschatological tension of the yet and the not yet and in the web woven between "anything goes" and "nothing goes," Paul affirmed his preference for celibacy, but also recognized the value of marriage, the goodness of sexuality and the needs for sexual responsibility. On the whole, then, his position is decidedly complex and even somewhat ambiguous.

What is not ambiguous, however, is Paul's option for sexual responsibility. There his basic anthropology, focusing on the body, led him to proclaim the nobility of the body-person and its consecration unto resurrection. On the basis of this anthropology, Paul developed his particular attitudes with respect to the different forms of sexual activity. Paul's doctrine of the body winds throughout much of his teaching. Women, too, are members of the body of Christ. They are one with men in Christ. That oneness is the source of the dignity and ecclesial function of both male and female, yet it does not obliterate social distinctions and cultural roles.

In this respect, Paul does not appear to be as much of an innovator as Jesus, whose association with women was truly amazing for a first century rabbi. Yet, it was not as rabbi that Jesus was the initiator. Even his getting-to-the-heart-of-the-matter explanation of the Decalogue's "Thou shalt not commit adultery" is paralleled by some rabbinic texts. Rather, what constituted the uniqueness of Jesus' attitude and teaching was his proclamation of the kingdom of God in word and in action. The kingdom's entrance into man's history meant that women are as men in being the recipients of God's justice. The coming of the kingdom also meant that sexual sins were like other sins in that they were to be forgiven by the prophet Son of God who came to call sinners (Mk 2:17).

Common to the teaching of both Jesus (Mk 10:6–7) and Paul (1 Cor 11:8–9) was the vision mediated by the ancient Priestly and Yahwistic authors. That was the vision of a fullness of humanity, created and yet to be redeemed, which exists by God's gracious will only in the condition of a creative relationship between male and female.

Expressing that relationship in a fully responsible and authentic way remains part of the eschatological task for these final times, present but yet to come.

## NOTES

1. Significantly, the Gospel ban on adultery is a reaffirmation of OT legal material. Cf. Mt 5:27; 19:18; Mk 10:19; Lk 18:20.

2. Cf. George F. Moore, *Judaism* 1, pp. 482–483.

3. *Yeb.* 6:6.

4. Cf. Joseph Bonsirven, *Palestinian Judaism at the Time of Jesus Christ* (New York, 1964), p. 101; R. A. Stewart, *Rabbinic Theology* (Edinburgh, 1961), p. 78.

5. Cf. R. A. Stewart, *o.c.*, p. 72.

6. Sifre Nm, 133.

7. In the Elephantine colony of Jews in Egypt, however, Jewish women enjoyed the same legal status as Egyptian women. Accordingly, a Jewish woman of Elephantine could obtain a divorce in her own right. Cf. Roland de Vaux, *Ancient Israel* (New York, 1961), p. 140.

8. Philo, *De Josepho*, 9.

9. This realization is more significant for an understanding of Jesus' attitude towards sexuality, as this can be gleaned from the pages of the Gospels, than the development of a sexual ethic based on the evangelical norm of agapeic love. Obviously, Jesus' teaching on agapeic love must be fully utilized in the formulation of a truly Christian sexual ethic. The formulation of sexual norms and the formation of sexual attitudes is not our present concern. Consequently, we must affirm that it is Jesus' concern for the kingdom that principally shaped His sexual attitudes.

10. Stephen Sapp, *art. cit.*, p. 115.

11. In form the Matthean addendum is parallel to the Markan version of the divorce logion itself. In contrast with the preceding material which has the form of a presumably public rabbinic debate, both Mt 19:11–12 and Mk 10:10–12 are presented as Jesus' teaching to His disciples.

12. Cf. Quentin Quesnell, "Made Themselves Eunuch for the Kingdom of Heaven," *CBQ* 30 (1968), 335–358.

13. Par. Mt 22:23–33; Mk 12:18–27.

14. There is no evidence that levirate marriage was, in fact, practiced in first-century Palestine.

15. Either to affirm or deny the sexual condition in the resurrection goes beyond the evidence of the text. Among recent writers who affirm that sexuality as such will not subsist in the resurrection, we can cite N. M. Loss; cf. Nicolo Maria Loss, "Bibbia e sessualità. Una situazione 'moderna' interroga la Parola di Dio scritta," *Salesianum* 38:2 (1976), 284–325, p. 291.

16. Commenting on the situation of women in first-century Palestine, Katherine Sakenfeld writes "It was into this worldview that Jesus was born and reared, and in this light, the Gospel record of Jesus' treatment of women seems remarkable, sometimes, even astonishing." Katherine D. Sakenfeld, "The Bible and Women: Bane or Blessing?" *Theology Today* 32:3 (1975), 222–233, p. 227.

17. Cf. Jn 11:1–12:8.

18. Par. Mt 19:18, Lk 18:20; comp Jas 2:8, Rom 13:9.

19. Cf. Edward Lohse, "Ich aber sage euch," in *Der Ruf Jesu und die Antwort der Gemeinde* (Jeremias Festschrift; Göttingen, 1970), 191–200.

20. Cf. R. Guelich, "The Antithesis of Matthew V. 21–48: Traditional and/or Redactional?" *NTS* 22 (1975–1976), 444–457, p. 454.

21. *Ahikar* (Sy) 2:5.

22. BT *Yom* 29a.

23. Cf. Bruce Malina, *art. cit.*, p. 12.

24. Cf. Raymond F. Collins, "The Representative Figures in the Fourth Gospel —1," *Downside Review* 94 (1976), 26–46, pp. 38–39.

25. Cf. Robert Jewett, *Paul's Anthropological Terms: a study of their use in conflict settings* (Leiden, 1971).

26. Cf. David R. Cartlidge, "1 Corinthians 7 as a Foundation for a Christian Sex Ethic," *The Journal of Religion* 55:2 (1975) 220–234.

27. The idea that spouses may refrain from sexual intercourse for but a limited period of time even when the abstinence is in the pursuit of religious purpose is also found in the teaching of the rabbis. Cf. Mishna, *Ket* 5:6.

28. Cf. Robin Scroggs, "Paul and the Eschatological Woman," *Journal of the American Academy of Religion* 40 (1972) 283–303, pp. 295–296; David R. Cartlidge, *art. cit.*, pp. 223–224.

29. The slogan is, most likely, the result of a misunderstanding, perhaps deliberate misunderstanding, of Pauline eschatology and Paul's preaching on Christian freedom. In a similar vein, David Cartiledge writes "that the chaos in Corinth is the result of an attempt by the Corinthians to establish new social patterns based on their understanding of Christian freedom. There patterns are grounded in the Pauline preaching." Cf. David R. Cartlidge, *art. cit.*, p. 223.

30. Cf. Rudolf Bultmann, *Theology of the New Testament* (London, 1965), 1, pp. 192–203; John A. T. Robinson, *The Body: A Study in Pauline Theology*, SBT 5, (London, 1952).

31. Cf. H. von Campenhausen, *Die Askese im Urchristentum*, p. 32.

32. Cf. Heb. 13:4.

33. Elsewhere I have developed more extensively the notion that Paul has, to a great extent, borrowed his ethical material from a variety of sources. See *supra*, essay 1.

34. In fact, the notion of the sanctification in marriage almost implies that Paul has a quasi-sacramental view of marriage.

35. Cf. David R. Cartlidge, *art. cit.*, p. 225.

36. Cf. Stephen Sapp, *o.c.*, p. 69.

37. George Bernard Shaw, "The Monstrous Imposition upon Jesus" in *The Writings of St. Paul* ed. Wayne A. Meeks (New York, 1972), p. 299.

38. Cf. Robin Scroggs, "Paul and the Eschatological Woman," *art. cit.;* "Paul and the Eschatological Woman: Revisited," *Journal of the American Academy of Religion* 42: 3 (1974) 532–537; Elaine H. Pagels, "Paul and Women: A Response to a Recent Discussion," *Journal of the American Academy of Religion* 42: 3 (1974) 538–549; Darwood C. Smith "Paul and the Noneschatological Woman," *Ohio Journal of Religious Studies*, 4: 1 (1976) 11–18.

39. Robin Scroggs, "Paul and the Eschatological Woman," p. 283.

40. W. Derek Thomas, "The Place of Women in the Church at Philippi," *The Expository Times* 83: 4 (1972) 117–120, p. 118.

41. Cf. Wayne A. Meeks, "The Image of the Androgyne: Some Uses of a Symbol in Earliest Christianity," *History of Religions* 13: 3 (1974) 165–208, pp. 180–183.

42. The use of *kai*, rather than the disjunctive *oude* used for the other two pairs, reflects the presence of *kai* in Gen 1: 27 (LXX).

43. Scroggs describes this as freedom from the performance principle.

44. Katherine Sakenfeld points out that 1 Cor suggests a double reason for a slowness of change in this regard. 1 Cor 10: 31–11: 1 indicates Paul's desire to present the attractiveness of the faith. 1 Cor 7: 17–24 shows that it "does not seem to make much difference." Cf. Katherine Sakenfeld, *art. cit.*, p. 230.

45. Robin Scroggs, "Paul and the Eschatological Woman: Revisited," p. 533.

46. Cf. John O'Donnell, "A Note on the Male-Female Relationship According to St. Paul," *Communio/International Catholic Review* 3: 1 (1976) 90–95, p. 91.

47. Cf. John O'Donnell, p. 93.

48. Cf. André Feuillet, "L'homme 'Gloire de Dieu' et la femme 'gloire de l'homme' (1 Cor., XI, 7b)," *Revue Biblique* 81: 2 (1974) 161–182; "La dignité et le rôle de la femme d'après quelques textes pauliniens: Comparaison avec l' Ancien Testament," *New Testament Studies* 21: 2 (1974–1975) 157–191, pp. 159–162.

49. André Feuillet, "L'homme 'Gloire de Dieu' et la femme 'gloire de l'homme' (1 Cor., XI, 7b)," p. 182.

50. A number of authors do, in fact judge 1 Cor 14: 34–35 to be inauthentic. One of the reasons cited is the tension between 1 Cor 14: 34–35 and 1 Cor 11: 5. Many authors, of course, do not admit the authenticity of Col. Thus the difficulty present in the household code is expurgated from the Pauline corpus.

51. Cf. 1 Pt 3: 1.

52. Cf. Markus Barth, *Ephesians IV–VI*. AB, 34A (Garden City, 1974), p. 656ff.

53. Cf. Ceslaus Spicq, *Agape in the New Testament* (St. Louis, 1965), 2, 76–82.

PART FIVE

# A New Testament Perspective

# 9

# The Unity of Paul's Paraenesis
# in 1 Thess 4:3–8:
# 1 Cor 7:1–7, A Significant Parallel

1 THESS 4:1–12 IS A particularly significant portion of the New Testament literature in that it constitutes our oldest documentary evidence of early Christian paraenesis. The passage is easily divided into three units: a general introduction in vv. 1–2, the exhortation of vv. 3–8, and the exhortation to brotherly love in vv. 9–12.

The presence of the third unit of material (vv. 9–12) in this earliest example of Pauline paraenesis gives substance to C. H. Dodd's claim that the pre-eminence of the love command is one of the characteristic features of Christian ethics.[1] The introductory unit of material (vv. 1–2) is noteworthy in that it serves as a significant indication of the fact that paraenesis was linked to the kerygma at a very early stage of the proclamation of the Gospel. Not only does Paul join moral exhortation to his reflection on the gospel in the letter itself, he has also made allusion[2] to the fact that he had shared at least the generalities of his paraenesis with the Thessalonians when he had been among them. The introductory verses also suggest the pastoral attitude with which the apostle exhorted the neophyte Christians at Thessalonica and provided them with a frame of reference within which to place their response to the apostolic appeal.

It is, however, with the central unit of this early paraenesis (vv. 3–8) that the present communication is principally concerned. The question which I would raise is whether these verses are topically concerned with but one subject matter, namely chastity, or whether two issues have been touched upon by the author, namely chastity and justice. The dilemma has been graphically expressed by the editors of the RSV[3] who have rendered the τὸ μὴ ὑπερβαίνειν καὶ πλεονεκτεῖν ἐν τῷ πράγματι τὸν ἀδελφὸν αὐτοῦ of v. 6a as "that no man transgress, and wrong his brother in this matter," while offering "defraud his brother in business" as an alternate rendition in the footnote. Since there are relatively few textual variants in vv. 3–6,[4] the issue is not that of determining a working version of the Greek text, it is rather that of interpreting the commonly accepted Greek text.

In the interpretative task, such authors as Rigaux, Maurer, Klaar, Baltensweiler, Martín Sánchez, Henneken, Grill, Rossano, Best, Friedrich, Adinolfi, and Rickards present chastity as the single topic of these verses; whereas von Dobschütz, Dibelius, Asting, Schlier, Merk, Wiederkehr, Laub, Beauvery, Marxsen, Koester, and Schade believe that Paul has addressed himself to the topics of chastity and justice in these verses. Indeed, a half century ago Regnar Asting suggested that the apostle traditionally paired the vices of sexual immorality and injustice to such a degree that v. 6a would represent Paul's own addition to his exhortation on chastity.[5]

Before entering upon the discussion of the issue at hand, we should take note of the fact that vv. 3–6 constitute but a single sentence in the Greek text. V. 3a serves as an introductory statement of principle, "For this is the will of God, your sanctification," while the remaining part of the sentence (vv. 3b–6), throughout which five infinitives are scattered, gives content to the general, introductory, exhortation. It must further be noted that a consensus within contemporary exegesis has been reached—a consensus to which authors such as Dibelius, Schrage, Eckart, Schmithals, Laub, Davis, and Schade bear witness—to the effect that the first six verses of 1 Thess 4 contain general ethical instruction.[6] Whence it is impossible to infer from these verses any specific reference to the real life situation of the Thessalonian community at the time of its being addressed by Paul.

## JEWISH TRADITION

One further element must be introduced in order that the context of the discussion be sufficiently clarified. That is the Jewish flavor of the Pauline paraenesis in 1 Thess 4:1–12.[7] Paul's first letter to the Thessalonians is distinctive[8] among the letters of the critical corpus in that it contains no explicit biblical citations. It is nonetheless a letter in which Paul's Jewish background is reflected at virtually every turn. Earlier studies, for example, have drawn our attention to the Jewish missionary sermon as the life situation of 1 Thess 1:9(–10),[9] and the homiletic benediction as the background for the wish prayers of 3: 11–13 and 5: 23.[10] Paul's manner of speaking about the faith of the Thessalonians certainly attests to a basically Jewish perspective. The faith of the Thessalonians is a faith in God,[11] the living and true God, to whom they have turned from their previous service of idols.[12]

The Jewish character of the letter as a whole seems to be intensified in its paraenetic section. Four Jewish motifs come immediately to the fore. 1) In the introductory unit (vv. 1–2), Paul makes reference to that which the Thessalonians had learned from him, making use as he does so of the verb παραλάμβανω. His usage reflects the Hebrew qibbel, the term technically used in rabbinic circles in connection with the faithful transmission of the tradition, particularly that concerned with moral instruction and the ethos of the people. 2) In the introductory unit there likewise appears a double use of the verb περιπατέω to describe the way of life of the Thessalonian Christians. The choice of this vocable reflects the rabbinic use of halak to denote one's way of life. 3) The notion of the ethos of the people of God, with whom Paul has assimilated the Thessalonian Christians by means of the term ἐκκλησία (1: 1) and the theme of election (1: 4),[13] comes to expression in 4: 4 wherein Paul contrasts the desired conduct of the Thessalonians with that of the "heathen who do not know God," τὰ ἔθνη τὰ μὴ εἰδότα τὸν θεόν.[14] The contrast between the conduct of God's people and the "ignorant" pagans is further elaborated by Paul in Rom 1, but it has biblical precedents not only in Wis 13–14 but also in the traditional refrain that certain behavioral patterns are not to be reproduced in Israel.[15] Finally, we must note that the notion of God's will, θέλημα τοῦ θεοῦ, the focal point of Paul's statement of principle in v. 3, was a major religious motif in late Judaism.[16] God's will was deemed to be a major source of motivation and a guiding light for faithful Jews.

The Jewishness of Paul's paraenesis seems, nonetheless, to be more intense in the exposition found in 4: 1–8 than in the exposition of vv. 9–12 where the Christian theme of brotherly love is the object of Paul's concern. This change of coloration suggests that there are two foci of interest in Paul's paraenetical exposé, rather than the three centers of interest proposed by those who see a reference to both chastity and justice in vv. 3–6. Moreover, the fact that Paul makes use of the parakalô formula[17] in v. 1, and again in v. 10, suggests that he is twice appealing to his apostolic authority as he offers his moral exhortation. The double use of this technical, introductory, formula indicates that Paul is making but two hortatory appeals.[18] Thus the *parakalô* formula of v. 1 is not only a part of the general introduction to the paraenetic section of the letter but also serves a specific function, namely as an introduction to his exhortation on chastity.

## STRUCTURE AND THEME

That exhortation (vv. 3–6) may be structured as follows:

A. Τοῦτο γάρ ἐστιν θέλημα τοῦ Θεοῦ
   B1. ὁ ἁγιασμὸς ὑμῶν
   B2. ἀπέχεσθαι ὑμᾶς ἀπὸ τῆς πορνείας
       C1. εἰδέναι ἕκαστον ὑμῶν τὸ ἑαυτοῦ σκεῦος κτᾶσθαι
           ἐν ἁγιασμῷ καὶ τιμῇ
       C1'. μὴ ἐν πάθει ἐπιθυμίας
           καθάπερ καὶ τὰ ἔθνη τὰ μὴ εἰδότα τὸν Θεόν
       C2. τὸ μὴ ὑπερβαίνειν καὶ πλεονεκτεῖν ἐν τῷ πράγματι
           τόν ἀδελφὸν αὐτοῦ
       C2'. διότι ἔκδικος κύριος περὶ πάντων τούτων
           καθὼς καὶ προείπαμεν ὑμῖν καὶ διεμαρτυράμεθα

The unity of the entire paraenesis on chastity, to which a three-fold statement of motivation has been appended in vv. 6b–8, is ensured by means of the sanctification (ἁγιασμός) motif.[19] The motif first occurs in the statement of principle: "This is the will of God, your sanctification (ὁ ἁγιασμὸς ὑμῶν)" (v. 3). It recurs in the exhortation "that each one of you know how to take a wife for himself in holiness (ἐν ἁγιασμῷ) and honor" (C1). It is likewise present in the second motivational element appended to the content of the paraenesis, i.e. "for God has not called us for uncleanness, but in holiness (οὐ γὰρ . . . ἐπὶ ἀκαθαρσίᾳ ἀλλ᾽ ἐν ἁγιασμῷ)" (v. 7). The motif of sanctification is not, however, absent from the third motivational reference (v. 8), namely in Paul's mention of "God who gives his Holy Spirit to you" (τὸν Θεὸν τὸν καὶ διδόντα τὸ πνεῦμα αὐτοῦ τὸ ἅγιον εἰς ὑμᾶς), a clause which forms something of an *inclusio* with v. 3a (Θέλημα τοῦ Θεοῦ ὁ ἁγιασμὸς ὑμῶν . . . τὸν Θεὸν τὸν καὶ διδόντα τὸ πνεῦμα αὐτοῦ τὸ ἅγιον εἰς ὑμᾶς).

The theme of sanctification recurs in Paul's first letter to the Corinthians in the section dealing with sexuality and marriage, specifically in his discussion on divorce (1 Cor 7:12–16). Within that context Paul speaks not only of the sanctification of spouses within marriage,[20] but also of a contrast between sanctification (ἅγια) and uncleanness (ἀκάθαρτα), and of the call of God (κέκληκεν ὑμᾶς ὁ θεός). Each of these three themes, sanctification, call, and uncleanness, were also used by Paul in his discussion on conjugal chastity in 1 Thess 4:3-8. That Paul speaks of the gift of the Holy Spirit in 1 Thess 4:8 is not, in my judgment, to be separated from his statement in 1 Cor 7:7 which implies that marriage itself is to be considered as a gift from God (χάρισμα ἐκ θεοῦ).[21] Thus Paul uses familiar motifs as he elaborates the basic theme of 1 Thess 4:3-8, namely that God's will is the sanctification of his people and that sanctification is to be found within a conjugal life lived in accordance with the will of God. This theme pervades the entire paraenesis with which the present communication is concerned.

## CHASTITY

Within this perspective we can further specify the content of Paul's exhortation in vv. 4-6, i.e. elements C1 and C2 of the sentence structured above. The principal exegetical discussion as to the interpretation of C1 centers on the problematic phrase ἕκαστον ὑμῶν τὸ ἑαυτοῦ σκεῦος κτᾶσθαι. Most recently J. Whitton[22] and James Reese[23] have opted for the opinion which interprets σκεῦος of the male organ.[24] They thereby have taken issue with the more commonly accepted exegesis which takes σκεῦος, metaphorically interpreted, to mean either wife[25] or body.[26] Consequently they see in v. 4 an exhortation to sexual restraint or sexual abstinence. Thus Whitton, who takes the phrase in the sense of "controlling one's sexual urge" or "mastering one's self" in a sexual sense, comments: "This interpretation . . . in indicating a specifically sexual connotation, would provide in 1 Thess 4:4 a positive statement of sexual abstinence and thus be applicable to unmarried as well as married men. Such an interpretation for 1 Thess 4:4 would more clearly parallel Paul's admonition in verse 3 to abstain from sexual sin (πορνεία) and would also reflect the ascetic ideal of celibacy which he advises in 1 Cor 7:7a (cf. v. 1b)."[27]

This line of reasoning seems, to me, to be fallacious on three counts. First of all, while it provides due consideration to Paul's use of the emphatic pronoun ἑαυτοῦ,[28] it does not sufficiently take into account the basically ingressive sense of κτᾶσθαι. Secondly, it is grounded on the assumption that an exhortation to marriage (and sexual intercourse within marriage) would be too limited an exhortation for the general paraenesis of vv. 3–6. Finally, it is deemed to be consistent with Paul's exhortation to "an ascetic ideal of celibacy" proposed in 1 Cor 7.

I would rely on the authority of the grammarians and lexicographers as to the ingressive nuance of κτᾶσθαι[29] and address myself to the faulty presuppositions of the reasoning. To suggest that v. 4a would be of limited reference were it to deal only with the married implies that the unmarried state was the normal condition of many among those to whom Paul is writing. In fact this would hardly be the case. At that time laws against childless persons and bachelors existed in the Hellenistic world. Moreover one must not neglect the Jewish coloration of Paul's paraenesis in 1 Thess 4. Within rabbinic circles it was handed down that "it is not he who marries who sins; the sinner is the unmarried man who spends all his days in sinful thought;"[30] and again that "he who has no wife is not a proper man."[31] Furthermore "be fruitful and multiply" (Gen 1:28) was considered to be the first among the commandments. Within this perspective it is quite normal that a general teaching of sexual instruction be addressed to the married.

Moreover, 1 Cor 7:1–7, rather than proposing "an ascetic ideal of celibacy," is an exhortation to marriage . . . lest one fall victim to immorality (πορνεία). Most recently Phipps[32] and Murphy-O'Connor[33] have argued—an argumentation with which I concur—that 1 Cor 7:1b, "It is well for a man not to touch a woman (καλὸν ἀνθρώπῳ γυναικὸς μὴ ἅπτεσθαι)," is Paul's summation of a position held by some of the Corinthian enthusiasts.[34] Subsequently Paul would offer a corrective to that position, just as he will later offer a corrective to their view on the spiritual gifts (πνευματικά) in 1 Cor 12. In 1 Cor 7, in response to the proposition of the celibate ideal, Paul argues that each one should be married (v. 2) and that the married should not refrain from sexual intercourse, except for a limited time and even then for reasons of prayer (v. 5). Paul makes this double plea lest the Corinthians succumb to immorality (πορνεία) because of their lack of self-control (ἀκρασία).[35] True, Paul might wish that they remain unmarried just as he was when he wrote to them (vv. 7a, 8), but Paul's gift was different from the gifts generally given to the Corinthians (v. 7b) and each one has his own special gift from God, by the working of the one Spirit who apportions to each one individually as he wills (1 Cor 12:11). In sum, 1 Cor 7:1–7 is indeed a text which can be cited as a useful parallel to aid in the interpretation of 1 Thess 4:4. The more accurate exegesis of the Corinthian passage would, however, incline the expositor of Paul's first letter to the Thessalonians to interpret σκεῦος in the sense of wife and the entire verse as an exhortation to marriage, indeed to marriage within which sexual activity has a normal and rightful place.

That this is indeed the correct interpretation of 1 Thess 4:4 is supported by a number of Jewish parallels. Maurer[36] cites as a parallel the biblical idiom ba'el 'ishah, which means "to take a woman sexually;" but there are also a number of rabbinic passages in which keli, the Hebrew equivalent of σκεῦος, designates a woman in a blatantly sexual context. Among such passages is a midrash on Est 1:10: "Some say that Medes are more beautiful, while others say that Persians are more beautiful. Then Assuerus said: The keli which I use is neither a Mede nor a Persian. Do you want to see her? Yes, they answered, provided that she is naked."[37]

To interpret σκεῦος as woman and v. 4 of marriage is to interpret the verse in a fashion which is consistent with the basic Jewish coloration of Paul's paraenesis at this point, that is consistent with rabbinic parallels, that is paralleled with a similar thought elsewhere in Paul— particularly the idea of marriage as a means of avoiding πορνεία, — that takes into account the use of the emphatic ἑαυτοῦ, and that is in accord with the fundamentally ingressive sense of κτᾶσθαι. In vv. 3–4 (5), Paul has spelled out the implications of God's will both positively (your sanctification) and negatively (abstain from immorality) and has cited a sexually active marital relationship as a means of fulfilling God's will.

Given the unity of vv. 3–8, achieved by means of the ἁγιασμός motif and the grammatical unity of the sentence found in vv. 3–6, can it be said that v. 6a introduces a foreign idea into Paul's exposition? Has he introduced the notion of greed into his argumentation because unchastity and greed are the major sins of the pagans?

The principal arguments for holding that Paul has introduced an extraneous topos in v. 6a are that sexual immorality and injustice are typically cited as vices of the pagans[38] and that Paul frequently uses within a single context both πλεονεξία and πορνεία, terminology borrowed from the catalogue of vices, with the result that the interpreter should distinguish one vice from the other. Those who maintain that v. 6 is therefore an injunction to abstain from greed take the expression ἐν τῷ πράγματι to be equivalent to "in business matters."

Any interpretation of v. 6a must, however, take into account the fact that the contrast between the desired behaviour of the Thessalonians and the presumed behaviour of pagans is specifically cited by Paul only in reference to the marital relationship itself.[39] Moreover, the term employed by Paul in v. 6a is not the noun πλεονεξία, a standard feature of biblical and extra-biblical catalogues of vices, but the verb πλεονεκτέω. The use of this verb is a Paulinism within the New Testament, occurring only in 1 Thess 4:6 and in the second letter to the Corinthians (four occurrences: 2:11; 7:2; 12:17, 18). Paul's use of πλεονεκτέω in 2 Cor 2:11 is similar to that of the classical authors who use the verb in reference to humans being outwitted or taken advantage of by the demon.[40] In the three other occurrences of πλεονεκτέω in 2 Cor, the verb has the general meaning "to take advantage of," specifically within the context of the apostolic *apologia*, as Paul proclaims that he has not taken advantage of the Corinthian Christians. In effect, Paul's use of the verb is both limited in its frequency and general[41] in its connotation.

It is only in 1 Thess 4:6 that Paul pairs πλεονεκτέω with ὑπερβαίνω. The latter verb, in a moral context, signifies "to transgress" or "to sin." The content of the transgression is, in 1 Thess 4:6, specified by πλεονεκτεῖν τὸν ἀδελφὸν αὐτοῦ, an expression used by classical authors[42] in the sense of taking advantage of someone. Therefore it redounds to the expression ἐν τῷ πράγματι of v. 6 to indicate the referent of the verbal expression ὑπερβαίνειν καὶ πλεονεκτεῖν. When πρᾶγμα is used in the general sense of "affairs," it is normally employed in the plural;[43] in 1 Thess 4:6, however, Paul employs the singular. Accordingly the phrase ἐν τῷ πράγματι ought to be rendered "in the matter," i.e. in the matter at hand, which is *in casu* chastity. Thus v. 6a can be paraphrased "in reference to chastity, let no one sin by cheating his brother."[44]

With this understanding of v. 6a, additional light is shed on Paul's use of the emphatic ἑαυτοῦ in v. 4. In v. 4 Paul writes of the attitude of the Christian towards his own marriage, while in v. 6 he writes of the Christian's attitude towards the marriages of his Christian brothers. In both instances Paul maintains a rather traditional attitude, marriage still being perceived in terms of the husband's rights over his wife, and adultery being considered as an offence against the aggrieved husband. Paul enjoins the Christian, in respect to his own wife, to take a wife and live with her in a sexually active manner "in holiness and honor."

In reference to the marriage of other Christians, the Christian man is enjoined not to violate a fellow Christian's marriage.

In sum, vv. 3-8 constitute Paul's reflection on a single topos, chastity. His reflections relate chastity to marriage. The chaste husband is one who honors his own wife and respects the marriage of his fellows. God who gives the Holy Spirit not only calls the Christian husband to a life of chastity; he also ensures the sanctification of faithful Christian spouses. This is Paul's major train of thought. Were his reflections prompted by some specific situation at Thessalonica? It is difficult to say. Paul's language is general and so it is not easy to establish conclusively that he has offered anything more than a general exhortation in 1 Thess 4:3-8. On the other hand, the fact that Paul has chosen to reiterate his earlier exhortation on chastity (vv. 1-2) and his manner of proceeding in other, later, letters suggest that there might be more than a casual connection between the apostle's paraenesis on chastity and the situation of those to whom he wrote his first letter.[45]

## NOTES

1. Cf. C. H. Dodd, *Gospel and Law. The Relation of Faith and Ethics in Early Christianity* (Cambridge: University Press, 1951), pp. 42-5.

2. 1 Thess 4:1-2.

3. Similarly, the NEB which reads "and no man must do his brother wrong in this matter, or invade his rights," but offers "must overreach his brother in his business (*or* in lawsuits)" in the footnote. Likewise the *Traduction oecumenique de la Bible* (Paris: Cerf, 1972) which reads "Que nul n'agisse au detriment de son frère en cette affaire" but notes that "D'autres traduisent *en affaires.*" The dilemma is also attested by *Die Bibel Einheitsübersetzung* (Freiburg-Basel-Wien: Herder, 1980) which offers a text similar to that footnoted by the RSV, NEB, and TOB as follows, "und dass keiner seine Rechte überschreitet und seinen Bruder bei Geschäften betrügt," and comments in a footnote: "Ander Übersetzungsmoglichkeit: und das keiner sich gegen seinen Bruder in der betreffenden Sache übergriffe erlaubt – In diesem Fall ware von Ehebruch die Rede."

4. Pertinent to the discussion which follows is only a rarely attested τινι in place of the τῳ of v. 6.

5. Cf. R. Asting, *Die Heiligtum im Urchristentum*. FRLANT 46 (Göttingen: Vandenhoeck & Ruprecht, 1930), p. 220.

6. Cf. M. Dibelius, *A Fresh Approach to the New Testament and Early Christian Literature* (New York: Scribner's, 1936), p. 39; *An die Thessalonicher I–II. An die Philip-*

per (Tübingen: Mohr, 1937), pp. 19–20; W. Schrage, *Die konkreten Einzelgebote in der paulinischen Paränese* (Gütersloh: Mohr, 1961), p. 42; K.-G. Eckart, "Der zweite echte Brief des Apostels Paulus an die Thessalonicher," ZTK 58 (1961), pp. 30–44, pp. 35–36; W. Schmithals, "Die Thessalonicherbriefe als Briefkompositionen," in *Zeit und Geschichte* (Bultmann Fs., Tübingen: Mohr, 1964), pp. 295–315, pp. 302–3. F. Laub, *Eschatologische Verkündigung und Lebensgestaltung nach Paulus. Eine Untersuchung zum Wirken des Apostels beim Aufbau der Gemeinde in Thessalonike. Münchener Universitäts-Schriften* (Regensburg: Pustet, 1973), pp. 51–2; R. H. Davis, Remembering and Acting: A Study in the Moral Life in Light of 1 Thessalonians (Yale Dissertation, Ann Arbor: University Microfilms, 1971), p. 187; H.-H. Schade, *Apokalyptische Christologie bei Paulus. Studien zum Zusammenhang von Christologie und Eschatologie in den Paulusbriefen. Göttinger Theologische Arbeiten*, 18 (Göttingen: Vandenhoeck & Ruprecht, 1981), p. 135.

7. Cf. G. F. Snyder, "Apocalyptic and Didactic Elements in 1 Thessalonians," in *1972 Proceedings, Society of Biblical Literature*, I, ed. by L. C. McGaughy, pp. 233–44, p. 238; "A Summary of Faith in an Epistolary Context. 1 Thess 1:9, 10," Ibid., pp. 255–365, p. 361; H. Koester, "1 Thessalonians—Experiment in Christian Writing," in *Continuity and Discontinuity in Church History. Essays Presented to George Hunston Williams on the Occasion of his 65th Birthday. Studies in the History of Christian Thought*, 19 (Leiden: Brill, 1979), pp. 33–44, p. 42.

8. Similarly, Phil., Phlmn. The twenty-fifth edition of Nestle–Aland identified several small citations of the OT in 1 Thess, for example, a citation of Jer 11:20 in 2:4, but those references have all been downgraded in the twenty-sixth edition.

9. Cf. G. Bornkamm, *Early Christian Experience. New Testament Library* (London: SCM, 1969), p. 32; J. Munck, "1 Thess i. 9–10 and the Missionary Preaching of Paul. Textual Exegesis and Hermeneutic Reflexions," NTS 9 (1963), pp. 95–110, pp. 101–2.

10. Cf. R. Jewett, "The Form and Function of the Homiletic Benediction," *Anglican Theological Review* 51 (1969), pp. 18–34.

11. 1 Thess 1:8.

12. 1 Thess 1:9. On the notion of faith in 1 Thess, see R. F. Collins, "The Faith of the Thessalonians," *Louvain Studies* 7 (1978–9), pp. 248–69.

13. Cf. R. F. Collins, "The Church of the Thessalonians," *Louvain Studies* 5 (1974–5), pp. 336–49.

14. Cf. W. Eichrodt, *Theology of the Old Testament, 2. Old Testament Library* (London: SCM, 1967), p. 317.

15. This notion has been developed by T. Korteweg in a paper, "De Wil van God als Religieuze Voorstelling in laat-Joodse en vroeg-Christlijke Geschriften," delivered at the annual meeting of the Conventus for New Testament Studies, Utrecht, May 15, 1981.

16. Cf. C. J. Bjerkelund, *Parakalô. Form, Funktion und Sinn der parakalô-Sätze in den paulinischen Briefen. Bibliotheca Theologica Norvegica*, 1 (Oslo: Universitetsforlaget, 1967).

17. Thus I would take issue with the point of view expressed by K. P. Donfried in a paper read during the New England sectional meeting of the Society of Biblical Literature, April 5, 1982. Donfried proffered the view that in the "response topics" of 1 Thess 4:1-12, there are three topoi, marriage, business, and public life.

18. Cf. M. Adinolfi, "La Santità del matrimonio in 1 Thess 4:1-8," *Rivista biblica italiana* 24 (1976), pp. 165-84, pp. 165-6. Although C. Roetzel has identified the judgment form in 1 Thess 4:3-8, an argument in favour of the topical unity of the passage can not be drawn from its form since several items can be encompassed within the "offense" element of the form. Cf. C. Roetzel, "The Judgment Form in Paul's Letters," JBL 88 (1969), pp. 305-12.

19. Koester has noted that "Paul brackets his interpretation by the traditional term ἁγιασμός "sanctification" (1 Thess 4:3 and 4:7)." He then sees 4:8 as an element of "sacred law." Cf. H. Koester, art. cit., pp. 42-3.

20. In their comments upon this passage, O. Cullman, G. Walther, and W. F. Orr-J. A. Walther write respectively of a "collective holiness," "contagious holiness," and a "kind of uxorial sanctification." Cf. O. Cullmann, *Baptism in the New Testament*, SBT, 1 (London: SCM, 1950), p. 44; G. Walther, "Übergriefende Heiligkeit und Kindertaufe im Neuen Testament," *Evangelische Theologie* 25 (1965), pp. 668-74; W. F. Orr-J. A. Walther, *1 Corinthians*, AB, 32 (Garden City: Doubleday, 1976), p. 213.

21. Cf. J. M. Cambier, "Doctrine paulinienne du mariage chrétien. Étude critique de 1 Co 7 et d'Ep 5:21-33 et essai de leur traduction actuelle," *Eglise et théologie* 10 (1979), pp. 13-59.

22. J. Whitton "A Neglected Meaning for SKEUOS in 1 Thessalonians 4:4," *NTS* 28 (1982), pp. 142-3.

23. Cf. J. Reese, *1 and 2 Thessalonians* (Wilmington: Michael Glazer, 1979), p. 44. Reese's commentary is based on the translation offered by the NAB, as follows, "each of you guarding his member in sanctity and honor."

24. Although Whitton argues from the use of σκεῦος as "a euphemism for the male organ," he clearly takes σκεῦος metaphorically and metonymically in the sense of "body."

25. Thus von Hofmann, Lünemann, Bornemann, von Dobschütz, Wohlenberg, Frame, Toussaint, Oepke, Rinaldi, Best, Nieder, Marxsen, Vogel, Schürmann, Schlier, Friedrich, Laub, and Adinolfi.

26. Thus Dibelius, Rigaux, Bahnsen, Martín Sánchez, Wolniewicz, Merk, Rossano, and Schade.

27. J. Whitton, *art. cit.*, p. 143.

28. On the importance of the pronoun, cf. W. Vogel, "Eidenai to heautou skeuos ktasthai. Zur Deutung von 1 Thess 4:3ff. im Zusammenhang der paulinischen Eheauffassung," *Theologische Blatter* 13 (1934), pp. 83-5.

29. Arndt-Gingrich, for example, render κτάομαι as "procure for oneself, acquire, get." Liddell-Scott offers "to procure for oneself, to get, gain, acquire" when the verb is used in the present, imperfect, future, and aorist. Even Béda Rigaux who

argued for the interpretation of σκεῦος in the sense of "body" noted that there is a nuance of taking possession in the use of the verb κτᾶσθαι, cf. B. Rigaux, *Les épîtres aux Thessaloniciens. Études bibliques* (Paris, Gabalda, 1956), pp. 505–6.

30. Kid 29b. Cf. Ben-Zion Schereschewsky, "Marriage," *Encyclopedia Judaica*, 11 (Jerusalem: Keter, 1971), 1025–1051, col. 1028.

31. Yev. 63a.

32. Cf. W. E. Phipps, "Is Paul's Attitude towards Sexual Relations Contained in 1 Cor 7:1?," *NTS* 28 (1982), pp. 125–31.

33. Cf. J. Murphy-O'Connor, "The Divorced Woman in 1 Cor 7:10–11," *JBL* 100 (1981), pp. 601–6, pp. 603–4.

34. For earlier interpretations of 1 Cor 7:1 along these same lines, see D. Smith, *The Life and Letters of St. Paul* (New York: Harper & Row, 1920), p. 262; J. M. Ford, "Levirate Marriage in St. Paul (1 Cor VII)," *NTS* 10 (1964), pp. 361–5, p. 361; C. H. Giblin, "1 Corinthians 7-a Negative Theology of Marriage and Celibacy," *The Bible Today* 41 (1969), pp. 2839–55, esp. pp. 2841–2; G. E. Harpur, "A comment on abstinence mentioned in 1 Corinthians," *Journal of the Christian Brethren Fellowship* 27 (1975), pp. 38–50; W. Schrage, "Zur Fronstellung der paulinischen Ehebewertung in 1 Kor 7:1–7," *ZNTW* 67 (1976), pp. 214–34; R. F. Collins, "Human Sexuality in the Christian Scriptures," *supra* essay 8. R. Puigdellers, "Notas para una interpretación de 1 Cor 7," *Revista Catalana de Teologia* 3 (1978), pp. 245–60. Econtra, K. Niederwimmer, "Zur Analyse der asketischen Motivation in 1 Kor 7," *TLZ* 99 (1974), pp. 241–8.

35. Cf. K. N. Papadopoulos, "Η σημασις της λεξεως 'ακρασια' εν 1 Κορ. 7, 5," *Deltion Biblikon Meleton* 8 (1979), pp. 135–7, who argues that the expression διὰ τὴν ἀκρασίαν means a lack of conjugal relations.

36. Cf. C. Maurer, "σκεῦος," *Theological Dictionary of the New Testament*, 7, ed. by G. Friedrich (Grand Rapids: Eerdmans, 1971), pp. 359–67, 362.

37. Cf. Pes 98b, San 22b, Taan 20ab.

38. Cf. H.-H. Schade, op. cit., p. 135; F. Laub, op. cit., p. 53.

39. 1 Thess 4:5.

40. Arndt-Gingrich cite Demosthenes (41, 25) and *Orientis Graeci Inscriptiones Selectae* (484, 27) ed. by W. Dittenberger, 2 vols., 1903–5.

41. Even W. Marxsen has drawn attention to the general language of v. 6a. He argues, however, that Paul is speaking about getting rich and that the verse must be interpreted in that sense. Cf. W. Marxsen, *Der erste Brief an die Thessalonicher. Zürcher Bibelkommentare*, 11/1 (Zurich: Theologischer Verlag, 1979), p. 61.

42. Thus Plutarch (*Marc.* 29, 7) and Pseudo-Lucian (*Armor.* 27), according to Arndt-Gingrich.

43. Cf. Liddéll-Scott and Arndt-Gingrich, ad loc.

44. Arndt-Gingrich write of πρᾶγμα that it is perhaps "a euphemism for illicit sexual conduct" in 1 Thess 4:6.

45. Cf. R. H. Davis, op. cit., p. 187.

# 10

# Christian Personalism and the
# Sermon on the Mount

WE ARE CONSTANTLY confronted with the temptation to project into the past something of the present. This temptation, when succumbed to, can only yield a false view of the past and, when the past at hand is the literary past, can only yield a distorted view of what an author intended to say. Yet, because the temptation is constant, we have frequently fallen and have obtained for ourselves a distorted view of many a literary work.

If this is generally true, it is particularly true insofar as the interpretation of the Scriptures is concerned. We have often failed to grasp their full meaning because we have read our meanings into them. We have taken our systems, theology, ethics, and read these into the pages of the Old and the New Testaments. If contemporary exegetical methods put the lie to such procedures, we still run the risk of reading into an earlier Scriptural passage something which represents a later, though oftentimes still Scriptural, phase of development.

We must be wary of the danger of falling into such a misguided methodology when we speak of Personalism and the Scriptures, or more particularly, Personalism and the Sermon on the Mount. By choosing this as a topic we do not intend to imply that Personalism as we know it is to be found in the Sermon on the Mount. Indeed, such a thought should repel us since the very mention of Personalism and the Sermon on the Mount implies a polarity in which the latter, Palestinian, pole is alien to the former. The Semitic mentality reflected in the very name of the Sermon on the Mount was not able to conceptualize personality as such and, *a fortiori*, was unaware of personalism, in our contemporary and philosophical understanding of the term.

This does not mean that the Sermon on the Mount does not give witness to values and realities which are fully at home in Christian personalism. Many of the aspects of personal existence to which personal-

223

ism so readily and so meritoriously calls our attention have already been highlighted in another language in the Sermon on the Mount. It is precisely these values and realities which we would like to cite in this article. These are the values and realities which correspond to the personalistic ideal and those aspects of the Christian ideal, as found in the Sermon, which must be even more fully integrated into personalism to make it Christian personalism.

## THE SERMON ON THE MOUNT: A POINT OF VIEW

To appreciate the personalistic values included within the Sermon on the Mount, we must first appreciate the Sermon on the Mount itself. There have been those who have sought to understand the Sermon on the Mount as a collection of ethical maxims. Inevitably, they evaluate the Sermon as a code of law. Subsequently they dispute among themselves as to the type of law contained in the Sermon. For some of these authors, such as Hans Windisch, the Sermon on the Mount is fundamentally a Jewish document, a code of abridged and edited Jewish laws, all of which can be found in the Bible and in post-biblical Judaism. For others, the Sermon on the Mount expresses an impossible legal ideal and is, therefore, a pedagogical device used by Christ to reveal to man that he is a sinner who stands in need of redemption. Such a point of view is undoubtedly neo-testamentary, since it is found in the Epistle to the Romans, but this does not warrant our interpreting Jesus' words in the light of Paul. Still another group, eschatologists such as Johannes Weiss and Albert Schweitzer, would have us see in the Sermon an interim ethic developed and proclaimed as a temporary way of life by Jesus under the pressure of an imminent Parousia.

The fallacy in all three approaches is that they isolate the Sermon on the Mount from its setting in the Gospel. They view it apart from the proclamation of the good news. But this is precisely the context which Matthew has chosen for the Sermon on the Mount. The Sermon on the Mount is not simply an ethical code; it is the Gospel ethic. This realization is vital to a proper understanding of the Sermon on the Mount. But the thought can be pursued further.

Even a cursory glance at the Sermon on the Mount makes us realize that the Sermon is, in reality, a collection of isolated *logia* of Jesus which have been juxtaposed by Matthew on the basis of similarity of content or verbal resonance. These *logia* could conceivably have been preserved and narrated by the Christian community which transmitted them in other circumstances. Indeed, a comparative reading of the Synoptics makes us realize that some of these *logia* were, in fact, narrated by the community in other settings. A prime example is the Lord's prayer, which Luke has inserted into his Gospel as Jesus' response to his disciples' question (Luke 11:1-4).

But why has Matthew isolated these several *logia* of Jesus and collected them into one discourse in such an artificial manner? Undoubtedly because he intended to contrast the Gospel ethic with that of the Torah as interpreted by the Scribes and as lived by the Pharisees. This Matthew makes very clear by coupling with the repeated reference to the mountain (Matt 5:1 and 8:1)—the phenomenon of inclusion which makes of the Sermon one whole—a reference to Christ, the teacher. At the opening of the Sermon, Matthew writes that Christ adopted the posture of the rabbi and taught: "There he sat down and was joined by his disciples. Then he began to speak. This is what he taught them: . . ." (Matt 5:1-2). By way of conclusion to the discourse he writes that "Jesus had now finished what he wanted to say and his teaching made a deep impression on the people because he taught them with authority, and not like their own scribes" (Matt 7:28-29). Christ, therefore, is the authoritative teacher. What he has conveyed to his disciples and to the crowds is his authoritative teaching—his *didache*.

Indeed, this Sermon is one of the classical examples of an early Christian *didache*. But the Christian *didache* was always delivered in context. Most probably the community *Sitz-im-Leben* of the Sermon on the Mount was a pre-baptismal or post-baptismal instruction. This means that in the life of the Christian community which transmitted the Sermon on the Mount with its manifest ethical content, the Sermon on the Mount was preceded by something else, viz., the proclamation of the kerygma, conversion, and baptismal regeneration. Such a consideration implies that the Sermon on the Mount was not an ethical program imposed from without, was not a categoric imperative, was not an external code of law. Rather, the Sermon on the Mount was considered, and is to be considered, as an illustrated program of living out that which had preceded it.

*Formgeschichtliche* considerations on the *logia* themselves lead to a similar conclusion. The isolated *logia* can be properly understood only in the light of something else, something which preceded them. Thus, for example, the words "if you do not forgive others, your Father will not forgive your failings either" (Matt 6:15) can best be understood in the other context in which they appear in the first Gospel, namely, as the conclusion to the debt-cancellation parable (Matt 18:35). In the light of this parable, the words of Matt 6:15 do not appear to be so much an example of *do ut des* justice as they appear to be a response to the divine initiative and an emulation of the forgiving Father. The thought expressed is not so much that of a bargain or a relationship of justice, but a paraenetic conclusion to the realization of redemption: God has forgiven so much, ought you not also to forgive?

Another example would be the instruction on divorce, the third of the Matthean antitheses. Because its form is different from that of the other antitheses, some scholars have rejected it as not original. It is undoubtedly difficult to understand—in itself, and in the setting in which Matthew has chosen to place it. Yet, seen as the conclusion to the controversy narrative of Mark 10 and Matt 19, it instances the radicalism of Jesus' demands, as do the other five antitheses.

Again the *logion* about loving one's enemies and praying for one's persecutors makes full sense only on the basis of a proclamation of the Father, a proclamation which is alluded to in Matt 5:45.

Other instances could be cited, but these three should illustrate that the *logia* of the Sermon on the Mount can only be understood in the light of something else. They are illumined by some reference to the kerygma itself or to a controversy revolving about the kerygma. Thus Joachim Jeremias has been led to comment:

> Every word of the Sermon on the Mount was preceded by something else. It was preceded by the preaching of the Kingdom of God. It was preceded by the granting of sonship to the disciples (Matt 5:16; 5:45; 5:48; etc.). It was preceded by Jesus' witness to himself in word and deed. The example of Jesus stands behind every word of the Sermon on the Mount. But this means: the instructions of the Sermon have been torn out of their original context, although in many cases . . . this context has been preserved in parallel passages. All of them are, as it were, apodoses, which cannot be understood without the protasis, and which would not have been understood without the protasis at the time Jesus spoke them.[1]

Should we turn our thoughts from considerations of form to considerations of content, it is equally obvious that the ethical demands of the Sermon on the Mount must be considered in the light of something else. The words "I have come" (Matt 5:17) introduce the "antitheses section" of the Sermon. These words, in fact, express Jesus' consciousness of his mission. They, therefore, indicate that the decisive point of view is that of the history of redemption. The same indication can be seen in the presence of the so-called ninth beatitude: "Happy are you when people abuse you and persecute you and speak all kinds of calumny against you on my account. Rejoice and be glad, for your reward will be great in heaven; this is how they persecuted the prophets before you" (Matt 5:11f.).

"Even when," writes Rudolph Schnackenburg, "the logia are viewed in themselves, the point of view of redemptive history is the dominant one."[2] Expressed somewhat differently it can be said that the perspective which dominates the entire Sermon is that of the kingdom of heaven. With Jesus the kingdom is present. The ethical demands of Jesus are but the indicated fashion for the disciple of Jesus to live out his participation in the kingdom: "Set your hearts on his kingdom first, and on his righteousness, and all these other things will be given you as well" (Matt 6:33).

Thus conceived, the fundamental approach to life expressed in the Sermon on the Mount concurs with the fundamental approach of the personalist. Personalism would view the ethical life as life in accordance with what one is, namely, a human person. The basic approach to the ethical life found in the Sermon is that of living the life of one implicated in the history of redemption, of expressing in action one's citizenship in the kingdom. As a baptismal paraenesis, the Sermon explains the life of the baptized person as a baptized member of the kingdom. It indicates the expression in life of what one is.


## THE PERSON: BEING IN RELATION

If the thought is pursued further, it appears that the Sermon presents the life of the Christian as a response to the vocation, the call, of Jesus. This is particularly apparent in the final pericope of the Sermon. The last four paragraphs of the Sermon have a single theme, namely, the contrast between the way that leads to destruction and the way that leads to life. The contrast of the two ways is a well-known Judaic theme, appearing in the rabbinic literature and in the sectarian literature of

Qumran. In the final pericope of the Sermon, however, Jesus specifies that the true contrast between the two ways is that between those who hear his words and act on them and those who only hear his words (Matt 7: 24–27). All who have heard his words have received his call; only those who have acted on them have responded to that call. Consequently we feel that the final pericope of the Sermon clearly conceives of the ethical life as a response to the message and call of Jesus. This response, moreover, must be the response of the total man, since a merely verbal response is not deemed adequate (Matt 7: 21–23). We shall return to this in a moment, but it must be appreciated that Matthew has understood the ethical life to be a true response to the call of Jesus.

The Christian therefore, is one who stands in a relationship, a relationship which we, in our terminology, would call a personal relationship, to Jesus. That relationship determines his ethical life.

Matthew particularly highlights this truth in that part of the instruction which deals with the suffering of persecution. It is explicitly stated in the ninth beatitude: "Happy are you when people abuse you and persecute you and speak all kinds of calumny against you *on my account*" (Matt 5: 11). But it is equivalently expressed in the eighth beatitude: "Happy are those who are persecuted in the cause of right" (Matt 5: 10). The similarity of *heneken dikaiosynes* to *heneken emou* of the following verse suggests that in some way Jesus is righteousness and recalls his words in Matt 3: 15: "It is fitting that we should, in this way, do all that righteousness demands."

Because he has thus identified himself with the demands of God, what is suffered on his account is suffered also for the sake of God. Moreover, even the *logion* on being struck on the cheek (Matt 5: 39) has overtones of the Isaian servant motif (Isa. 50: 6) and thus can be indicative of a real relationship between Jesus and the Christian. The ethical life is not merely a response to the call of Jesus or the acceptance of his ethical teaching; it is a following of Jesus, discipleship.

Yet, the Christian is not only one who stands in relation to Jesus, he is also one who stands in relation to the Father. The Sermon indicates the care of God for men of faith, albeit little faith (Matt 6: 30), in the pericope which describes the care which God demonstrates for the birds and the lilies (Matt 6: 25–33). If God manifests his loving Providence for these creatures, how much more is the care and concern which he has for those who are his children! Elsewhere God's care for his children is indicated by the fact that God so loves his children that he knows their needs even before these needs are expressed in prayer (Matt 6:8).

God manifests such care for the man of faith because of his relationship with that man. But this relationship is that of a Father to his children: "If you then, who are evil, know how to give your children what is good, how much more will your Father in heaven give good things to those who ask him!" (Matt 7:11).

Matthew especially capitalizes on this relationship in the context of prayer. But it is a relationship which pervades the entire Sermon. The man of faith, the Christian, is a child of his Father. It is for this reason that the words of the Christian redound to the glory of his Father in heaven: "In the same way your light must shine in the sight of men, so that, seeing your good works, they may give the praise to your Father in heaven" (Matt 5:16).

There is no contradiction between this statement and the *logia* on the three characteristic works of piety. The Christian does not act in order to be seen by men, and thus be praised for his activity. When the Christian acts as a Christian, he acts always as a child of the Father. Consequently when he acts as a Christian, his activity necessarily redounds to the glory of the Father of whom he is the child.

The climax of Matthew's expression of the relationship between the Father and the Christian is, however, to be found in the *logion*, "You must therefore be perfect just as your heavenly Father is perfect" (Matt 5:48). In many ways, this *logion* is the positive highlight of the ethics found in the Sermon on the Mount. This positive epitome of the Sermon's ethics comes at the close of the "antitheses section." In contrast, the negative epitome of the Sermon's ethics immediately precedes the antitheses: "For I tell you, if your virtue goes no deeper than that of the scribes and Pharisees, you will never get into the kingdom of heaven" (Matt 5:20). Between these two *logia* the contrast is manifest. The ethic of the Christian is not to be that of the scribes and Pharisees, a righteousness of works performed in view of reward. Rather the ethic of the Christian must be the lived expression of his sonship.

Commenting on this extraordinary ideal, C. Spicq has written:

> Although the Old Testament required the Israelites to be holy (Lev 11:44–45; 19:2) and perfect before God (Deut 18:13) because he himself is holy, these prescriptions were entirely negative; they cautioned men to avoid sin. Not one text conceived of charity under its most gen-

erous form of love of enemies, much less as the love proper to sons who
show that they have in their own hearts the charity of their Father in
heaven. Charity's extension to all, demanded of men because exempli-
fied in God, implies a unique and deeply mysterious quality in the Christian, as St. John and St. Paul later made clear. Christians are distinguished
from pagans and from publicans by more than their belonging to the
Lord whose orders they execute and whose spirit they imitate. Their
relation with God goes beyond the moral order of obedience and fidelity
and even beyond the order of religious consecration envisaged in the
Pentateuch; the relation, we would say today, is of a divine order.

In other words, to love both neighbor and enemy as God loves
them, they must actually be sons of God in the strictest sense of the
word. Only those who have God for their Father share his love and
are able to do what he does — include all men in his charity. The fullness
of love in the disciple's heart displays itself in love's universal extension. Whoever loves universally is perfect because he does what is prescribed in verse 45: "Therefore prove yourselves children of your Father
in heaven."

Yet, the Christian is the Christian in the world. He stands in a
relationship to other men. His ethical relationship with them is not
one predetermined in a code of law; it is not the carrying out of $x$
number of minute prescriptions in a meticulous fashion. Rather, it is
living with others a relationship which is that of the disciple of Jesus
and the son of the Father. This idea could be developed in some detail,
but two examples will have to suffice.

First, the Christian must live his relationship to others as the disciple
of Jesus. This understanding is eminently useful for an appreciation of
Matt 5:13–16: "You are the salt of the earth. But if salt becomes taste-
less, what can make it salty again? It is good for nothing, and can only
be thrown out to be trampled underfoot by men. You are the light of
the world. A city built on a hill-top cannot be hidden. No one lights
a lamp to put it under a tub; they put it on the lamp stand where it
shines for everyone in the house. In the same way your light must shine
in the sight of men, so that, seeing your good works, they may give
the praise to your Father in heaven." Israel had been likened to salt,
but this salt had lost its taste. Christ is the new Israel, the new salt.
The Christian, disciple of Christ, must fulfill his salting role. Similarly,
it is Christ, not the Torah, not Israel, who is the light of the world.

The Christian, disciple of Christ, must in turn be a light to the world. These verses, therefore, which emphasize the universal task of the disciples of Jesus not only contrast the old Israel with the New but also demonstrate that the mission of Jesus is fulfilled in the life of his disciples precisely because and insofar as they are his disciples.

Similarly, the relationship between the Christian and any other person must be a living out of his relationship with the Father. This is what differentiates the relationship between an individual and the Christian from the relationship that exists between that same individual and the publican, faithful Jew, or Gentile (Matt 5:47). His love for all, even his enemies as expressed in prayer (Matt 5:44) is the Christian's manner of living as a son of the Father who loves all, just and unjust alike.

## THE PERSON: INTEGRAL HUMAN

There is, however, one aspect of the relational ethic of the Sermon on the Mount which we cannot afford to overlook in this somewhat rapid overview, and that is the unity and integrity of the Christian who answers his call and lives his relational life. Man is a totality. There can be no dichotomy between his heart and his action, no separation between his word and his work, no disjunction of his relationship with one from his relationship with another if he is to be truly ethical.

Thus we find in the Sermon, as elsewhere in the Synoptics, that Jesus demanded interior disposition as the decisive factor in moral action. He made the heart the center of moral personality. He called those who are pure of heart, that is, the simple-minded and simple, "happy" (Matt 5:8). Our hearts are not to be fixed on earthly treasures, but are to be wholly concerned with God in heaven (Matt 6:21). By a lustful look at another's wife, a man has already committed adultery with her "in his heart" (Matt 5:28). Man is one, and if his heart is not ethical, he is not ethical.

Similarly, Jesus demanded sincerity. This is apparent in the antithesis on oaths: "But I say this to you: do not swear at all, either by heaven, since that is God's throne; or by the earth, since that is his footstool; or by Jerusalem, since this is the city of the great king. Do not swear by your own head either, since you cannot turn a single hair white or black. All you need say is 'Yes' if you mean yes, 'No' if you mean no; anything more than this comes from the evil one" (Matt 5: 34–37).

Hypocrisy has no place in the life of a Christian, either in the response that he would give to the Lord (Matt 7:21–23) or in his relationship to his brethren (Matt 7:2–5), as the *mashal* of the splinter and the plank illustrates so well.

Finally, the Sermon on the Mount graphically emphasizes the unity of the life of the Christian. "So then, if you are bringing your offering to the altar, and there remember that your brother has something against you, leave your offering there before the altar, go and be reconciled with your brother first, and then come back and present your offering" (Matt 5:23–24). One relationship cannot be separated from another because the Christian has not two lives, but a single life. For "no one can be the slave of two masters: he will either hate the first and love the second, or treat the first with respect and the second with scorn. You cannot be the slave both of God and of money" (Matt 6:24).

## PERSONAL DEMAND

These considerations bring us to the charge that has been frequently laid to Matthew's account, namely, that he has introduced rabbinism into the Sermon on the Mount and made of it a code of law. Indeed, some authors, such as W. D. Davies, speak of the neo-legalism of the Sermon on the Mount and see in this the beginning of legalistic moralism within the Church.

Since a detailed response would mean that this article would become too long, I would offer just three considerations. First, the Sermon on the Mount is not intended to be a complete code of law. Its incompleteness and its, at least at times, seemingly apparent contradictions make it impossible for the Sermon to be considered as a legal document, inculcating a juridical, canonical type of morality. In this regard, I would willingly quote the words of Jeremias:

> What Jesus teaches in the sayings collected together in the Sermon on the Mount is not a complete regulation of the life of the disciples, and it is not intended to be; rather, what is here taught are symptoms, signs, examples of what it means when the Kingdom of God breaks into the world which is still under sin, death and the devil. Jesus says, in effect: I intended to show you, by means of some examples, what

the new life is like, and what I show you through these examples, this you must apply to every aspect of life. You yourselves should be signs of the coming Kingdom of God, signs that something has already happened. Through every aspect of your lives, including aspects beyond those of which I speak, you should testify to the world, that the Kingdom of God is already dawning. In your lives rooted and grounded in the *basileia*, the Kingdom of God, the victory of the Kingdom of God should be visible.[4]

Thus the mere fact of the incompleteness of the Sermon's ethical indications should make us realize that it is not to be viewed as a legal document. Indeed, legal documents normally exclude incompleteness by the adoption of an apodictic type of law and/or the casuistic "if-then" law form.

Secondly, where there is contact between the ethic inculcated in the Sermon and matters dealt with by "civil" law, the intention of Jesus to bypass the strict requirements of law is manifest. As an example we might cite Matt 5:40–41, since this pair of verses gives evidence of contact with both Jewish and Gentile law. The text reads: "If a man takes you to law and would have your tunic, let him have your cloak as well. And if one orders you to go one mile, go two miles with him." The intention is certainly to draw a contrast between juridically directed conduct and the voluntary conduct of the disciple of Jesus. Not only has Matthew phrased the protasis of each clause in legal terminology; he has also juridicized the taking of the coat, an incident which appears in Luke with the wrongdoer seizing the coat by violence. According to the social legislation of Ex 22:26, and Deut 24:12–13, a plaintiff could sue for the tunic, but not for the cloak. Jesus' words indicate that that which is legally statuted is not a sufficient directive for a Christian's dealing with his neighbor. Similarly, the second portion of the cited text, whose vocabulary[5] recalls the commandeering of service for public use, indicates that the Christian's duty toward his neighbor extends beyond that of his legal obligation.

Thirdly, the attitude of Jesus toward the law of Moses is not that of the legal approach. This is quite apparent in Mark 2:27: "The sabbath was made for man, not man for the sabbath," but is likewise visible in the introduction to the antitheses in which Jesus contrasts the righteousness, that is, the ethico-religious conduct, of his disciples with that of the scribes and Pharisees. In addition, the stark contrast between "You have learnt how it was said to our ancestors" and "But I say this

to you" of Matt 5 indicates that Jesus has radicalized his demands. On
this point, Bultmann has commented:

> God does not lay claim to man only so far as conduct can be deter-
> mined by formulated laws (the only way open to legalism), leaving man's
> own will free from that point on. What God forbids is not simply the
> overt acts of murder, adultery, and perjury, with which law can deal,
> but their antecedents: anger and name-calling, evil desire and insincerity
> (Matt 5:21–22, 27–28, 33–37). What counts before God is not simply
> the substantial, verifiable deed that is done, but how a man is disposed,
> what his intent is. As the laws concerning murder, adultery and perjury
> are thus radicalized, so others which were once meant to restrict arbi-
> trary action but now are conceived as concessions defining an area of
> leeway for permissive acts, are from the point of view of God's intention
> altogether abolished: the provision for divorce, the law of retaliation,
> the limitation of the duty to love one's neighbor alone (Matt 5:31–32,
> 38–41, 43–48).[6]

Expressed in this radical demand of Jesus is his zeal to win acknowledge-
ment for God's will in its original totality. Such radicalism pertains more
to the order of demand than it does to the order of law. Indeed, it can
hardly be supposed that the demands of Jesus, as expressed in the Matthew antitheses, are of the order of law, since the examples cited by
Jesus are in no wise exhaustive, but merely illustrative.

Is, therefore, the Sermon on the Mount to be considered as Law?
I think not. It is rather an exhortation in view of the kingdom—an
exhortation to which man can respond because of the coming of the
kingdom.

With this thought our rather summary study of the Sermon on
the Mount can be terminated. In it we have found a number of elements which can and should be integrated into a personalistic ethic:
viz., 1) an ethic which is based on what one is; 2) the call to discipleship; 3) the relationship with the Father; 4) a view of the total person;
and 5) an ethic of demand, not one of law.


## CHRISTIAN PERSONALISM

By way of conclusion, it might well be said that a study of the
Sermon on the Mount can offer a true refinement to personalism. Such

a study allows us to reject as Christian personalism some forms of so-called personalism. These types of "personalistic philosophy" would have to be rejected because they do not adequately correspond to the Christian Ideal as expressed in the Sermon on the Mount.

First to be abandoned would be that personalism which absolutizes the individual, that personalism which endeavors to make absolute the parts at the expense of the whole. Aristotelian eudonism and the Cartesian ideal of self-realization would have to be rejected. Any so-called personalism which centers on the individual rather than viewing the person as an openness to others, as a being-in-relationship, would not satisfy the Christian ideal. Thus a personalism which is only apparently open to others, but which, in reality, sees others as a means to self-realization, is non-Christian. The Sermon on the Mount clearly indicates that a Christian personalism cannot be neo-individualism, for it demands that the openness to the "other" be not based on what the "other" can offer to the self, but on what the other "is." In different words, self-centered personalism cannot be Christian personalism.

Secondly, the Sermon on the Mount requires that any personalism which describes man merely in light of the function of his citizenship in this world be set aside. Social personalism and, *a fortiori*, collectivism cannot be described as Christian personalism, because their *Weltanschauung* neglects the coming of the kingdom among men. They deny, at least by implication, if not by explicit affirmation, man's personal vocation as a disciple of Jesus and his existence as a child of the Father. Man is not immersed in a totality; he does not merely serve the collectivity; he has a personal call.

Yet, if a study of the Sermon on the Mount allows us to reject some so-called personalistic views as Christian personalism because they are not in accord with the Christian ideal, it also enables us to baptize personalism and make personalism Christian personalism. In this sense the Sermon on the Mount can offer a dimension or precision to our understanding of personalism.

It has been written that the person can be described according to its three dimensions: vocation, incarnation, and communion.[7] The Sermon on the Mount offers some insights into each of these dimensions, thereby enabling us to have a Christian description of the person —a description which serves as the basis for Christian personalism.

The *vocation* of the Christian man is to be a disciple of Jesus. The Christian must respond to the call of Jesus. He must do what he does for the sake of Jesus. The existence of man and, consequently, his vocation must be described in the light of the kingdom. Since the kingdom is come, the Christian is called to act as the disciple of Jesus, reflecting to others the attitude of Jesus.

Nonetheless, it must be remembered that the Sermon offers a teleological view of man insofar as it implicates man in the kingdom which is come, but which is "not yet." Thus the Christian can pray "your kingdom come" (Matt 6:10). The coming of the kingdom is not yet fulfilled. When it is accomplished, "the Father who sees all that is done in secret will reward you" (Matt 6:4, 6, 18). But the Christian's involvement in the fulfilled Kingdom is itself the reward. The Christian is called to see God (Matt 5:8). He is called to communion with God. This is the kingdom and that is the reward, as is apparent from the synonymous expressions of the beatitudes.

Furthermore, the *incarnation* of man in time and space is adequately reflected in the Sermon, since the demands of Jesus are concretized and illustrated by frequent reference to the contemporary practices of Pharisees and Gentiles. Yet even more important is Jesus' demand that the disposition of man be incarnate in his actions. Hypocrisy and verbalism are totally rejected. The whole approach of the Sermon to man is its appeal to the total man, the whole man, whose dispositions cannot be separated from his actions. The Sermon on the Mount admits of no dualism, no angelism, no formalism. Its man is the whole man, incarnate and situated in time and space. Its appeal is to the incarnate man, and it is for this reason that the demands of Jesus are illustrated in the Sermon.

Finally, the Sermon describes man in *communion* with the Father and with Jesus. The Christian community, of which the individual Christian is a member, is not formed exclusively of man to man relationships. The Christian is in communion with the Father, of whom he is the child, and with Jesus, of whom he is the disciple. The "other" with whom the Christian is in relation is not merely another human but the Father, and Jesus in whom the kingdom comes.

Yet, the Christian is not in isolated communion with the Father and with Jesus. He is also in relationship with others, described in the Sermon as his brother (Matt 4:22; 7:22 *et passim*), his neighbor (Matt 5:43), his wife (Matt 5:31), his enemy (Matt 5:43), and such neutral terms as woman (Matt 5:27), and men (Matt 5:16). It is his outgoing relationship toward these others that determines the Christian's full relation to the kingdom. Moreover, from the Sermon it is apparent that no man is excluded or able to be excluded from among those with whom the Christian is in communion.

Thus the Sermon on the Mount is able to offer a Christian dimension to personalism, insofar as it presents a three-dimensional view of human communion (the Christian—others—the Father and Jesus), a true incarnationalism, and the vocation of the Christian as the disciple of Jesus and child of the Father.

## NOTES

1. J. Jeremias, *The Sermon on the Mount* (Philadelphia, 1963), p. 29.

2. R. Schnackenburg, *The Moral Teaching of the New Testament* (New York, 1964), p. 59.

3. C. Spicq, *Agape in the New Testament* (St. Louis, 1963), 1, pp. 14–15.

4. J. Jeremias, *op. cit.*, p. 31.

5. The Greek verb *aggareuō* means to compel a person to perform some public service.

6. R. Bultmann, *Theology of the New Testament* (London, 1965), 1, p. 13.

7. Cf. F. C. Copleston, *Contemporary Philosophy* (London, 1956), p. 110. The description is taken from the writings of Emmanuel Mounier.

# 11

## "And Why Not Do Evil
## That Good May Come?"

THESE WORDS FROM PAUL'S letter to the Romans (Rom 3:8) have become a focal point in the debate on proportionalism among Roman Catholic ethicists. Commenting on the passage, Germain Grisez has stated that "Proportionalists deny the relevance of this verse of St. Paul as a proof text against their position. They claim that Paul only excludes the choice of a moral evil, not of a premoral evil proportionalism seeks to justify. However, the preceding verse is raising precisely the question whether what otherwise would be evil—a lie or refusal of the truth—might not be justified if it promotes God's glory."[1]

In the exposition of his own position on the significance of the passage, Grisez unabashedly cites Rom 3:8 as a proof text or Scriptural warrant for the moral adage that the end does not justify the means. The adage sums up the eighth mode of moral responsibility, namely that "One should not be moved by a stronger desire for one instance of an intelligible good to act for it by choosing to destroy, damage, or impede some other instance of an intelligible good."[2] Grisez explains that whatever limitations the Old Testament attached to the dictum — that is, that the end does not justify the means, *unless God commands and authorizes otherwise*—have been removed in the New Testament. In support of this claim he invokes Rom 3:7-8, along with 2 Cor 4:2 and Eph 4:14-15 as teaching that Paul excludes rationalizations which would seek to justify evildoing for the sake of religion.[3]

In Grisez's judgment the moral adage is the consequence of a significant theological truth. ". . . we must trust God. We do not have the same responsibility God has for the good he wills. That is why St. Paul teaches that we may not do evil that good may come of it (see Rom 3:8)."[4]

Arguing for the validity of the moral principle on the basis of the Roman Catholic ethical tradition, Grisez has cited the authority of Pope

Paul VI, who "firmly teaches that 'it is never lawful, even for the gravest reasons, to do evil that good may come of it' and cites St. Paul (see Rom 3:8) on this point."[5] Indeed in his encyclical letter *Humanae Vitae* Pope Paul VI did teach that "it is never lawful, even for the gravest of reasons, to do evil that good may come of it." In support of this position the encyclical made a footnoted reference to Rom 3:8.[6]

In similar fashion, John R. Connery has argued against the acceptability of proportionalism by Roman Catholic ethicists, has used Rom 3:8 as a scriptural warrant for his own position, and supported the use of that Scripture by citing an authoritative figure within Roman Catholic tradition.[7] Connery's authority is Thomas Aquinas, who paraphrased Rom 3:8 in his discussion on the recipients of baptism. The specific topic under consideration by Thomas was "Can a child still in the womb be baptized."[8] Responding to a hypothetical negative answer to this question, Thomas observed that "Evil should not be done that good may come, according to St. Paul. Therefore a man should not kill the mother in order to baptize the child."[9] Connery makes reference to this response as a clear indication that Thomas does not consider it legitimate to do wrong as a means to the accomplishment of a good end. Indeed Connery highlights the fact that Thomas had made use of Rom 3:8 in his consideration of the liceity of doing a caesarean section in order that the fetus may be baptized.[10]

It does not behoove the exegete to attempt to find a solution to the discussion among ethicists as to the acceptability of proportionalism. Nonetheless an exegetical reflection on Rom 3:8 might help to clarify at least some aspects for the moralists' discussion. The Romans passage does not lend itself to easy interpretation as the subsequent remarks shall certainly indicate. Moreover in an essay such as this it is impossible to make an adequate exegesis of the passage within its proper context. However some attempt to understand Paul's words should be made if, indeed, those words are to be cited in ethical discussion. It is in an attempt to shed some light on the meaning of Paul's own words that the following remarks are offered.

Before entering upon the exegesis of Rom 3:8, however, it might be useful to highlight by means of a series of questions those elements on the discussion on proportionalism which have to do with the meaning and use of Rom 3:8. Did St. Paul actually *teach* that it is never lawful to do evil that good may come of it? Did he, in other words, teach that the end does not justify the means? To what extent did Paul's language belong to the register of moral discourse? In other words, as Paul uses the terms "evil" (*ta kaka*) and "good" (*ta agatha*) in Rom 3:8, do these terms denote ethical concepts? Thirdly, does the language of verse 7 belong to the register of moral discourse? In other words, when Paul writes of "my falsehood" (*tē emō pseusmati*) is he speaking of a lie in the ordinary sense of the deliberate and willful communication of an untruth? Finally, to what extent does the use of a scriptural passage taken out of its context constitute a legitimate use of the text? In other words, does the appeal of various scriptural passages as proof-texts truly respond to the call of Vatican Council II that the teaching of moral theology be more thoroughly nourished by the Sacred Scriptures?[11]

It is beyond the scope of the present essay to respond specifically to each of the four questions which have been raised. What this essay will do is to offer a few exegetical reflections so that we might better understand what Paul meant when he was writing his letter to the Romans and raised the question "And Why Not Do Evil That Good May Come?"

## CONTEXT

The context of this question is a short pericope, Rom 3:1–8, which Ernst Käsemann entitles "Objections."[12] It comes towards the end of a lengthy section of the letter[13] in which Paul has been treating of the righteousness of God. While Paul's argumentation has been generally universalist, it takes a particularist turn in 3:1–8.[14] The passage is somewhat difficult to understand, but it seems to admit of division into two major parts.[15] Verses 1–2 present the advantage of the Jews. In fact, Paul cites but a single advantage of the Jews, namely their possession of the divine oracles. He will return to the topic in Rom 9:4–5, where he will list a series of privileges which belong to the Israelites. That exposition begins the climax (Rom 9–11) of the first part of the letter to the Romans (Rom 1–11). Thus Rom 3:1–8 should be seen as an integral and significant part of the epistle's dominant line of thought, despite the fact that a series of objections is presented in vv. 3–8.[16] These verses constitute the second major part of our pericope. The underlying motif is the covenant. Paul is expressing the fact that the judgment of God upon the Jews, as described in chapter two, does not contradict the covenant. The Scriptures themselves attest that the divine judgment is consistent with divine righteousness; moreover if God were not to exercise eschatological judgment, unacceptable moral consequences would result.

## KEY CONCEPTS

Despite this facile division, Rom 3:1–8 remains one of the more obscure passages in the New Testament and is generally recognized as such by those who choose to comment upon it. According to no less an authority than C. H. Dodd "the whole argument of Rom 3:1–8 is obscure and feeble."[17] Part of the difficulty apparently lies in the fact that Paul is attempting to reconcile two apparently inconsistent ideas, namely God's covenant fidelity to Israel and God's impartiality towards Jew and Gentile.[18] The notion of God's righteousness would seem to be the mediating concept. The theme of covenant fidelity is introduced in v. 3 with the mention of faithlessness (*apistia*) and faithfulness (*pistin*). Subsequently the covenant provides the framework for Paul's reflections. Is that covenant grounded in the promises (thus Goppelt) or is it grounded in creation (thus Käsemann)?

The theme of God's righteousness is explicitly introduced into the pericope—as an eschatological concept—in verse 5. What Paul has to say about divine righteousness in the letter to the Romans remains an abiding concern of exegetes. John Piper is among those who have entered into a discussion of the matter, specifically with regards to the passage under consideration. According to his analysis of Rom 3:1–8 it emerges that

> God's righteousness is neither a strict distributive justice nor a merely saving activity. It is more fundamental to God's nature than either of these and thus embraces both mercy and judgment. It is God's faithfulness to his own name, his unwavering commitment to preserve and display his glory. . . . Thus God manifests his righteousness in keeping his promises to those who believe, for in this he displays the value of his glory by blessing those whose stance of faith renders his glory most conspicuous (Rom 4:20). But he also manifests his righteousness in punishing those who remain in unbelief because unbelief is the gravest assault on God and to bless it indefinitely would be to deny the infinite value of his glorious trustworthiness. God's righteousness is his faithfulness to

his own name, his unwavering commitment to preserve and display his own glory in salvation and in judgment.[20]

## LITERARY FORM

If the major themes of covenant and righteousness are integral to the exposition of Paul's thought in Rom 3:1-8 and if there is no little ambiguity in the understanding of these concepts—especially as they pertain to the passage under consideration—it is clear that the pericope presents a challenge to the interpreter. Yet the obscurity of the passage and the challenge to the exegete do not merely derive from conceptual ambiguity. There is also some ambiguity in determining the literary form adopted by Paul in these verses. Typically scholars think of the diatribe as providing the key insight into Paul's choice of style. Within the perspective which this option provides the series of questions which dominate Rom 3:1-8 are perceived as rhetorical questions.

Since Bultmann's 1910 study the diatribal features of Romans have generally been acknowledged in scholarly circles.[21] Rhetorical questions are a typical feature of the diatribe,[22] as is the citation of an authority as a proof.[23] The diatribe is, of course, essentially a pedagogical device which features censure and protreptic. Its purpose is to persuade. If the essential features of the diatribe were consistently present in 3:1-8 its main line of argumentation would be relatively easy to delineate.

In recent times, however, serious objections have been raised against the simple classification of Rom 3:1-8 as an example of Paul's use of the diatribe.[24] These objections fall into two basic categories. On the one hand, there are those who note the absence from Rom 3:1-8 of significant features of the diatribe. For example, Paul does not use the classic formulae which typically introduce a rhetorical objection. They are normally in the second or third person ("You say," "they say"), whereas Paul's expression in v. 5 is in the first person—"what shall we say?" David R. Hall has brought this part of the discussion into distinct focus by stating that "if Paul is really using the diatribe style in this passage, he is using it in a very strange way. Normally, in the diatribe, the objector's point is stated briefly, and replied to in detail. But in Romans 3:1-8, as commonly interpreted, the objections are stated in detail, and Paul's replies are brief and inadequate."[25]

Moreover there are those who object that Paul is dealing with real rather than imaginary opponents as he formulates objections to his position in Rom 3:3–8.[26] A classic proponent of the second objection is Ernst Käsemann who has discerned a shift in the nature of Paul's argument after verse 4.[27] According to this view, vv. 5–8 reflect Paul's wrestling with real objections which had been raised against him. In any case the parenthetical expressions of v. 8 "as some people slanderously charge us with saying"—an expression which specifically qualifies the passage under our immediate consideration—seems to indicate that Paul is dealing with a real objection rather than one which he has himself formulated for didactic purposes.

## STRUCTURE

Given the weight of these objections it would seem preferable to evaluate Rom 3:1–8 as a pericope in which there is a suggestion of diatribal style rather than consider it simply as an example of Paul's use of the diatribe without further qualification. Paul Achtemeier has, nonetheless, noted that some constructions are repeated in the pericope.[28] From his analysis he has concluded that a basic rhetorical structure appears in the passage. Simply stated, the structure consists of a question, introduced by *ei* ("if") and conceded to be true, a possible inference introduced by *mē* (variously translated) and considered to be false, an emphatic asseveration of its falseness (*mē genoito*, "by no means"), and the reason why it is false. This structure clearly appears in vv. 3–4 and 5–6. It is somewhat modified in vv. 7–8, the very verses whose significance is the object of the present essay.

In this pair of verses Paul has modified his basic structure in two fundamental ways. First of all, Paul cites two false inferences. Secondly, there is the absence of the dramatic *mē genoito* ("by no means"), its place having been taken by the second of the false inferences. Achtemeier has suggested that the reason for Paul's modification of his structure at this point is that the issue of the possibly good consequences of evil acts was familiar to him. His interruption of the structure results from his need to deny that his proclamation of grace legitimized such an inference.

The verses in question (vv. 7–8) seem to be lacking in the subtilities of theological reflection. Paul is no longer the biblical scholar citing the Scriptures to indicate that the outpouring of God's wrath upon the unfaithful, but covenanted people, is not without precedent.

Rather he is the preacher and teacher who not only has grounds to fear that his message might be misunderstood; he is also one who has already had the experience of having his message misconstrued. He is agitated that this be so because, in his estimation, what is really at stake is the proclamation of God's salvific righteousness for all.

## CONSTRUCTION AND GRAMMATICAL DIFFICULTIES

The agitation has led to a somewhat awkward construction in vv. 7–8, a construction whose irregularity is only somewhat relieved by the consideration that "as some people slanderously charge us with saying" is a parenthetical clause.[29] It should be well known that every translation of a text is an interpretation of it. The editors of the Revised Standard Version have offered "But if through my falsehood God's truthfulness abounds to his glory, why am I still being condemned as a sinner? And why not do evil that good may come?—as some people slanderously charge us with saying. Their condemnation is just." as their English translation of Rom 3:7–8. This translation resolves in a very acceptable fashion some of the major exegetical problems affecting the interpretation of verses 7–8.

Initially two problems come to the fore. The first is reflected in the way the text is to be punctuated.[30] The punctuation found in the RSV and the New American Bible[31] is the most natural.[32] It implies that verse 8 is some sort of a response to the question posed in verse 7. A second initial interpretative problem concerns the parenthetical remark—which, incidentally, is found at the beginning of the verse in the Greek text. Essentially the technical discussion[33] related to the parenthesis is reflected in two possible translations, that found in the RSV: "And why not do evil that good may come? *as some people slanderously charge us with saying?*"[34] and one which might be rendered: "And why should we not say 'let us do evil that good may come?'—*as some people slanderously charge.*"[35]

The problems to which reference has just been made are quite technical; let the reader be spared the details of the grammatical discussion. Mention of the discussion has been introduced in order to show that the interpretation of "And why not do evil that good may come?" is not quite as simple as a rapid reading of a modern English translation of Rom 3:8 would lead one to believe. What seems to be clear, upon interpretation of a clumsy Greek text, is that Paul is referring to an allegation that he taught an antinomianism which could be summed up as "why not do evil that good may come"[36] and that he is determined to reject that allegation. In fact, if it is virtually certain that Paul's opponents accused him of antinomian teaching, it must also be acknowledged that even some members of the churches which he established so misunderstood his teaching as to think that he was proclaiming that moral evil did not matter.[37]

## PAUL'S THOUGHT

Having passed in review some of the conceptual, structural, and grammatical problems affecting the interpretation of Rom 3:3-8, we can briefly summarize the main lines of the development of Paul's thought in an attempt to shed some further light on the meaning of verses 7 and 8. In the first structural unit, i.e., vv. 3-4, Paul raises the objection that the Jews have become unfaithful. For Paul the climax of their infidelity is their rejection of the Gospel; yet he affirms that their infidelity ultimately makes no difference. God remains faithful to the covenant which he has established. Indeed the Scriptures attest that God remains faithful despite the infidelity of his people. Paul alludes to two verses of the Psalms, Ps 115:2 and 50:6 (in the Greek version), in order to provide a scriptural basis for his position. God's fidelity is not destroyed by the infidelity of his people.

In the second structural unit, i.e. vv. 5-6, Paul sharpens his thought. Does Paul's teaching on justification and/or his scriptural exposition on the fidelity of God imply the justification of the unjust? At this point in his exposition Paul links God's eschatological judgment, God's wrath, with his righteousness. Paul's argumentation supposes a moral order. If sin provides God with the opportunity to manifest his wrath, and thus, his righteousness, does this not mean that God should justify the sinner? After all, sin seems to be in the service of God. Paul rejects this notion as being a merely human way of reasoning.[38] The righteousness of God[39] includes his judgment—his eschatological wrath which is an ultimate manifestation of his goodness.

In the third structural unit, i.e. vv. 7-8, Paul's thought is sharpened still further and given a personal twist. He asks: "But if through my falsehood God's truthfulness abounds to his glory, why am I still being condemned as a sinner?" The issue is basic infidelity.[40] Even though the question is one which each individual might well pose, the "I" of verse 7 is not autobiographical. From Paul's polemical vantage point, the question is raised as proceeding from Jews[41] or Jewish Christians. It is the sinfulness of the Jews which provides the broad context for Paul's discussion at this point. It was moreover the situation of "the Jew" (see verse 1) which has given rise to Paul's digression in vv. 3–8.[42] However it is not to be excluded that Paul has the Jewish Christian more specifically in mind as he writes v. 7.

If in the face of infidelity God remains faithful and nonetheless manifests his glory, why should the Jew be considered a sinner and thus worthy of eschatological condemnation? Does not the covenant ensure the Jew's ultimate salvation? Paul does not give an analytical response to this objection but responds with a kind of *reductio ad absurdum*. "Why not do evil that good may come? Does God's fidelity imply that we should be antinomian or libertine?

In the context of Paul's argumentation, "good," which usually expresses the essential goodness of God,[43] denotes the eschatological manifestation of his glory.[44] The mere suggestion that God's goodness, his righteousness, his fidelity should lead to libertinism and antinomianism is rejected by Paul not only as a false inference from his[45] teaching on justification but as blasphemy.[46] It is tantamount to the rejection of the Gospel itself. Hence Paul concludes his exposition by proclaiming that the justice of God will effect the condemnation[47] of those who so pervert his gospel. He utters a curse[48] on those who make a parody of the gospel.

The objection which Paul has summed up in the phrase "Why not do evil that good may come from it" is a real objection to the manner in which Paul proclaimed the gospel. Mostly likely the objection came from Jewish Christians who were disturbed by Paul's proclamation of salvation for Gentile "sinners?" If those sinners can be saved, why not live without moral scruples? The very idea, says Paul, is contrary to the Gospel. To suggest this is to insult Paul and blaspheme against God.

## A SIGNIFICANT PARALLEL

A pseudonymous commentator on Paul's writings has told us that "there are some things in them hard to understand."[49] Paul himself was well aware that his words could be misunderstood. In his letter to the Romans he repeatedly draws false inferences from his own exposition. Most characteristically he uses "By no means!" (*mē genoito*) to summarily dismiss the erroneous inference.[50] Only then does Paul proceed to the further exposition of his ideas. The emphatic phrase "By no means!" occurs in our passage in vv. 4 and 6. In sequence, the formula reappears in chapters six and seven. For our purposes, the first two of these occurrences are enlightening. In Rom 6:1 Paul asks "What shall we say then? Are we to continue in sin that grace may abound?" and then vigorously replies "By no means!" (v. 2). Similarly in Rom 6:15 Paul queries "What then? Are we to sin because we are not under law but under grace?" and responds "By no means."

In some respects these two passages might be cited as parallels to Rom 3:7-8. Granted they speak of sin (*hē hamartia*) rather than evil (*ta kaka*), but they do seem to speak of the mandate and/or freedom to sin in the context of the proclamation of the gospel of grace, and they do make use of language which echoes the diatribal style.[51] In Rom 6, the context is not merely ethical; it is theological. Indeed of the two verses under consideration in chapter six, Rom 6:1 provides the closest parallel[52] with Rom 3:8 but sin may well be cited as a power[53] rather than as an offense in 6:1.

When further consideration is given to this verse (6:1) it appears that the objection raised by Paul, namely, "Are we to continue in sin that grace may abound?" is the logical sequence to Paul's thesis in 5:20b, namely, "where sin increased, grace abounded all the more." Indeed Paul has picked up on his own language in 6:1. To the objection that one can infer that believers ought to remain in sin from his proclamation of the gospel of grace, Paul simply retorts "By no means!" Paul does not enter into a lengthy discursive argument as to why the inference is false.[54] He merely denies the legitimacy of the inference and affirms the incompatibility of sin and life under grace. In no way should his proclamation of the gospel of grace be taken to mean that it is proper for sin to continue or, still worse, increase. The reality of the gospel is not a warrant for remaining in sin. The mere suggestion that it might be so is to be excluded out of hand. This having been said, Paul pauses to reflect on the significance of Christian baptism, the foundation of life in Christ Jesus. Later in the letter, especially in Rom 12:1-21, Paul will turn his attention to the way of life that is singularly compatible with the gift of God's grace. There he will briefly summarize the life-style of the Christian, a life-style which ought to flow from and express a new relationship with Christ.

## POSTSCRIPT

These exegetical remarks have been formulated in order to clarify the thought of Paul in Rom 3:8. His words bespeak his personal intensity as he rejects a number of false inferences which might be drawn from his proclamation of the gospel which had been entrusted to him.[55] In context Rom 3:8 contains a final objection raised by Paul and he summarily dismisses it.

Paul's words have been co-opted into a contemporary ethical debate by various ethicists. Without wishing to enter into a discussion of proportionalism, my purpose was to ask whether Rom 3:8 should be taken as a Scriptural warrant for the ethical dictum "the end does not justify the means." To that end I initially raised a series of questions whose answers belong to the background material of the ethical debate. As this essay is brought to a close, it might be useful to return to those questions and offer a brief suggestion as to the proper response.

First, in Rom 3:8 did Paul actually teach that it is never lawful to do evil that good may come of it? What Paul did was to reject unequivocally the idea that antinomianism and libertinism are the logical consequences of his proclamation of the gospel.

Secondly, does Paul's language in v. 8 belong to the register of moral discourse? In Rom 3:1–8 Paul is concerned with the moral order as of verse 5. In v. 8, "evil" (*ta kaka*)[56] is an ethical term, but "good" (*ta agatha*) has to do with eschatological salvation rather than the moral good.

Thirdly, does Paul's language in v. 7, specifically his use of "falsehood" (*pseusma*), belong to the register of moral discourse? It is clear that in v. 7 Paul is not talking about a lie in the ordinary sense of that term; rather he is dealing with a basic infidelity.

Fourthly, is the teaching of moral theology more thoroughly nourished by the Sacred Scriptures when texts are taken out of their context? Our analysis of Rom 3:8 reveals that, at least in this instance, Paul's words are easily misconstrued when they are taken out of context. And he had, indeed, some harsh words to address to those who misconstrue his message!

## NOTES

1. G. Grisez, *The Way of the Lord Jesus*, vol. 1: *Christian Moral Principles* (Chicago: Franciscan Herald Press, 1983), p. 168, n. 32.

2. Ibid., p. 216.

3. Ibid., p. 220.

4. Ibid., p. 155.

5. Ibid., p. 185.

6. See Claudia Carlen, ed., *The Papal Encyclicals 1958–1981* (Wilmington: McGrath, 1981), pp. 227, 233.

7. See J. R. Connery, "Catholic Ethics: Has the Norm for Rule-Making Changed?" *Theological Studies* 42 (1981), 232–250, p. 235.

8. *Summa Theologiae*, III, 68, 11.

9. St. Thomas Aquinas, *Summa Theologiae*, 57 (London: Eyre & Spottiswoode, 1974), p. 115. The citation is taken from the *Ad tertium*, which begins "Ad tertium dicendum quod *non sunt facienda mala ut veniant bona*, ut dicitur Rom 3." Thomas' citation is not, in fact, a literal citation of Rom 3:8. The Vulgate reads: "Et non (sicut blasphemamur, et sicut aiunt quidam nos dicere) faciamus mala ut veniant bona: quorum damnatio iusta est."

10. J. R. Connery, *art. cit.*, p. 235.

11. *Optatum Totius*, 16. See Walter M. Abbott, ed., *The Documents of Vatican II* (New York: America Press, 1966), p. 452.

12. E. Käsemann, *Commentary on Romans* (London: SCM, 1980), p. 77.

13. Rom 2:1–3:20. Some would, however, prefer to identify the unit as 1:18–3:20. See, for example, F. Stagg, "The Plight of Jew and Gentile in Sin: Romans 1:18–3:20," *Review and Expositor* 73 (1976), 401–413. Stagg identifies four major subunits: 1) the wrath of God (1:18–22); 2) the righteous judgment of God (2:1–16); 3) the Jew and the Law (2:17–3:8); 4) both Jew and Greek under sin (3:9–20).

14. Thus J. Christiaan Beker who sees Rom 3:1–8 as a particularist argument, similar to Rom 1:16b and 2:9–10, picked up after its apparent demise in 2:21–26. See J. Christiaan Beker, *Paul the Apostle: The Triumph of God in Life and Thought* (Philadelphia: Fortress, 1980), p. 78.

15. See David R. Hall, "Romans 3.1–8 Reconsidered," *New Testament Studies* 29 (1983), 183–197.

16. On the significance of Rom 3 for the interpretation of the letter see W. S. Campbell, "Romans iii as a Key to the Structure and Thought of the Letter," *Novum Testamentum* 23 (1981), 22–40. According to Campbell the two question and answer sections of Rom 3 (viz., 1–8 and 27–31) are useful for discerning the structural center of Paul's letter.

17. C. H. Dodd, *The Epistle of Paul to the Romans* (London: Hodder and Stoughton, 1932), p. 46. David Hall begins his article on the passage with the striking statement that "Romans 3.1–8 is one of the most puzzling passages in the epistle," while

Paul J. Achtemeier has included his analysis of the passage in an article entitled "Some Things in Them Hard to Understand." See D. R. Hall, *art. cit.*, p. 183. Paul J. Achtemeier, "'Some Things in Them Hard to Understand' Reflections on an Approach to Paul," *Interpretation* 38 (1984), 254–267, esp. pp. 259–263.

18. See D. R. Hall, *art. cit.*, p. 183.

19. See M. T. Brauch, "Perspective on God's Righteousness in Recent German Discussion," in E. P. Sanders, *Paul and Palestinian Judaism* (Philadelphia: Fortress, 1977), pp. 523–542.

20. John Piper, "The Righteousness of God in Romans 3:1–8," *Theologische Zeitschrift* 36 (1980), 3–16, p. 15.

21. R. Bultmann, *Der Stil der paulinischen Predigt und die Kynischstoische Diatribe.* Forschungen zur Religion und Literatur des Alten und Neuen Testaments, 13 (Göttingen: Vandenhoeck & Ruprecht, 1910). See further, with special emphasis on Rom, Stanley Kent Stowers, *The Diatribe and Paul's Letter to the Romans.* Society of Biblical Literature Dissertation Series, 57 (Chico: Scholars Press, 1981).

22. R. Bultmann, *op. cit.*, p. 67.

23. Ibid., p. 95.

24. Noteworthy in this respect is the fact that Stowers examines Rom 2:1–5; 2:17–27; 9:19–21; 11:4; and 11:17–24 in his analysis of Romans but does not treat Rom 3:1–8. See S. K. Stowers, *op. cit.*, pp. 93–100.

25. D. R. Hall, *art. cit.*, p. 183.

26. Thus, for example, while C. H. Dodd holds that "the Jewish objector" is in Paul's own mind, C. K. Barrett holds that Paul is dealing with real objections. See C. H. Dodd, *op. cit.*, p. 43; C. K. Barrett, *A Commentary on the Epistle to the Romans.* Black's New Testament Commentaries (London: A. & C. Clark, 1962) p. 61. See also Isaac J. Canales, "Paul's Accusers in Romans 3:8 and 6:1," *The Evangelical Quarterly* 57 (1985) 237–245, esp. pp. 238, 242.

27. See E. Käsemann, *op. cit.*, p. 83.

28. See P. J. Achtemeier, *art. cit.*, p. 261.

29. See C. E. B. Cranfield, *A Critical and Exegetical Commentary on the Epistle to the Romans,* vol. 1: *Introduction and Commentary on Romans I–VIII,* The International Critical Commentary (Edinburgh: T. & T. Clark, 1975), pp. 186–187.

30. Cranfield proffers four different ways of punctuating vv. 7–8. See C. E. B. Cranfield, *op. cit.*, pp. 185–186.

31. "If my falsehood brings to light God's truth and thus promotes his glory, why must I be condemned as a sinner? Or why may we not do evil that good may come of it? This is the very thing that some slanderously accuse us of teaching; they will get what they deserve." With the RSV and the NAB, one might compare the punctuation utilized in the Jerusalem Bible for these verses, namely, "You might as well say that since my untruthfulness makes God demonstrate his truthfulness and thus gives him glory, I should not be judged to be a sinner at all. That would be

the same as saying: Do evil as a means to good. Some slanderers have accused us of teaching this, but they are justly condemned."

32. Thus C. E. B. Cranfield, *op. cit.*, p. 186.

33. The parenthesis obviously begins with the first *kathōs*. The technical problems concern *legein hoti*. Does *legein hoti* belong to the parenthesis or not? Even if *legein* belongs to the parenthesis, does it necessarily follow that *hoti* belongs? Might not *hoti* be construed with *mē*, thus lying outside the parenthesis? See C. E. B. Cranfield, *op. cit.*, pp. 186–187.

34. With regard to the question of the interpretation of the parenthesis, the position adopted in the RSV's translation is essentially reflected in the Authorized Version, the New American Bible, and the New English Bible. According to this view *legein hoti* belongs to the parenthesis.

35. My own translation is offered in an attempt to preserve the language of the RSV. Essentially this translation's manner of resolving the problem of the parenthesis is reflected in the translations found in the Jerusalem Bible (see above, note 31), Today's English Version, and the New International Version. The approach reflected in these translations basically interprets *legein hoti* as lying outside the parenthesis.

36. See also E. P. Sanders, *Paul, the Law and the Jewish People* (Philadelphia: Fortress, 1983) pp. 31, 94, 149. Whether the clause represents Paul's summation of the opponents' allegations or whether it is a slogan which the opponents themselves bandied about (as is that found in 1 Cor 7:1b) is not entirely certain.

37. Cf. 1 Cor 5:1–6, where Paul's teaching about the gift of the Spirit has been misconstrued as a warrant for licentiousness. Käsemann notes that "libertinism really could develop out of Paul's view of justification, and his adversaries claim that it is an unavoidable result." See E. Käsemann, *op. cit.*, p. 84.

38. Cf. Rom 6:19; 1 Cor 9:8; Gal 3:15. John A. T. Robinson notes that vv. 6 and 8 are typical of Paul's argument in this sort of case. He further notes that Paul is "content to point to the 'infinite qualitative difference' (Kierkegaard) between God and man. The mere suggestion that human standards of judgment can be applied to God is anthropomorphic." See J. A. T. Robinson, *Wrestling with Romans* (Philadelphia: Westminster, 1979) p. 33.

39. D. R. Hall states succinctly in this regard that "God's righteousness means his right dealing with people according to their various relationships with himself." See D. R. Hall, *art. cit.*, p. 189.

40. In context "falsehood" (*pseusmati*) signifies infidelity rather than a mere lie. In the writings of Plato *pseusma* denotes a lie or an untruth. In the New Testament, *pseusma* is used in no other place; it therefore is to be considered as a *hapax legomenon*.

In the context of v. 7, the contrast is between God's truthfulness (*alētheia*, his fidelity) and human falsehood (*pseusma*, his/her infidelity). Paul's use of abstract language in v. 7 has been prepared for by v. 4 where Paul writes of God as "true" and

252 A NEW TESTAMENT PERSPECTIVE

every man as "false" (*pseustēs*). Although *pseustēs* is found in John 8:44, 55; 1 Tim 1:10; Ti 1:12; and 1 John 1:10; 2:4, 22; 4:20; 5:10, *pseustēs* is a *hapax legomenon* within the critical Pauline corpus. It contrasts with *alethēs* ("true") a notion which reflects the biblical concept of covenant fidelity (*emeth*). That this is indeed the case is clearly indicated by the context of verse 4a.

41. "Nevertheless," writes Käsemann, "it is clear . . . that Paul is no longer debating with the Jews but is simply taking the Jews as examples of mankind and extending the idea of the covenant to creation." See E. Käsemann, *op. cit.*, p. 83.

42. According to Käsemann, p. 83, "Jewish-Christians are most probably mangling Paul's message in v. 8." If the objection of v. 8 specifically comes from Jewish Christians, one ought to further refine the question raised above in note 36. We might not be dealing merely with an ideological confrontation; rather the phrase "why not do evil that good may come" might be a commentary on the libertine conduct of some of those who have accepted Paul's proclamation of the gospel.

43. See Walter Grundmann, "*agathos*, ktl.," in Gerhard Kittel, ed., *Theological Dictionary of the New Testament*, 1 (Grand Rapids: Eerdmans, 1964) 10–18, p. 15.

44. Thus, André Viard, *Epître aux Romains. Sources bibliques* (Paris: Gabalda, 1975) p. 91. Jörg Baumgarten also notes that Paul often uses "good" (*ton agathon*) in the letter to the Romans in the sense of eschatological salvation. See J. Baumgarten, "*agathos*," in Horst Balz and Gerhard Schneider, eds., *Exegetisches Wörterbuch zum Neuen Testament*, 1 (Stuttgart: Kohlhammer, 1980) 11–17, c. 13.

45. Paul is writing in the first person plural. However commentators are in general agreement that Paul is writing about himself. See Barclay M. Newman and Eugene A. Nida, *A Translator's Handbook on Paul's Letter to the Romans.* Helps for Translators, 14 (Stuttgart: United Bible Societies, 1973) p. 57. One who departs from the consensus is André Viard who believes that Paul is writing about himself and his companions. See A. Viard, *op. cit.*, p. 91.

46. Paul uses the verb *blasphēmoumetha*, from *blasphēmeō*. He rarely uses the word, having employed it only four times in the extant literature (Rom 2:24; 3:8; 14:16; 1 Cor 10:30). In Rom 2:24 Paul cites Is 52:5 and uses the verb in its religious sense. Although the verb, in both secular and New Testament usage, can mean "to speak slanderously of," some suggestion of divine insult is not to be avoided in the interpretation of v. 8. See, likewise, E. Käsemann, *op. cit.*, p. 84.

47. "Their condemnation is just" is open to some ambiguity. A first question concerns the subject of the condemnation; are those who condemn humans or God? (See Newman and Nida, *op. cit.*, p. 57.) In fact, the entire context would imply that it is God, the judge of v. 6, who will effect the condemnation. A second question concerns the object of the condemnation. Although a relatively few interpreters assume that it is the arguments of Paul's opponents which stand condemnable, the overwhelming majority of commentators link "their" (*hōn*) of v. 7b with "some people" (*tines*). The condemned are those persons who pervert his Gospel.

48. See Otto Michel, *Der Brief an die Römer.* Kritisch-exegetischer Kommentar

über das Neue Testament, 5, 12th ed. (Göttingen: Vandenhoeck & Ruprecht, 1963)
p. 97; see also Otto Kuss, *Der Römerbrief* (Regensburg: Pustet, 1958) pp. 104–105.

49. 2 Pet 3:16.

50. Rom 3:4, 6, 31; 6:2, 15; 7:7, 13; 9:14.

51. See C. K. Barrett, *op. cit.*, p. 121; and E. Käsemann, *op. cit.*, p. 163.

52. See J. A. T. Robinson, *op. cit.*, p. 67.

53. See E. Käsemann, *op. cit.*, p. 163. Indeed it is well known that in the Pauline
writings *hē hamartia*, in the singular, generally designates a super-human force. It
is, moreover, significant that in 6:1 Paul writes of "remaining in sin" (*epimenōmen
tē hamartia*) rather than "sinning" or "committing sin."

54. Robinson has commented: ". . . here he [Paul] takes no more space to
counter it [the objection] than in chapter 3. He does not meet it at the logical level—
it cannot be so met. . . . He appeals to the faith-experience of the new relationship
with Christ." See J. A. T. Robinson, *op. cit.*, p. 67.

55. See 1 Thess 2:4.

56. My understanding of the debate between deontologists and proportionalists is that it concerns a determination of the criteria by which a given reality is to
be characterized as "evil." In Rom 3:8 Paul does not give any indication of what
specific realities he considers to be "evil" (*ta kaka*).

# Index

254